WRITER'S MARKET LIBRARY

FORMATTING & SUBMITTING YOUR MANUSCRIPT

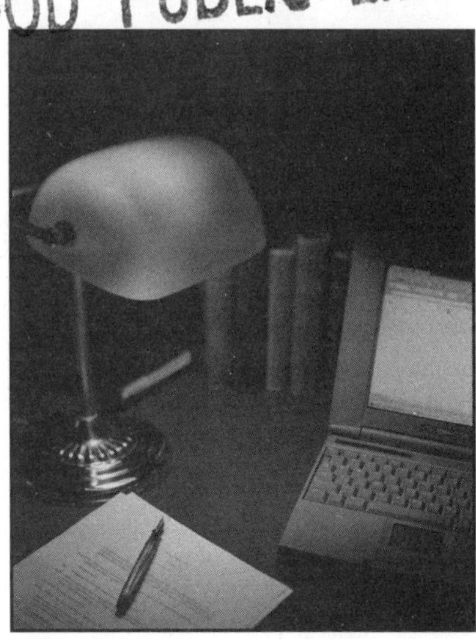

JACK & GLENDA NEFF, DON PRUES
AND THE EDITORS OF WRITER'S MARKET

WRITER'S DIGEST BOOKS
CINCINNATI, OHIO
www.writersdigest.com

 Published by Writer's Digest Books, an imprint of F&W Publications, Inc., 1507 Dana Avenue, Cincinnati, Ohio 45207. (800) 289-0963. First edition.

04 03 02 01 00 5 4 3 2 1

Library of Congress Cataloging-in-Publication Data

Neff, Jack
Formatting & submitting your manuscript / by Jack Neff, Glenda Neff, Don Prues, and the editors of Writer's Digest.—1st ed.
p. cm.
Includes index.
ISBN 0-89879-921-X (pbk.: alk. paper)
1. Manuscript preparation (Authorship). 2. Authorship—Marketing. I. Title. II. Title: Formatting and submitting your manuscript. III. Neff, Glenda Tennant IV. Prues, Don
PN160.N44 1999
808'.02 21—dc21 99-043650
CIP

Editors: Kirsten Holm and Michelle Howry
Designer: Sandy Kent
Production coordinator: Kristen D. Heller

ABOUT THE AUTHORS

JACK NEFF has been a freelance business writer since 1989. He writes regularly for *Advertising Age*, *How* and other national business and trade publications. He is also author of *Make Your Woodworking Pay for Itself*, a contributing author of *The Writer's Essential Desk Reference* and co-author of *The Insider's Guide to Greater Cincinnati.*

GLENDA TENNANT NEFF is former editor of *Writer's Market* and *Novel and Short Story Writer's Market.* She was also editor and contributing author of *The Writer's Essential Desk Reference.* She is now program director for educational outreach and business training at University of Cincinnati–Clermont College.

DON PRUES is a writer and editor living in Cincinnati, Ohio. Former editor of *Guide to Literary Agents* and assistant editor of *Writer's Market*, Don now spends most his time staring at screens (first the movie theater's, then his computer's!) as managing editor for three movie-related Web sites: critics.com (a critical consensus of national reviews); kids-in-mind.com (reviews for parents); and mediascreen.com (DVD and laserdisc reviews).

TABLE OF CONTENTS

Introduction

"It's the content that counts."

Those five words probably best sum up the opinions of editors and agents concerning manuscript formats.

Proper formatting helps you to distinguish yourself as a professional and get your point across clearly and cleanly. Beyond that, format really doesn't mean much. Perfect margins and ideal spacing won't prevail over dull, poorly written work in the mind of an editor. On the other hand, editors have been known to forgive a few formatting glitches when a great story or concept shines clearly through the clutter.

What, then, is the point of this book?

This is simply a tool to keep you from sweating the details. With a complete set of manuscript formats in hand, you can confidently set about the real work of writing without having to worry whether your header is in the right place or your indentation is proper. No one should let formatting worries stand in the way of creativity, or let sloppy formatting stand in the way of great work. Beginning writers, especially, often get caught in a trap—either letting the minutiae of manuscript formats bog down and frustrate their creativity, or throwing all caution to the wind and submitting work so poorly organized that editors can't follow it or summarily reject it. Each mistake is a mark of an amateur.

Beyond the mechanics of page formatting, this book also takes you through the finer points of how to structure your submissions, from query letters through books and screenplays. This information is more important than the look of a page, because it addresses the fundamental issues of how your work is organized. The organization has a tremendous impact on whether your work captures the attention of readers, starting with the most important one—the editor.

Keep in mind that the models presented here are only models, not divine archetypes. They are meant only as starting points that give you the confidence to go forward with your own projects. You will find, over time, variations that work better for you and your editor. You'll also find that different editors and applications require variations.

Ultimately, do what works for you. Don't mangle or otherwise abuse your work in order to fit it into some set format you find in a book. Especially avoid trying to mimic the style of the models you see here. Besides disliking poorly organized, sloppy submissions, most editors also grow tired of formulaic writing once they've encountered the same formula dozens of times. You'll find that most editors value freshness, creativity and insight above slavish adherence to a formula. Even in highly formulaic genres, your ability to bring a fresh approach within the confines of the genre is highly prized.

You'll also find some forms at the end of the book meant to help you organize your work and your submissions. Look at these as suggested solutions, not burdensome mandates. These are only offered to make your life easier. If you have a computer and a large enough hard drive that you can store everything you do, many of these forms aren't necessary. Time-saving alternative methods of recordkeeping are also suggested when appropriate. By no means feel that you have somehow violated some tenet of an imaginary writer's code if you don't religiously fill out these forms.

A few guidelines, of course, are set in stone. (Don't misspell the editor's name. Don't misspell the name of the publication.) But precise margins, placement of page headers and diligent keeping of submission logs are not among the cardinal rules.

This book assumes that the writer is working with a computer, word processing software, fax machine, on-line access and E-mail. These are simply tools of the trade that most editors expect you to have these days. If money is an issue, you can buy a used computer system for the cost of a new typewriter. For many writers, the investment in these gadgets will pay for itself in a matter of weeks.

In an age of electronic submissions and electronic publishing, how you format the printed page has become largely irrelevant for many articles and short forms. But there are new issues connected with electronic submissions of which you should be aware, and this book will detail those in the appropriate places.

General Tips on Submitting Manuscripts

Paper

Generally use clean, white laser or inkjet paper for manuscripts and good quality 20-pound bond letterhead for letters. Recycled paper may present a poor appearance. But it may be appropriate in some cases, such as with environment-conscious publishers.

Type Size

Use 10- or 12-point type for body copy.

Printers

Laser or inkjet printers are both perfectly acceptable. Letter-quality dot matrix output will also do, but is not preferred.

Headers

Generally, slugs and page numbers go in headers, which your word processing software will allow you to set up fairly easily. Page numbers are usually found in the top right-hand corner, but centering them at the top or placing them bottom-center or bottom-right is acceptable. Just be consistent.

Margins

Generally allow for a 1″ margin around letters and manuscript pages. You're free to go up to 1½″, but you'll be shorting yourself room for letters and spend more on paper.

Attaching Pages

Use paper clips, or, in the case of book-length manuscripts, submit loose-leaf. Staples are OK for clippings.

Part One
NONFICTION

CHAPTER ONE

ARTICLES

What You Need to Submit

Submitting articles is a sequential process that starts with sending a query to an editor, continues through getting acceptance to do the article, and ends with submitting the article. Barring some bumps along the way, the process is that simple.

Before you write an article, you should sell it. You can submit finished articles, but this is usually a recipe for disappointment. Most editors want queries before assigning articles. And even if the editor likes the article, he's likely to want to provide some guidance before it's written. Working on spec is usually an unprofitable habit for freelancers.

The query letter is the time-honored traditional method for selling an article. Articles do get sold with telephone pitches, but that's usually only after the writer has developed a relationship with an editor. Just as you don't like to be interrupted at dinner with unsolicited telemarketing pitches for replacement windows or Florida time-share condominiums, editors don't like to be interrupted from their work with pitches for stories.

> **"If you have a query that's of real interest and deliver it in a way that you know fits that magazine, and you have the writing ability to back it up, that's much more important than if you have fancy letterhead or paid attention to whether your margins are one inch. They may even come through E-mail."**
>
> —Joni Praded, editor, *Animals*

The Query Letter

Submission Tips

The query should serve several primary purposes:

- Sell your idea through a brief, catchy description.
- Tell the editor how you would handle the lead and develop the article.
- Show that you're familiar with the publication and how your article would fit with it.
- Indicate why you're qualified to write this article.

When applicable—and when possible within space constraints—the query should also:

- State the availability of photography or other artwork. (If this is a key selling point, you should definitely include such information. If it's not, these details can be discussed when the editor contacts you about an assignment.)
- Provide a working title that succinctly and enticingly sums up your idea for the editor.
- Estimate an article length. (The article should be as long as you think is necessary to cover the topic, keeping in mind the typical length of pieces in the publication. Remember: the editor may think otherwise.)
- Outline possible sidebars.
- Summarize the supporting material, such as anecdotes, interviews, statistics, etc.
- State when the article will be available.
- Indicate if you're submitting this idea simultaneously to other publications.

A side benefit for the writer is that preparing the query helps define the project and develop a lead and a strategy for completing the assignment well before you actually have to do it. The down side is that a query letter can take longer to write, word-for-word, than the article itself.

Query letters are something of a genre unto themselves. Writing them successfully requires considerable attention to detail, and tight editing to fit within the one-page standard, which is a widely observed rule for article queries.

Formatting Specs

- Use a standard font or typeface (avoid bold, script or italics, except for publication titles).
- Your name, address and phone number (plus E-mail and fax, if possible) should appear in the top right corner or on your letterhead.
- Use a 1″ margin on all sides.
- Address the query to a specific editor, preferably the editor assigned to handle freelance submissions or who handles the section you're writing for. (Call to get the appropriate name, and make sure you know the gender, too.)
- Keep it to one page. If necessary, use a resume or list of credits attached separately to provide additional information.
- Include an SASE or postcard for reply, and state in the letter you have done so, either in the body of the letter or in a listing of enclosures. (The postcard is cheaper and easier for everyone involved. You can have them printed in bulk.)

- Use block format (no indentations, extra space between paragraphs).
- Single-space the body of the letter and double-space between paragraphs.
- When possible, mention that you can send the manuscript on disk or via E-mail.
- Thank the editor for considering your proposal.

Other Dos and Don'ts

- Do mention previous publishing credits that pertain to the article you're proposing.
- Don't take up half a page listing credits of little interest to the editor. If you have extensive credits that pertain to the query, list them on an enclosed sheet.
- Do indicate familiarity with the publication. It's OK to make a positive comment, too, if it's sincere and appropriate. But don't get obsequious.
- Don't request writer's guidelines or a sample copy in your letter. This clearly indicates you're not familiar enough to query, and you should do it before you send a query (see the Request for Guidelines letter on p. 23).
- Don't overpromise. If you can't deliver, it will soon become obvious to the editor.
- Don't tell the editor the idea already has been rejected by another publication. Such full disclosure does you no good and isn't necessary.
- Do enclose clippings, especially when they're applicable to the idea you're proposing. No more than three are necessary, or even desirable.
- Do send copies, not originals, of your clippings. They can always get lost, even if you include an SASE. Photocopied clips are assumed to be disposable; if you want them back, make sure you include an SASE with sufficient postage and say so in your letter.
- Don't discuss payment terms. It's premature.

ARTICLE QUERY LETTER #1: NONFICTION

Jack Neff
555 W. Fourth St.
Cincinnati, OH 45200
(513) 555-9000
writer@email.com

One of many letterhead styles you can use.

December 10, 2000

1 line

Always address a specific editor.

Edward Fictitiousman
Managing Editor
Inc.
1200 Sixth St.
Boston, MA 01655

Not necessary; easy to remove if you need an extra line of space.

1 line

Dear Mr. Fictitiousman:

1 line

A two-paragraph comparison contrast lead. Also shows you have anecdotes ready to use.

Custom Cleaner Inc.'s doom was sealed before the company's first home dry cleaning kit reached stores. Procter & Gamble Co. already was preparing a competing product. And when P&G announced its plans, retailers wouldn't stock Custom Cleaner.

1" margin

1 line between paragraphs

Clean Shower, another upstart cleaning product, seemed headed for a similar fate. After a promising initial reception in the market, the no-scrub daily shower cleaner inspired knockoffs from such well-heeled rivals as Clorox Co. But Automation Inc., maker of Clean Shower, fought back successfully, increasing sales by boosting advertising even as four competing brands hit the market.

Estimated word count

Explains how the article would be developed.

In a 1,000-word article, I would like to use such case studies to explore how entrepreneurs respond, and sometimes even prevail, when established competitors invade their turf. I believe this would strongly appeal to *Inc.* readers who invest in new products—and usually harbor deep fears of sudden ruin at the hands of giant foes.

Shows familiarity with publication and its readers.

Use one or two sentences to highlight qualifications.

I am a freelance business writer who has published two books on start-up businesses, and for eight years I've covered the consumer products industry for *Advertising Age* and other national business publications. In this work, I've encountered numerous start-up companies that have launched novel products only to face potentially fatal competition.

Be polite.

Thanks for your time and consideration. I look forward to hearing from you.

Be positive without being pushy.

Sincerely,

Signature

Jack Neff

Detail enclosures. (If space is tight, mentioning enclosures in the body of the letter is OK.)

Encl.: Reply postcard
Clippings

ARTICLE QUERY LETTER #2: NONFICTION

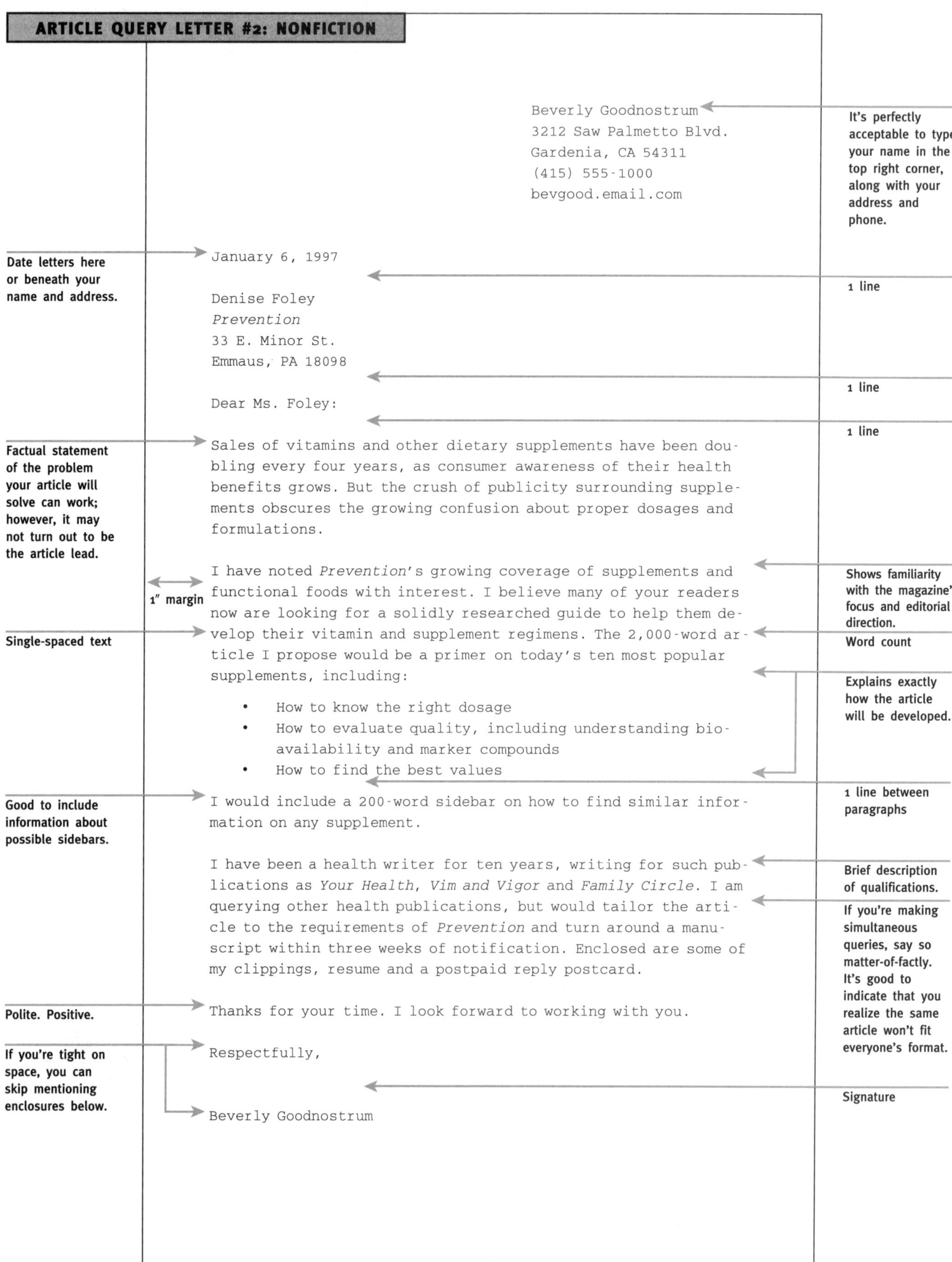

Beverly Goodnostrum
3212 Saw Palmetto Blvd.
Gardenia, CA 54311
(415) 555-1000
bevgood.email.com

January 6, 1997

Denise Foley
Prevention
33 E. Minor St.
Emmaus, PA 18098

Dear Ms. Foley:

Sales of vitamins and other dietary supplements have been doubling every four years, as consumer awareness of their health benefits grows. But the crush of publicity surrounding supplements obscures the growing confusion about proper dosages and formulations.

I have noted *Prevention*'s growing coverage of supplements and functional foods with interest. I believe many of your readers now are looking for a solidly researched guide to help them develop their vitamin and supplement regimens. The 2,000-word article I propose would be a primer on today's ten most popular supplements, including:

- How to know the right dosage
- How to evaluate quality, including understanding bioavailability and marker compounds
- How to find the best values

I would include a 200-word sidebar on how to find similar information on any supplement.

I have been a health writer for ten years, writing for such publications as *Your Health*, *Vim and Vigor* and *Family Circle*. I am querying other health publications, but would tailor the article to the requirements of *Prevention* and turn around a manuscript within three weeks of notification. Enclosed are some of my clippings, resume and a postpaid reply postcard.

Thanks for your time. I look forward to working with you.

Respectfully,

Beverly Goodnostrum

It's perfectly acceptable to type your name in the top right corner, along with your address and phone.
Date letters here or beneath your name and address.
1 line
1 line
1 line
Factual statement of the problem your article will solve can work; however, it may not turn out to be the article lead.
1" margin
Shows familiarity with the magazine's focus and editorial direction.
Single-spaced text
Word count
Explains exactly how the article will be developed.
1 line between paragraphs
Good to include information about possible sidebars.
Brief description of qualifications.
If you're making simultaneous queries, say so matter-of-factly. It's good to indicate that you realize the same article won't fit everyone's format.
Polite. Positive.
If you're tight on space, you can skip mentioning enclosures below.
Signature

ARTICLE QUERY LETTER: NONFICTION COLUMN

Jack Neff
555 W. Fourth St.
Cincinnati, OH 45200
(513) 732-9000
Fax: (513) 555-9091

March 2, 2000

1 line

Mr. Peter Stephano
Better Homes and Gardens Wood
P.O. Box 1212
Des Moines, IA 55155-1212

1 line

Dear Mr. Stephano:

1 line

If editor is already familiar with you, certainly note that.

An opportunity to make a call that isn't so cold.

As you may remember from our interview last month, I am the author of the book *Make Your Woodworking Pay for Itself*. You mentioned that you might be interested in a column on ''The Business Side of Woodworking,'' so I'm writing to offer possible topics. Here are three ideas I have for initial columns:

1" margin

1 line between paragraphs

Brief descriptions of several column ideas show you can deliver more than once.

1) Getting free publicity for your work and your business. This would cover the basics of getting free media attention, which actually can be more effective than advertising. I would cover such basics as crafting press releases, developing relationships with local media, and taking advantage of any promotional opportunities.

2) Selling direct to consumers. This column would examine the fine points both of making a sale (obviously more of an issue with higher-ticket items) and dealing with the public (e.g., difficult and demanding customers). I would draw heavily on experience from woodworkers who are very good at this, including one with a storefront business, one who makes a living selling very high-ticket wood carvings to business executives, and a cabinetmaker who does a lot of custom work.

Single-spaced text

3) Taxes for woodworkers. If you have a woodworking business, particularly if you're a hobbyist/woodworker, many complex tax issues arise. I'd highlight some of the key ones, such as the hobby/business distinction and deducting expenses for home workshops.

Thanks again for your interest. I look forward to hearing from you.

Respectfully,

Signature

Jack Neff

Encl.: SASE

QUERY LETTER MISTAKES TO AVOID

Joseph Getajob
555 Goingnowhere Lane
Misadventure, IA 60116

No phone number.

August 12, 1999

Colombia Journalism Review
1235 W. Fifty-fifth St.
New York, NY 10022

Misspelling the magazine's name is a killer.

To whom it may concern:

Shows he didn't even do the basic research to find an editor's name.

I am a formerly unemployed journalist interested in writing an expose about one of the least credible news organizations in America—my former employer. This would also be an inspirational tale about my comeback as a successful writer of action-adventure novels.

Raises red flags of ax-grinding, potential libel suit.

No indication of how he would hook readers.

I would also provide anecdotes about how other journalists have overcome similar bad experiences and gone on to bounce back in other jobs or occupations.

Don't promise anecdotes or research you don't have. If you have them, briefly describe them.

Enclosed, please find a self-addressed stamped envelope for your writer's guidelines and $4 for a sample copy.

Never ask for the guidelines or sample copy in a query. One more sign of no research.

Please reply within fourteen days, or I will need to look elsewhere. I look forward to your reaction.

Probably not.

Don't adopt an attitude.

Sincerely,

Joseph Getajob

Electronic Queries

Submission Tips

The digital age has brought an air of informality to communications between editors and writers. Keep in mind, however, that the computer did not redefine manners. Communications with a new editor should still be formal and respectful whether you make contact by mail, fax or E-mail. Once you've developed a relationship, you can afford to become less formal. Because the editor is familiar with your writing experience and ability to develop an article, you might pitch story ideas over the phone or in one- or two-sentence E-mails. But rarely will an editor make a judgment based on casual contact with a new writer.

Thus, the basic format and tone of an electronic query shouldn't be much different than for a query on paper, but certain features of E-mail do dictate different strategies.

Formatting Specs

- Include the same information you would in a paper query, including your name, address, phone and fax, etc. The top right-hand corner or top center position is fine for this, in keeping with the paper tradition, though you can also include this information in a signature line at the end. It isn't necessary to include your E-mail address in the body of the E-mail, however, since the editor can reply with the click of a button and your E-mail address will be preserved along with the E-mail if he saves it for later response.
- Fill in the subject line of the E-mail with a description of your query. This gives you an extra selling line and can be a good place for the proposed title of your work.
- Follow the same format you would with a paper query, including the date, salutation and block paragraph format. Leaving out these formalities isn't unusual, but there's no good reason to do away with them just because it's an E-mail. The information could be useful to the editor, and it never hurts to be polite.

How to Include Clips With E-Mailed Queries

When you send an E-mail query, you can provide clips five ways. There are no generally accepted standards yet for which is best, but the pros and cons of each method are described below:

1. **Include a line telling the editor that clips are available on request.** Then, mail, fax or E-mail clips according to the editor's preference. This is a convenient solution for the writer, but not necessarily for the editor. The clips aren't available immediately, so you potentially slow the decision process by adding an additional step, and you lose any speed you've gained by E-mailing the query in the first place.

2. **Include electronic versions of the clips in the body of the E-mail message.** This can make for an awfully long E-mail, and it doesn't look as presentable as other alternatives, but it may be better than making the editor wait to download attachments or log on to a Web site.

3. **Include electronic versions of the articles as attachments.** The disadvantage here is the editor has to download the clips, which can take several minutes. Also, if there's a format disparity, the editor may not be able to read the attachment. The safest bet is to

attach the documents as ".rtf" or ".txt" files, which should be readable with any word processing software, although you will lose formatting.

4. **Send the clips as a separate E-mail message.** This cuts the download time and eliminates software-related glitches, but it clutters the editor's E-mail queue.

5. **Set up a personal Web page and include your clips as hypertext links in or at the end of the E-mail** (e.g., http://www.aolmembers.com/jackneff/smallbusinessclips). Setting up and maintaining the page takes a considerable amount of effort, but it may be the most convenient and reliable way for editors to access your clips electronically. Most Internet access providers provide personal Web page services, but you'll have to learn how to set up your own page. Don't bother with high-graphic bells and whistles. Editors who click on your clips don't want to wait for the graphics to download.

Most editors will accept your original, unedited manuscripts (unless you want to retype articles that have appeared in print). These provide a much more accurate reading of what the editor can expect. Simply indicate the publication and issue date where they appeared.

When your clips are available on-line, you may be able to include a link directly to a clip at a publication's Web site or Web edition. Only do this, however, if you can provide a URL that will take the editor directly to your work. It's unreasonable to expect an editor to click and browse to find your clip.

Other Dos and Don'ts

- Don't use all caps or exclamation points in the subject line. These are among the dreaded earmarks of spam and will cause some editors to summarily delete your E-mail.
- Don't submit an E-mail query unless you know it's welcome. Listings in *Writer's Market* or *Writer's Digest* will indicate whether electronic queries are accepted. If you can't find a listing, call the publication to check.
- Don't send an E-mail query to the editor's personal E-mail address unless expressly directed to do so. Many publications maintain separate E-mail addresses for queries.
- Don't insert clip-art graphics or other images.
- Do attach or provide links to photos or graphics when you already have digital versions stored on your computer and their availability will help sell your article. They may take a long time to download, but the editor only needs to do it if she's interested.
- Do indicate how you'll make your clips and other supporting material available.

If you were wondering about the future of communications with editors, consider this: Americans sent seven times as many pieces of E-mail than regular first-class mail in 1998, according to Internet research firm eMarketer Inc. The company estimated 766.5 billion pieces of E-mail were sent during the year, compared to 107 billion first-class items. eMarketer's estimate did not include commercial E-messages, whose volume it estimates at 7.3 billion daily.

E-MAIL QUERY

TO: editor@fastcompany.com CC:

SUBJECT: Brain wedgies for bug spray marketers

Jack Neff
555 W. Fourth St.
Cincinnati, OH 45200
(513) 555-9000
Fax: (513) 555-9001
writer@email.com

March 17, 1998

Bill Breen
Senior Editor
Fast Company
77 N. Washington St.
Boston, MA 02114-1927

Dear Mr. Breen:

Despite toiling in such unglamorous businesses as bug spray and toilet bowl cleaners, S.C. Johnson & Son has had three of the top-ten new product concepts in the past two years, as rated by AcuPOLL, a Cincinnati market research firm.

How do they create fresh ideas for very old product categories? ''Brain wedgies.'' That's what Marc Marsan, president of Sawtooth Invention Company, calls tactics he uses to shock corporate clients out of creative complacency. Sample brain wedgies include having male executives walk around wearing sanitary napkins or masked marketing executives describe how they use toilet paper. Marsan also mixes into his sessions thinkers from other fields, such as former football coach Sam Wyche, inventor of the no-huddle offense.

I've been invited to go through one of Marsan's product development sessions with S.C. Johnson—on the ground rules that I can't discuss specific product ideas before they go to market. Still, I believe the story of a seemingly staid company using shock tactics to spark creativity would fit with *Fast Company*'s focus on how smart companies work.

I'm a Cincinnati-based freelance business writer who covers consumer goods for *Advertising Age* and other business publications. I know it's pushy to get demanding in a story pitch, but, because of the imminent approach of the session and S.C. Johnson's natural suspicion about reporters without firm assignments, I would like to hear from you by March 20. I can provide clips by E-mail or fax if you're interested.

Thanks for your time. I look forward to hearing from you soon.

Best wishes,

Jack Neff

Annotations:

You can use this space for your working title. (→ SUBJECT line)

1 line (after subject)

1 line (after date)

This fits on one printed page, too. Don't abuse the formlessness of E-mail to become verbose.

1 line (before salutation)

1 line (after salutation)

An attempt to hook a magazine that focuses largely on high-tech companies with a story about a low-tech one.

1 line between paragraphs

Describe your special circumstances.

Always address qualifications.

Provides justification for a quick response.

In this case, if they don't like the concept, the clips aren't necessary.

You can save an electronic version of your signature in E-mail programs, but it's not vital.

Fax Queries

Why Not to Fax Queries

It's relatively quick and easy to slip a query on the fax—but this is the least reliable and potentially most annoying way to pitch your article. Even if the publication accepts faxed queries, you'd be advised to try a letter or E-mail instead.

What's wrong with faxed queries?

- Faxes tend to get lost or misrouted within organizations more frequently than letters or E-mails.
- The fax machine is an extremely unreliable technology. At times faxes get jammed, shredded and stretched to the point of illegibility. They can easily fall prey to fax paper jams, get stuck in a fax machine's computer memory, or just thrown out along with scads of other unsolicited offers that clog the fax pile. Even when your fax machine or software indicates a fax has gone through, sometimes it hasn't.
- You'll frequently end up faxing your query to the wrong fax machine in an organization, increasing the likelihood that it won't even get to the editor's desk.
- If the editor's fax uses thermal paper, your query will end up on a curly, poorly reproduced sheet that may fade before the editor has had a chance to consider it.
- Reproduction quality of faxes can be very poor, making them hard to read.
- You can't enclose a self-addressed stamped envelope or postcard with a fax or provide the convenience of a quick E-mail response. Unless you include a toll-free number for response, you're making the customer bear the time and financial burden of response. Thus, editors are much less likely to respond.
- It's harder to attach clips with a fax than to either a mail or E-mail query. Once you've pushed all those clips through a fax machine, you've consumed a lot of your time and your editor's fax paper. People seldom appreciate twenty-page unsolicited faxes.

Before E-mail became widespread, faxed queries often made sense for time-sensitive topics. These days, however, editors mostly expect you to have E-mail if you're pressed for time.

That said, you may still find times when a faxed query is appropriate—such as when a topic is time sensitive and either you or the editor doesn't have access to E-mail. But such situations become rarer all the time.

Formatting Tips

In those rare cases when a faxed query is called for, here are some tips for making them work as well as possible.

- Keep the format the same as a letter query, unless you're also faxing clips. If you're just faxing the letter, you don't need a cover sheet announcing the letter is coming.
- If you do fax a clip, fax only one, preferably of no more than three pages. Less is better.
- If you fax a clip, use a cover page to indicate the total page count of the transmission. Avoid Post-it-style fax notes that clutter the page.
- Try a sans serif font, which should make it easier to read on the other end.

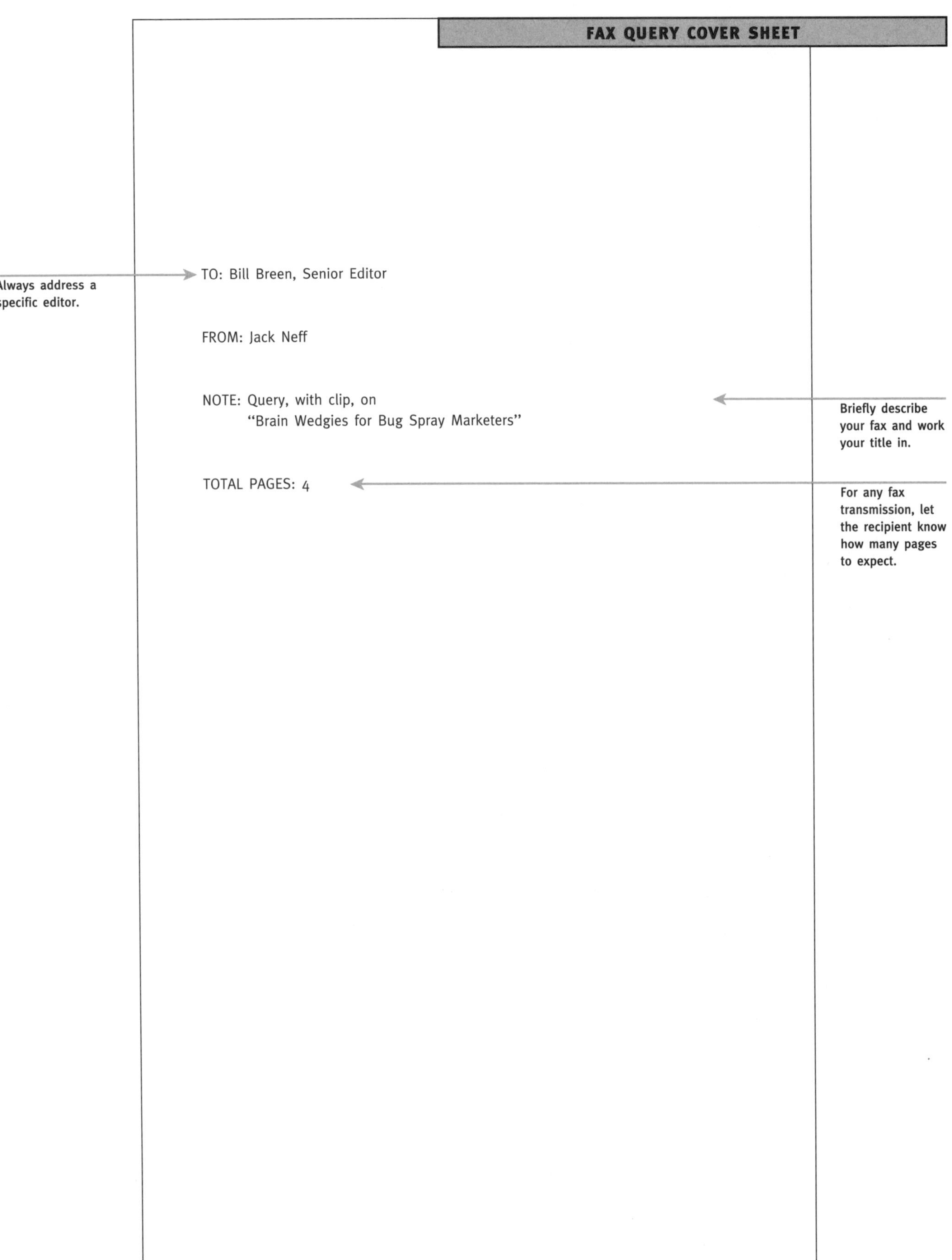
FAX QUERY COVER SHEET

TO: Bill Breen, Senior Editor

FROM: Jack Neff

NOTE: Query, with clip, on
"Brain Wedgies for Bug Spray Marketers"

TOTAL PAGES: 4

Always address a specific editor.
Briefly describe your fax and work your title in.
For any fax transmission, let the recipient know how many pages to expect.

FAX QUERY

Jack Neff
555 W. Fourth St.
Cincinnati, OH 45200
(513) 732-9000
Fax: (513) 555-9001
writer@email.com

March 17, 2000

1 line

Bill Breen
Senior Editor
Fast Company
77 N. Washington St.
Boston, MA 02114-1927

1 line

Dear Mr. Breen:

1 line

Despite toiling in such unglamorous businesses as bug spray and toilet bowl cleaners, S.C. Johnson & Son has had three of the top-ten new product concepts in the past two years, as rated by AcuPOLL, a Cincinnati market research firm.

Sans serif font may work better on a fax.

How do they create fresh ideas for very old product categories? "Brain wedgies." That's what Marc Marsan, president of Sawtooth Invention Company, calls tactics he uses to shock corporate clients out of creative complacency. Sample brain wedgies include having male executives walk around wearing sanitary napkins or masked marketing executives describe how they use toilet paper. Marsan also mixes into his sessions thinkers from other fields, such as former football coach Sam Wyche, inventor of the no-huddle offense.

1″ margin

1 line between paragraphs

I've been invited to go through one of Marsan's product development sessions with S.C. Johnson—on the ground rules that I can't discuss specific product ideas before they go to market. Still, I believe the story of a seemingly staid company using shock tactics to spark creativity would fit with *Fast Company*'s focus on how smart companies work.

Single-spaced text

I'm a Cincinnati-based freelance business writer who covers consumer goods for *Advertising Age* and other business publications. I know it's pushy to get demanding in a story pitch, but, because of the imminent approach of the session and S.C. Johnson's natural suspicion about reporters without firm assignments, I would like to hear from you by March 20.

If you fax a query, by all means explain why your article is so time sensitive that you can't wait.

Thanks for your time. I look forward to hearing from you soon.

Best wishes,

Signature

Jack Neff

Follow-Up and Update Letters

Occasionally lines get crossed, mail gets lost and plans change. Sometimes, editors are just plain rude. For whatever reason, your postcard or SASE is never returned, the article you submit never appears, or you don't get paid. You may need to follow up on an article submission. Here are some polite, gentle ways to go about it.

Submission Tips

When you haven't heard back from a publication within a reasonable time, such as sixty days or the reporting period cited in *Writer's Market*, send a brief, businesslike inquiry.

Formatting Specs

- As with queries, address it to the correct editor and use proper greetings and salutations.
- Enclose a reply postcard or SASE, in case your original was lost.

Other Dos and Don'ts

- Do be businesslike and polite.
- Do briefly explain the history behind your request (e.g., "I sent you a query with a prepaid reply postcard on . . .).
- Don't be emotional or accusatory or jump to conclusions about what happened.

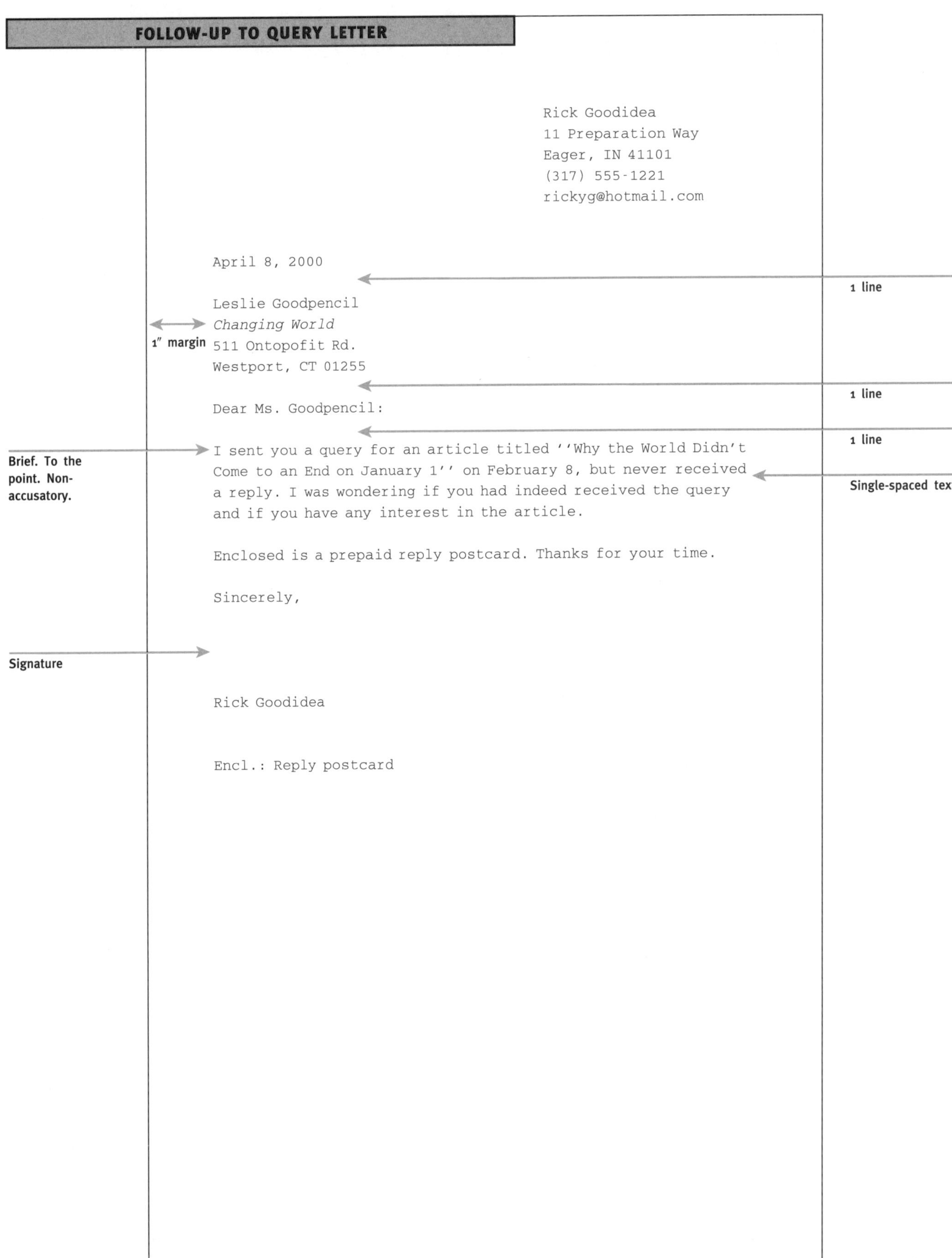
FOLLOW-UP TO QUERY LETTER

Rick Goodidea
11 Preparation Way
Eager, IN 41101
(317) 555-1221
rickyg@hotmail.com

April 8, 2000

Leslie Goodpencil
Changing World
511 Ontopofit Rd.
Westport, CT 01255

Dear Ms. Goodpencil:

I sent you a query for an article titled ''Why the World Didn't Come to an End on January 1'' on February 8, but never received a reply. I was wondering if you had indeed received the query and if you have any interest in the article.

Enclosed is a prepaid reply postcard. Thanks for your time.

Sincerely,

Rick Goodidea

Encl.: Reply postcard

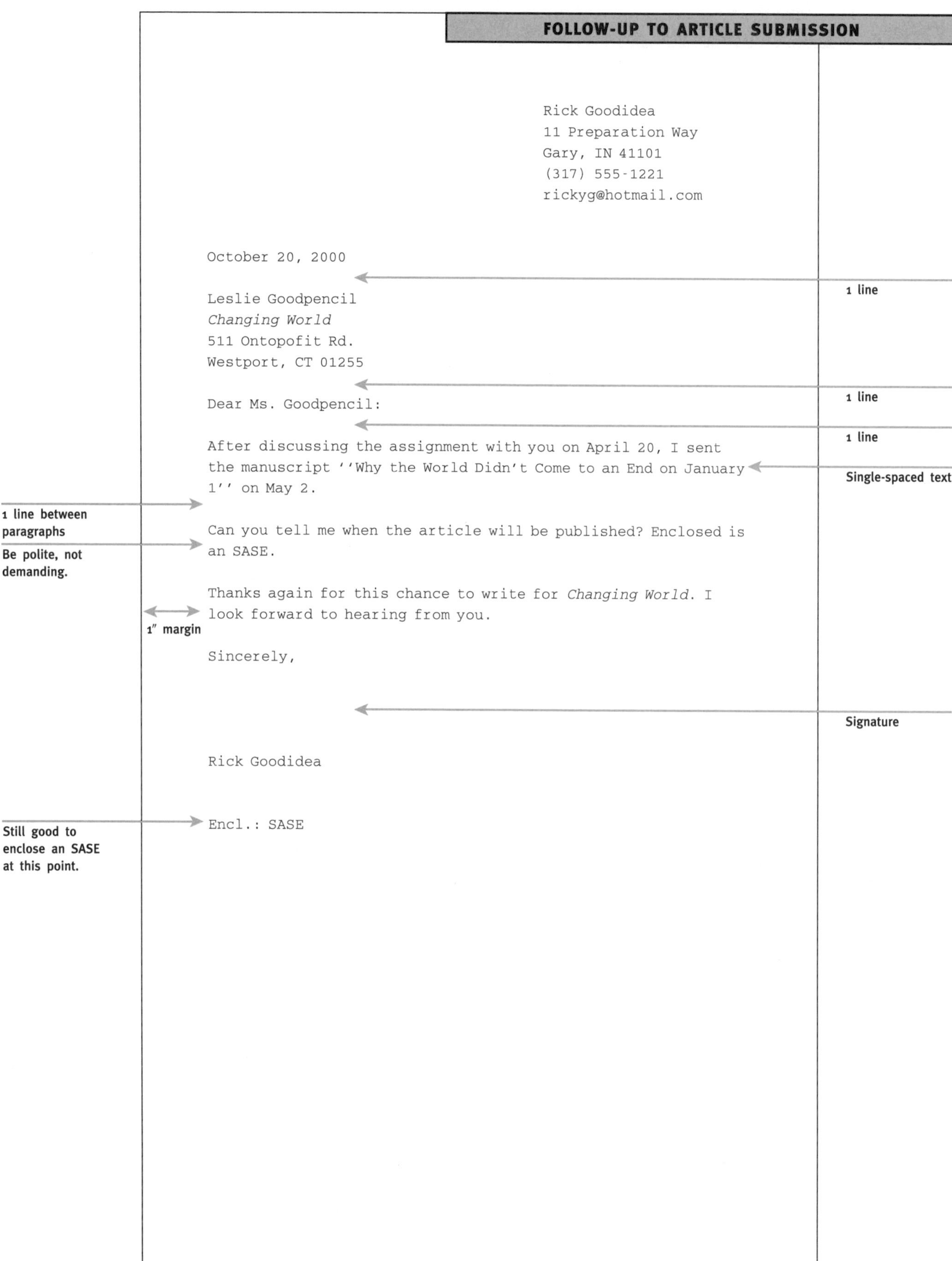
FOLLOW-UP TO ARTICLE SUBMISSION

Rick Goodidea
11 Preparation Way
Gary, IN 41101
(317) 555-1221
rickyg@hotmail.com

October 20, 2000

Leslie Goodpencil
Changing World
511 Ontopofit Rd.
Westport, CT 01255

Dear Ms. Goodpencil:

After discussing the assignment with you on April 20, I sent the manuscript ''Why the World Didn't Come to an End on January 1'' on May 2.

Can you tell me when the article will be published? Enclosed is an SASE.

Thanks again for this chance to write for *Changing World*. I look forward to hearing from you.

Sincerely,

Rick Goodidea

Encl.: SASE

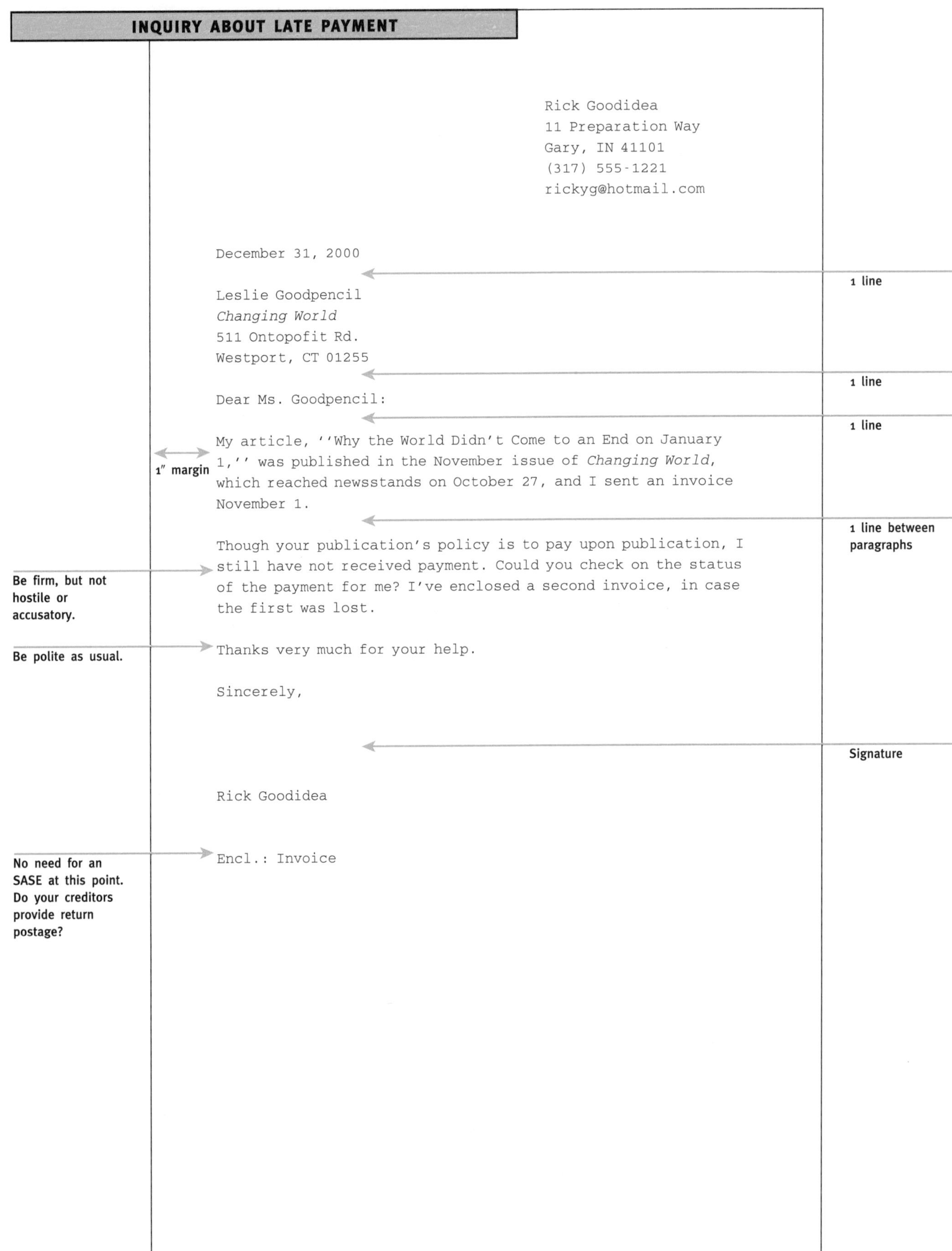

INQUIRY ABOUT LATE PAYMENT

Rick Goodidea
11 Preparation Way
Gary, IN 41101
(317) 555-1221
rickyg@hotmail.com

December 31, 2000

Leslie Goodpencil
Changing World
511 Ontopofit Rd.
Westport, CT 01255

Dear Ms. Goodpencil:

My article, ''Why the World Didn't Come to an End on January 1,'' was published in the November issue of *Changing World*, which reached newsstands on October 27, and I sent an invoice November 1.

Though your publication's policy is to pay upon publication, I still have not received payment. Could you check on the status of the payment for me? I've enclosed a second invoice, in case the first was lost.

Thanks very much for your help.

Sincerely,

Rick Goodidea

Encl.: Invoice

1 line
1 line
1 line
1" margin
1 line between paragraphs
Be firm, but not hostile or accusatory.
Be polite as usual.
Signature
No need for an SASE at this point. Do your creditors provide return postage?

Letter Offering Reprint Rights

Submission Tips

Just send a brief letter describing the article and where it ran. Since the article is enclosed, don't give it a glowing send-off—it should sell itself. If you can provide any follow-up information on the article's impact or how it was received in its original market, however, that could help you sell reprint rights. Also offer any ideas you might have on how the article could be adapted to the publication's needs.

Formatting Specs

- Use similar format to follow-up and query letters.
- Keep it short. Two or three brief paragraphs will do.
- Enclose a reply postcard.

Request for Guidelines Letter

Submission Tips

Just send a brief letter stating that you want to receive the publication's writer's guidelines. Before you send the letter, use a search engine, such as www.yahoo.com, to find whether the publication has a Web site and whether writer's guidelines are included on the site.

Formatting Specs

- Address the letter to the correct editor. Check *Writer's Market* listings when available, or use the phone (you needn't ask for the editor—just get the name and address).
- Use block or semiblock format.
- Keep it simple. One paragraph will do.
- Include your name, address and phone number (including fax and E-mail where possible).
- Enclose an SASE.

Other Dos and Don'ts

- Don't try to pitch yourself or a story at this point. This may not even be read by an editor, and all you need are the guidelines, anyway.
- Don't use "Dear Sir," "To whom it may concern" or other indications that you don't know who the editor is.

LETTER OFFERING REPRINT RIGHTS

Jason Secondcycle
333 Rapid Run Rd.
Spin City, NY 14011
(914) 555-1400
Fax: (914) 555-1500
jason2@xt.net

September 20, 2000

1 line

Richard Smartbuyer
The Daily Planet
Planet, IA 51556

1 line

Dear Mr. Smartbuyer:

1 line

Single-spaced text

Enclosed is a copy of my article titled "The 10 Best Spelunking Destinations in America" as it appeared in the August issue of *Cavedweller* magazine.

1 line between paragraphs

Mention positive results in the initial publication when possible.

This article produced more positive mail than any other in the magazine's history. I believe it would also be of interest to readers of your Sunday travel section, few of whom subscribe to *Cavedweller*.

You still need to tell why the article would work for this publication.

1" margin

It doesn't hurt to offer ways to add value by reslanting/revising the article.

Please call or return the enclosed prepaid reply postcard if you're interested. Please also let me know if I can revise the article in any way to make it of more use to your readers.

Sincerely,

Signature

Jason Secondcycle

Encl.: Reply postcard

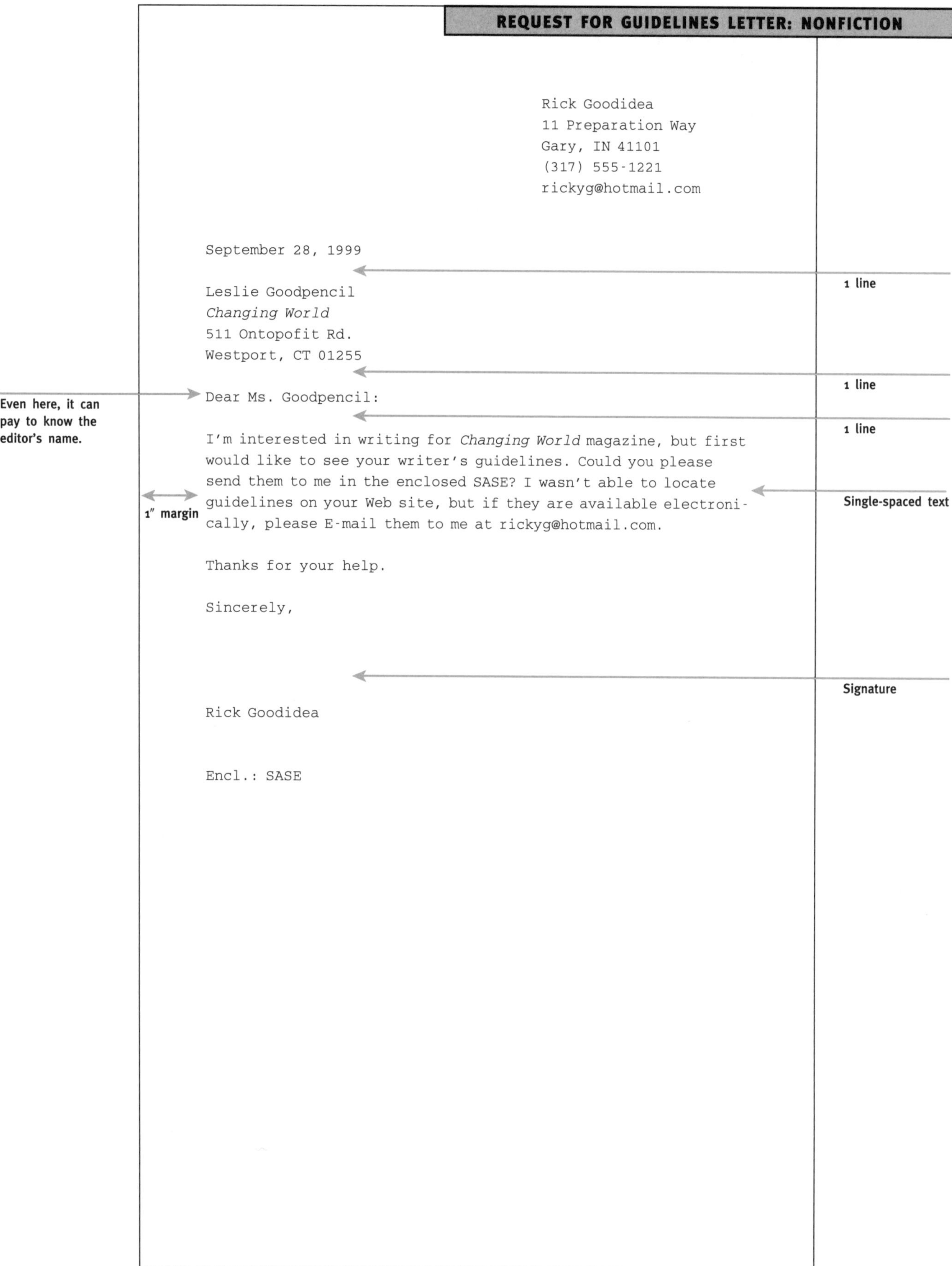

REQUEST FOR GUIDELINES LETTER: NONFICTION

Rick Goodidea
11 Preparation Way
Gary, IN 41101
(317) 555-1221
rickyg@hotmail.com

September 28, 1999

Leslie Goodpencil
Changing World
511 Ontopofit Rd.
Westport, CT 01255

Dear Ms. Goodpencil:

I'm interested in writing for *Changing World* magazine, but first would like to see your writer's guidelines. Could you please send them to me in the enclosed SASE? I wasn't able to locate guidelines on your Web site, but if they are available electronically, please E-mail them to me at rickyg@hotmail.com.

Thanks for your help.

Sincerely,

Rick Goodidea

Encl.: SASE

Reply Postcard

If you're a bit paranoid about whether your article actually makes it to the publication, you may send a reply postcard along. Having it signed by the editor (or someone on the staff) and sent back to you will alleviate any worries that the package didn't make it to its destination. Two caveats: 1) Not all editors are gracious enough to send your reply postcards back—but most do; 2) Just because you receive a postcard reply from a publication, you cannot assume your story has been read or will be read in the next few days or even weeks. Your reply postcard's only function is to let you know your submission has been received.

Your best bet to ensure an editor will return your reply postcard is to make it neat and simple to use. That means typing your postcard and not asking the editor to do anything other than note your submission has been received. Although it's okay to leave a small space for "Comments," keep the space very small and never expect it to be filled in—most editors simply don't have the time or a reason to write anything in it. You'll turn off an editor if you ask him to do too much.

Creating a suitable and functional reply postcard is easy. If you create a reply postcard similar to the one on the following page you'll be just fine. Above all, remember to keep things short and sweet—and, of course, always be sure the postcard has a stamp in the top right corner on the side with your address.

"Though it helps to express strong qualifications to write about a topic in a query, somebody who seems to know everything about a topic can be a problem, too," says Robin Dolch, senior editor of *ICON Thoughtstyle* magazine. "They may be the most expert person in the world. But if they come off as didactic that's a problem. The process of writing needs to be about inquiry."

REPLY POSTCARDS

Jack Neff
555 W. Fourth St.
Cincinnati, OH 45245

Front of card.

Your query was received on ____________________ .
We need more time to consider your query and will be in touch. ☐
Yes, we are interested in your idea. An editor will be in touch soon. ☐
No, we are not interested in your article at this time. ☐
Please send the following additional information (see below). ☐
Comments: ____________________

Back of card — submitted.

Date ____________________
Yes, your article was received on ____________________
We need more time to consider you query and will be in touch. ☐
No, we are not interested in your article at this time. ☐
Please send the following additional information (see below). ☐
Comments: ____________________

Back of card — follow-up.

I would like to reprint your article. Please call me. ☐
No, we are not interested in your article. ☐
Please send the following additional information (see below). ☐
Comments: ____________________

Back of card — letter offering reprint rights.

The Article

What You Need to Submit

Compared to the query letter that leads up to the article, formatting the article itself is relatively easy. The style and approach of each article is different, of course, and beyond the scope of this book. However, the layout of the printed page and the information is relatively clear-cut. All you need is:

- A cover letter
- Your article

This section will guide you through the cover letter and the article itself, including information on faxing articles and the differences between magazine and newspaper-style articles.

Cover Letter

Submission Tips

By the time you send the article, the editor should already know who you are and about the article. The cover letter accomplishes a few additional purposes:

- It provides details that may be important in the editing and fact-checking process, including names, addresses and phone numbers of sources.
- It informs the editor of the status of photographs and graphics that will accompany the article (whether they're enclosed or coming from another party).
- It provides information about how you can be reached for questions.

Formatting Specs

- Use a standard font or typeface (avoid bold, script or italics, except for publication titles).
- Put your name, address and phone number (include E-mail and fax) on the top right-hand corner or in your letterhead.
- Use 1″ margins on all sides.
- Address it to a specific editor (call and get the appropriate editor's name, and make sure you know the gender).
- Use block letter format (no indentations, extra space between paragraphs).
- If you need more than a page, use it. The editor will need this information in handling your manuscript.
- Provide a word count.
- Provide contact names of sources if needed.
- Mention any details the editor should know in editing the manuscript, such as difficulty in reaching a particular source or conflicting data you received and how you resolved the conflict.
- Tell about the status of photography or other artwork when appropriate.
- Thank the editor for the assignment and express your interest in writing for the publication again.

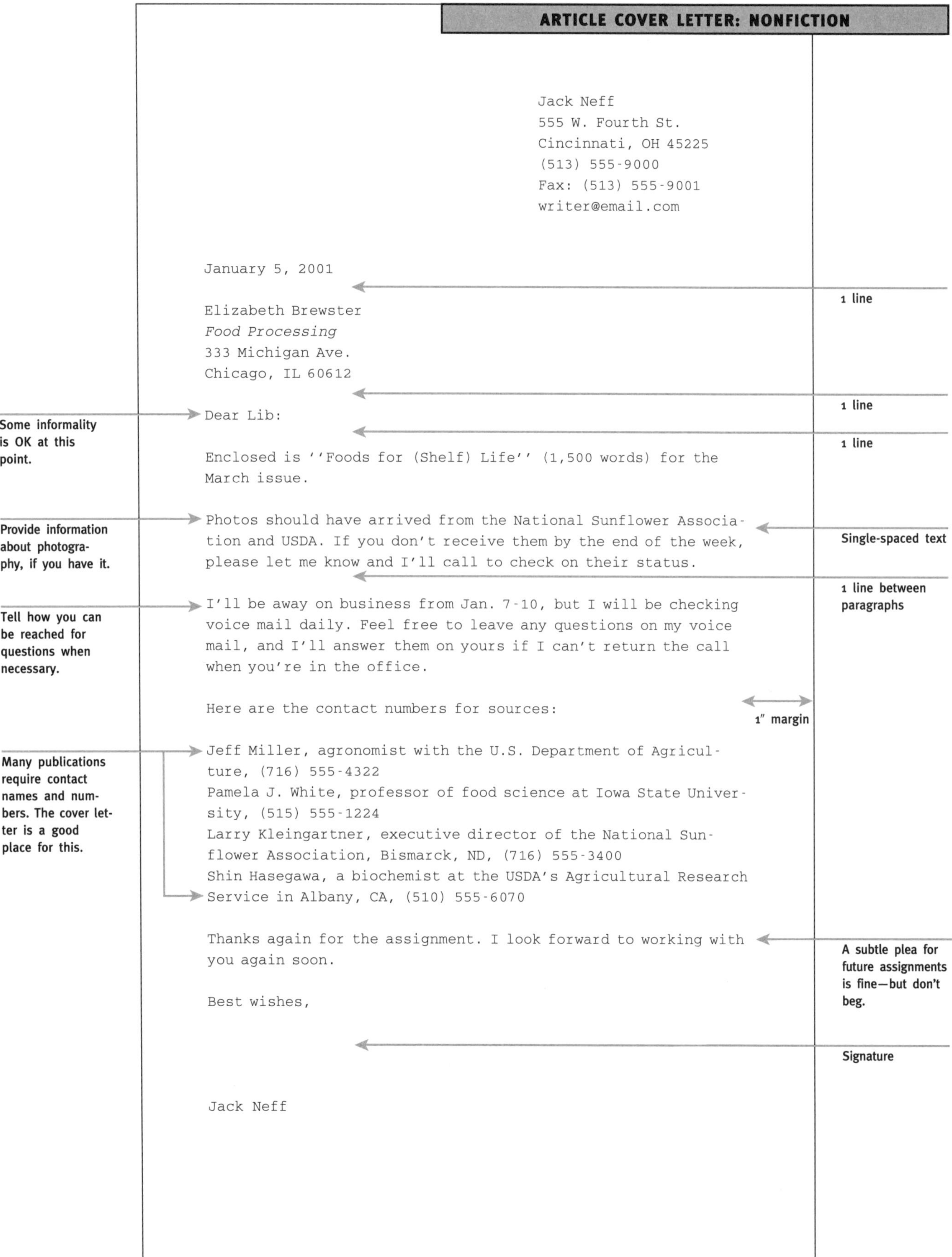

ARTICLE COVER LETTER: NONFICTION

Jack Neff
555 W. Fourth St.
Cincinnati, OH 45225
(513) 555-9000
Fax: (513) 555-9001
writer@email.com

January 5, 2001

Elizabeth Brewster
Food Processing
333 Michigan Ave.
Chicago, IL 60612

Dear Lib:

Enclosed is ''Foods for (Shelf) Life'' (1,500 words) for the March issue.

Photos should have arrived from the National Sunflower Association and USDA. If you don't receive them by the end of the week, please let me know and I'll call to check on their status.

I'll be away on business from Jan. 7-10, but I will be checking voice mail daily. Feel free to leave any questions on my voice mail, and I'll answer them on yours if I can't return the call when you're in the office.

Here are the contact numbers for sources:

Jeff Miller, agronomist with the U.S. Department of Agriculture, (716) 555-4322
Pamela J. White, professor of food science at Iowa State University, (515) 555-1224
Larry Kleingartner, executive director of the National Sunflower Association, Bismarck, ND, (716) 555-3400
Shin Hasegawa, a biochemist at the USDA's Agricultural Research Service in Albany, CA, (510) 555-6070

Thanks again for the assignment. I look forward to working with you again soon.

Best wishes,

Jack Neff

1 line
1 line
Some informality is OK at this point.
1 line
Provide information about photography, if you have it.
Single-spaced text
1 line between paragraphs
Tell how you can be reached for questions when necessary.
1″ margin
Many publications require contact names and numbers. The cover letter is a good place for this.
A subtle plea for future assignments is fine—but don't beg.
Signature

Article Manuscript

Submission Tips

Show you're a professional by submitting a clean, grammatically correct and properly spelled manuscript that hews as closely as possible to the style of the publication.

Formatting Specs

- Use a 1″ margin on all sides.
- Don't number the first page.
- Include rights offered or negotiated and a word count in the top right corner of the first page.
- If you have one or more sidebars, indicate this in the top right corner of the first page, along with the word count for each sidebar.
- Include your name, address and phone number (include fax and E-mail, when applicable) in the top left corner of the first page.
- Put the working title in all caps or boldface and the subtitle underlined or in italic centered, about one-third of the way down the page from the top margin.
- Skip one line and write "by" in lowercase, then skip another line and put your name. (If using a pseudonym, put that name in all caps, and then on the next line put your real name in parentheses.)
- Drop four lines, indent and begin the article.
- Double-space the entire text of the story.
- Put a slug, a one- to two-word name, at the top left corner of the header in the second and preceding pages.
- Put page numbers (2–the end of the article) in the top right-hand corner of the header.
- Keep type size 10–12 points.
- Optional: At the article's end, put a "–30–" or "–###–" notation. This is more of a relic in publishing than a necessity, but some writers feel insecure without it. It won't hurt to do it or leave it out.
- To submit articles by fax, use the same guidelines. Simply use the fax cover sheet to replace the mail cover sheet version. Consider using a sans serif font and 12-point type to make the manuscript more legible.

Other Dos and Don'ts

- Do use paper clips in the top left corner of your manuscript (butterfly clips or paper clamps for articles of more than ten pages).
- Don't use staples, since most editors prefer clips.
- Don't clip, and especially don't staple, your cover letter to the manuscript.
- Don't use a separate cover page. It's pretentious for an article-length manuscript and wholly unnecessary.
- Don't justify text or align the right margin. Ragged right is fine.
- Don't insult the editor's intelligence or intentions by putting a copyright notice on the manuscript. It's copyrighted as soon as you write it.
- Don't use unusual fonts. A simple Times Roman will do fine.
- Do include suggested subheads in the body of your manuscript if the magazine's

style is to use subheads; however, don't rely on subheads as a substitute for transitions. Subheads may need to be removed for layout/page composition purposes. Besides, they're an editor's prerogative. Don't count on them staying where you put them.

Winning Style Points

Virtually all newspapers and many magazines use some variation of Associated Press style. Other magazines and most books use *The Chicago Manual of Style.* Thus, two books that should be on the shelves of freelancers include *The Associated Press Stylebook and Libel Manual* and *The Chicago Manual of Style*, from The University of Chicago Press. The latter provides useful general guidance on grammar and usage issues in addition to strictly style points.

The most common style questions concern such areas as numbers, localities, abbreviations and capitalization. Style manuals also cover such fine points as the difference in usage between *lawyer* and *attorney.* It's a good idea to at least skim through the style manuals to become familiar with the usage issues they cover, in addition to using them as references when unsure about a style issue.

Most publications have style rules of their own that deviate from whichever standard they use. Freelancers can't realistically be expected to know all the rules before first being published in a magazine, but try to be familiar with the publication's basic style standards.

"I'm always a little nervous when queries come in and go into 'what I will talk about . . . ' or 'I'll go try and track down someone who will be the perfect lead.' We can always tell when people are going to be very hard to work with. It's when they're willing to do very little work up front before getting a contract . . . . No attitude please."

—Robin Dolch, senior editor, *ICON Thoughtstyle*

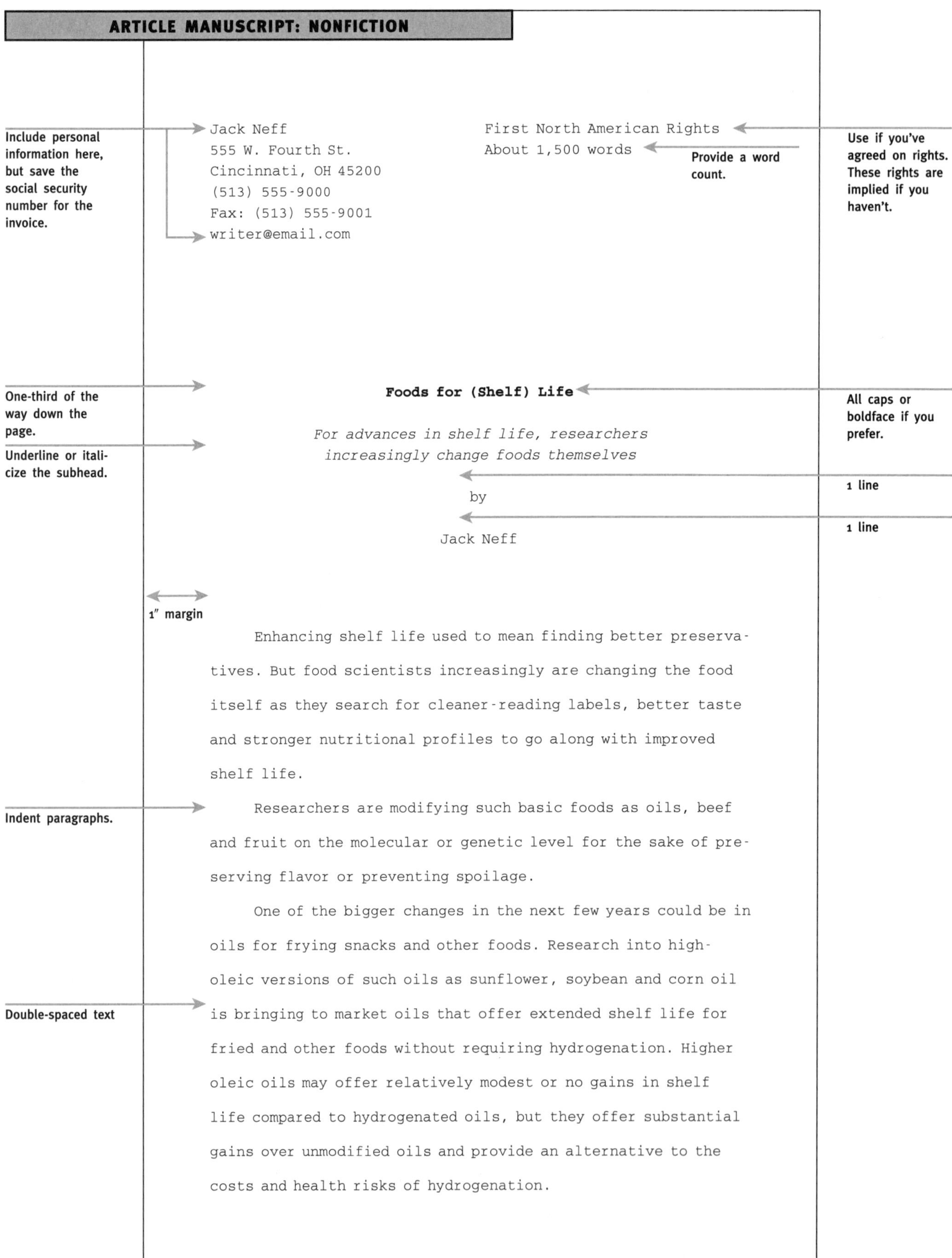
ARTICLE MANUSCRIPT: NONFICTION
Include personal information here, but save the social security number for the invoice.
Jack Neff
555 W. Fourth St.
Cincinnati, OH 45200
(513) 555-9000
Fax: (513) 555-9001
writer@email.com
First North American Rights
About 1,500 words
Provide a word count.
Use if you've agreed on rights. These rights are implied if you haven't.
One-third of the way down the page.
Foods for (Shelf) Life
All caps or boldface if you prefer.
Underline or italicize the subhead.
For advances in shelf life, researchers increasingly change foods themselves
1 line
by
1 line
Jack Neff
1" margin
Enhancing shelf life used to mean finding better preservatives. But food scientists increasingly are changing the food itself as they search for cleaner-reading labels, better taste and stronger nutritional profiles to go along with improved shelf life.
Indent paragraphs.
Researchers are modifying such basic foods as oils, beef and fruit on the molecular or genetic level for the sake of preserving flavor or preventing spoilage.
One of the bigger changes in the next few years could be in oils for frying snacks and other foods. Research into high-oleic versions of such oils as sunflower, soybean and corn oil is bringing to market oils that offer extended shelf life for fried and other foods without requiring hydrogenation. Higher oleic oils may offer relatively modest or no gains in shelf life compared to hydrogenated oils, but they offer substantial gains over unmodified oils and provide an alternative to the costs and health risks of hydrogenation.
Double-spaced text

ARTICLE MANUSCRIPT, INSIDE/END PAGE: NONFICTION

Slug at the top left.

Shelf Life 5

Page number

A side benefit of the enzyme may be prevention of tumor formation. Separate studies at Baylor University and the University of Western Ontario found the enzyme inhibited oral cancer tumors in hamsters and human breast cancer cells in mice.

It's OK to include subheads, but make sure your article will work without them here.

Vitamin E as Beef Preservative

Consumers also won't have to wait so long to see the benefits from the addition of megadoses of vitamin E to the diets of beef cattle.

Food processors have long used vitamin E as a natural preservative in some foods. In recent years, agricultural research in U.S. and England has found that adding vitamin E to the diets of both forage and grain-fed cattle one hundred days before slaughter can increase the shelf life of the beef.

In one study in Britain, among cattle given 1,500 international units of vitamin E a day, compared with a natural diet supplying 30-40 international units, shelf life was improved by two to three days. In the U.S., inclusion of vitamin E in animal feed is becoming increasingly standard practice, as supermarket buyers begin to specify it. Use of vitamin E cuts waste in the meat supply chain by thirty dollars per head of cattle at a cost of only two to three dollars per head, according to the USDA.

''By changing the cattle's diet, we can extend shelf life for retailers and potentially increase profit margins for growers and processors, too,'' says Richard Wilson, spokesman for the USDA Agricultural Research Service. ''You don't find many technologies so cheap and so effective.''

No need to mark the end. Especially avoid using "The End" in nonfiction articles. Use "—30—" or "—###—" if you must.

Sidebars

Submission Tips

For sidebars included with articles, start the sidebar on a new page immediately following the last page of the main bar. Don't include all the front page information you put at the beginning of the main bar. Simply use a header that says "Sidebar: (Same slug you used for the article)" in the top left corner and a word count in the top right corner.

Formatting Specs

- With the exception just noted, follow the same formatting specs used with the article manuscript.
- Don't number the first page of the sidebar, but do number subsequent pages, if any.
- Use the sidebar slug in the header of the second and following pages, along with a page number, in the same format as a regular article.

> **"If something looks so unprofessional that it seems to be hastily prepared, that might be a little bit of a red flag. But essentially I'm looking for content and writing ability and not a particular style a writer might have read in a style guide somewhere."**
>
> —Joni Praded, editor, *Animals*

ARTICLE MANUSCRIPT WITH SIDEBARS: NONFICTION

Jack Neff
555 W. Fourth St.
Cincinnati, OH 45200
(513) 555-9000
Fax: (513) 555-9001
writer@email.com

First North American Rights
About 1,500 words, plus side-bars of 225 and 150 words

Indicate the side-bars separately here as part of the package.

One-third of the way down the page.

Timid Steps Toward Brave 'Nute' World

Boldface

1 line

Major food players get feet wet but produce few patents so far

Italicized

1 line

by

1 line

Jack Neff

4 lines

Indent paragraphs

Nutraceuticals may have captured the interest and imagination of major food companies. But at least based on patent activity, they don't appear to have captured many research and development dollars yet.

A *Food Processing* review of patents granted in the 1990s shows that major food companies have received fewer than sixty patents for nutraceutical products. One company alone, Procter & Gamble Co., accounts for more than half of those. Even P&G, however, denies it has a ''nutraceutical'' business.

1" margin

That doesn't necessarily mean the food industry's R&D or patent activity in nutraceuticals is slack. But it does show that functional foods research has yet to produce the types of breakthroughs that can be easily patented. That could change quickly as interest in the area grows.

Double-spaced

ARTICLE SIDEBAR: NONFICTION

Sidebar slug on the first page.

Sidebar: Nutraceuticals About 225 words

Repeat the word count for the sidebar.

Patents From Major Food Companies

Here's how the major food companies rank by number of nutraceutical-related patents, and a roundup of products for which they hold patents.

1. Procter & Gamble Co. 37

1" margin

Psyllium and other cholesterol-lowering drinks and compounds, tea extracts, fortified drink mixes, enhanced bioavailability of nutrients and system for physiological feedback in administration of nutrients.

Double-spaced, just like manuscript text.

2. Kellogg Co. 7

Psyllium and other cholesterol-lowering foods, improved iron fortification.

3. Unilever NV 4

Probiotic for treating irritable bowel syndrome, antioxidant tea extracts.

4. Quaker Oats Co. 2

Cholesterol lowering through beta-glucans.

5. Mars Co. 1

Antioxidant sports bar.

6. General Mills Inc. 1

Psyllium muffin mix.

7. Nabisco Foods Co. 1

High-oleic rice oil.

8. Suntory 1

Fermented tea products added to foods for prevention of tooth decay and gum disease.

ARTICLE SIDEBAR, PAGE 2: NONFICTION

Slug

Sidebar: Nutraceuticals 2

Paginate the sidebar separately, starting on the second page.

9. Campbell Soup Co. 1

Marketing research system for measuring effectiveness of diet programs.

10. PepsiCo 1

Hunger-suppressing food.

11. Wrigley Co. 1

Cavity- and gingivitis-fighting chewing gum.

Note: Counted as nutraceutical patents were foods manipulated to provide some kind of positive health benefit, or dietary supplements designed for addition to foods and enhanced to provide a health benefit. Not counted were foods or additives manipulated to decrease negative health effects, such as fat replacers.

Source: U.S. Patent and Trademark Office, Food Processing Research

Electronic Article Manuscripts

Submission Tips

Submitting articles electronically isn't so much about what you do as what you *don't* do. Don't sweat the details of an electronic manuscript format, because all the details will likely be worked out in-house at the publication.

For the most part, preparing an electronic manuscript is a matter of unformatting what you've already got.

Of course, the key consideration is whether the publication takes electronic submissions, and if they do, whether they want them on disk or via E-mail.

If the publication has a dial-in modem that allows you to send files directly to its computer system, you'll need to find out how to configure your communications software. This is relatively difficult. You'll have to understand how your communications software works, and talk with a systems manager on the other end to make the transaction work. Fortunately, most on-line article submissions these days are via E-mail, which is more user-friendly.

Formatting Specs

- Find out from the editor how she prefers to get files—in a particular word processing software format or as a generic file.
- The safest way to E-mail an article is as a text attachment. Saving the article as text strips out all the formatting and reduces the chances it will come out as gibberish on the other end.
- When in doubt, and when the editor doesn't specify, attach the article to the E-mail or save it to disk two ways: in your native word processing software format and as a text file.
- If the article isn't too large and the editor isn't using some kind of rare proprietary software, you also can include the article as part of the E-mail message, allowing the editor to cut and paste it. This is a bit awkward, but can work.
- Beyond these rules, formatting is mainly a matter of removing potential glitches from your copy. For instance, don't put two spaces after a sentence. Typesetters automatically handle the space, and your extra spaces may need to be removed by an editor.
- Likewise, don't double- or triple-space electronic files, as the spacing could also foul up production. An editor who wants a double-spaced printout to edit will probably request a manuscript on paper.
- For similar reasons, don't include headers, footers or page numbers on the electronic file. They can only cause problems in editing and production.
- Otherwise, include the name, address, rights and word count information at the top of the article, as you would with a paper manuscript.
- Your copyright remains intact, whether your manuscript is printed out or not.
- Generally, put all the information you would normally include in the cover letter into your E-mail and attach the article as an E-mail attachment.
- If you mail a disk, use the same kind of cover letter you would with a paper manuscript. Include a paper manuscript as well in the envelope, just as a point of reference if glitches appear in the electronic copy.

Filing Newspaper and Newsmagazine Submission Tips

Standards for filing stories to newspapers and weekly newsmagazines may vary somewhat from those for longer-cycle publications. Since these publications are so time sensitive and their staff so pressed for time, electronic submissions are the norm. Thus, the manuscript chosen for this section will be a story filed for a weekly business newsmagazine (other than some of the preceding "de-formatting" steps, format your regular magazine articles the same as paper transmissions).

Formatting Specs

- Put information you might normally include in a cover letter or E-mail body in a note on top of the file for newspaper or newsmagazine filings. This includes information about photos, unusual spellings and how you can be contacted with questions.
- Preferences vary widely among publications, but it's usually a good idea to note the editor who should see the file first when you're sending an article directly to a publication's editorial computer system. This can help avoid confusion.
- Some editorial systems, such as Atex, use "desks" in headers that help send articles to various departments of the publication and have special codes to tell the computer when articles begin and end. Make sure you follow the publication's coding guidelines precisely so the article goes to the right place.
- Generally, send only text files and make sure you've taken steps detailed earlier to remove formatting that could cause problems.

Other Dos and Don'ts

- Do call after you've sent a file to make sure it can be received. Electronic transfers are notoriously unreliable, and deadlines for news publications are tight.
- Do note at the top of the file where you can be reached if you're not going to be close to the phone, especially if your editor is working on a daily deadline.
- Don't use "–30–" or "–###–" to mark the end of your article. Only use the appropriate code here, if there is one.
- Do try to learn the style, especially with news publications. On tight deadlines, copyeditors get very testy about having to make style changes.
- Do include a suggested headline. It isn't necessary, and it probably won't fit, but it could be a starting point for the editor.

"I would say we reject about 50 percent of the queries we get for formatting or organization errors. Usually they reflect a lack of focus on our readers."

—Brenda Follmer, editor, *Wealth Building*

ELECTRONIC MANUSCRIPT SUBMISSION

TO: JUDY POLLACK
FROM: JACK NEFF, (513) 555-9000, Pager: (513) 555-2800

Credit information.

Use a note at the top of the file to convey key information.

Note: I gave our Wichita stringer a contributor mention. For art, a bottle of Physique should arrive via FedEx on your desk this morning. I'll be out of the office this afternoon, but you can page me at the number above and I'll get right back to you. Please leave any questions on my voice mail, so I can answer them on yours if you're not there when I call back. FYI, the line includes three kinds of conditioners, four shampoos, three gels and four hair sprays.

Art information.

How to get in touch.

Anticipate questions and confirm unusual spellings.

Suggested headline.

P&G hair line touts style over stiffness

There is no reason to center elements in an electronic submission. Write it as it will appear in an article.

by Jack Neff

Procter & Gamble Co. is launching a test of Physique, a fourteen-item premium-priced hair care line for men and women positioned as offering styling benefits without causing ''stiff, sticky hair.''

P&G is hoping consumers' wallets won't be sticky, as either product retails for $7-$8 each in their Wichita, Kan., and Little Rock, Ark., test markets.

A marketing campaign from Saatchi & Saatchi, New York, including TV, print, sampling and in-store and local event promotion, breaks this week.

Text is flush left.

Ads with the tag line: ''Physique for phenomenal style'' will feature models Mark Vanderloo and Esther Candace and focus on the brand's combination of ''science and style,'' a P&G spokeswoman said.

Single spaced

Physique's sleek, silver packaging features a prominent sigma symbol and ellipse shape as a play on the application of physics to hair styling—and particularly on breaking the law that styled hair has to be stiff and sticky.

''Our consumer research found style-conscious people don't want to settle for hair care products that leave their hair stiff or sticky,'' said Lisa Napolione, director of Physique product development.

Physique incorporates two points P&G has used to position its Pantene brand in the past year—a simultaneous appeal to men and women and flexible-hold technology. That leaves the question of how Physique will set itself apart from P&G's top hair care brand.

1 line between paragraphs

''The product lines are really going after two different consumer needs,'' the spokeswoman said. Physique is aimed at ''the styling-driven consumer'' while Pantene targets consumers who just want ''healthy, shiny hair.''

But she acknowledges Physique's effect on sales of P&G's other hair care lines—particularly Pantene and Vidal Sassoon—will be among factors monitored in test markets.

Though a major mass-market brand priced on par with salon-only brands may be unprecedented, salon-only marketers haven't had much success keeping their products off mass-market shelves, undermining that point of difference, says Tom Vierhile, president of Marketing Intelligence Ltd., a Naples, N.Y., new product research firm.

ELECTRONIC MANUSCRIPT SUBMISSION CONT'D.

Pantene's flexible-hold technology has had strong appeal to consumers, he said, but he doesn't see anything in the Physique packaging that differentiates the brand from dozens of others on the market.

''What they do with the advertising is really going to be key,'' Mr. Vierhile said.

The stakes for P&G are potentially huge. Hair care has been among P&G's fastest-growing global categories in recent years, but Salomon Smith Barney analyst Holly Becker characterizes the sector as ''strong but slowing'' in the U.S.

P&G's share of the $1.5 billion shampoo category slipped to 35.4% last year from 36.6% in 1996 and fell to 33.8% in the first quarter of 1998, according to Salomon Smith Barney.

P&G faces growing competition from Clairol, which, behind the performance of its Herbal Essences brand, has built its share from 4.1% in 1996 to 9.6% in the first quarter of 1998, and Unilever, with its recent $82 million launch of Thermasilk heat-activated shampoo.

In the $855 billion conditioner category, P&G's share slipped from 18.5% in 1996 to 16.6% in the first quarter of 1998.

For first-quarter numbers to be down is unusual, since P&G generally loads much of its promotional effort into the first quarter.

''P&G needs another Pantene,'' Ms. Becker said in a recent report, ''and one may be on the way.''

The outlook has never been better globally. Pantene, Pert Plus and Head & Shoulders have been among P&G's strongest international brands. Analysts and agency executives say P&G looks to Physique as the next global hair care brand.

Physique had been among key P&G new-business projects at Wells Rich Greene BDDP before the company fired the roster shop in January. Agency executives say two top staffers who worked on the project at Wells moved on to Saatchi, continuing their work there.

Responding to critics who said P&G had lost its edge, Chairman-CEO John Pepper has vowed to bring new brands and categories to market, and Physique is the latest example.

It's the third new brand P&G has launched into test in the past six months, following test launches of the Dryel home dry cleaning system and ThermaCare disposable heat pads.

In the same span, the company has rolled two brands from test to national distribution–its Olean fat replacer and Febreze fabric deodorizer.

P&G also is expected to relaunch the Eagle Snacks brand it purchased in 1996 from Anheuser-Busch into a test market soon.

Contributor lines for this publication. → Contributing: Judann Pollack, Laura Petrecca, Lauri O'Toole.

Submitting Photos and Graphics With Your Article

Submission Tips

When submitting photos, graphics and information graphic material for your article, it's important to give editors as much information as possible. Few things are as frustrating for an editor—or as common—as scrambling to find artwork or information about artwork at the last minute.

Formatting Specs for Photos and Graphic Submissions

- Provide suggested captions for photo(s) on a separate page at the end of your manuscript (or appended to the end of an electronic file).
- Captions should be brief, descriptive, action-oriented and in the present tense. Ultimately, caption writing is an editor's job, but she probably won't mind your help.
- Attach a form to the back of prints with key information (see Photo and Graphic Identification Form, p. 41).
- Use tape to attach the form to prints (never use staples).
- Use a code on the margin of slides, put the slides in an envelope and attach the envelope to the necessary form(s) with tape or staples.
- Put each transparency in its own coded envelope with the code corresponding to the information form.
- Blessed is the digital photograph and graphic, which does away with most of this paper shuffling. The digital photo can be E-mailed, attached to an E-mail that also includes your manuscript, and downloaded directly into the editorial graphic system by the techno-savvy graphics or design editor. If you take your own photographs or work with a photographer, use digital files whenever you can.
- If the photo needs to be returned, provide a pre-addressed, stamped mailer with sufficient strength and postage to get it through the mail intact. Preferably, allow the publication to keep prints when possible.
- If you have more than one photo or slide, use a coding system to keep captions and identifications straight.

> **"The worst thing (in a query) is when it's really clear (writers) haven't read the magazine—when they ask for guidelines as part of the query. We don't even have guidelines. If you read the magazine, it should be clear what kind of articles we want."**
>
> —Robin Dolch, senior editor, *ICON Thoughtstyle*

CAPTION LIST

Slug for the article.

Captions: Nutraceuticals

Use codes with more than one photo.

Photo A:

Researchers at Procter & Gamble Co.'s Sharon Woods laboratory display tea beverage.

Credit: Procter & Gamble Co.

Always include a credit, even when it's simply the company that provided the photo.

Photo B:

Double-spaced text

Bill Mayer, president and general manager of Kellogg Co.'s Functional Foods Division, discusses strategies for capitalizing on the company's recent Food and Drug Administration approval for health claims on psyllium-based cereals.

1″ margin

Credit: Andy Goodshot, Associate Press

Graphic

Kellogg Co. wasted no time getting its health claims into advertising copy, placing this ad in women's and health magazines within two weeks of FDA approval.

Reproduction of an ad also needs a caption for context.

PHOTO AND GRAPHIC IDENTIFICATION FORM

Date: ______________ Code: ______________
Slug: ______________
Subject (in artwork): ______________
____
Editor: ______________
Date article submitted: ______________
Credit: ______________

Direct questions to:
Jack Neff
555 W. Fourth St.
Cincinnati, OH 45200
(513) 555-9000
Fax: (513) 555-9001
E-mail: writer@email.com

Please return after use ☐
Keep this for your files ☐

Submitting Information Graphic Material With Your Article

Submission Tips

Providing information graphics isn't part of your job as a writer, but providing the information that goes into those graphics is. Since *USA Today* debuted in 1982, information graphics—with or without articles attached—have become a staple of journalism.

If you and your publication has the know-how, one of the best ways to submit information graphic material is in the form of a spreadsheet. A variety of word processing and graphics programs can create simple graphics using spreadsheet information.

If you're like most writers, and not familiar with any of the functions of Microsoft Word or Works that don't have to do with word processing, you can also submit your information in tabular form on a separate page appended to the end of your article (or attached at the end of the electronic text file).

Because of the hundreds of ways such information can be presented, you'll have to tackle each situation on a case-by-case basis. Here are a few simple formatting specs.

Formatting Specs

- Use a slug atop the printed page that links the graphic information to the article, i.e., "Graphic Information: Storyslug."
- Always include a line citing the source, even if it's only your own research (usually cited in the name of the publication, i.e., "Source: Yourpublication Research").
- Take special care to double-check the numbers and make sure the columnar material is properly matched. A relatively simple miscue can render an informational graphic useless, ludicrous or embarrassing.

INFORMATION GRAPHIC TEXT

Story slug

Graphic information: DTC-Direct

This could be used in a bar chart or a graph.

Table 1

New database and direct-response pharmaceutical drug marketing programs by year:

1995	108
1996	201
1997	258
1998	38 (through mid-February)

Source: John Cummings and Partners

Table 2

Top drug companies in database marketing:

1. Glaxo Wellcome
2. Merck
3. Pharmacia-Upjohn
4. Schering-Plough

Cite the source of the information.

Source: John Cummings and Partners

CHAPTER TWO

BOOKS

What You Need to Submit

Selling a nonfiction book can be an arduous process every bit as lengthy, if not quite as time-consuming, as actually writing the book. Writing a good proposal is not a project for the fainthearted. You can spend hours of time only to ultimately find your project rejected by agents or publishers who had encouraged your efforts. Indeed, despite the lure of the potential five-figure advance, writing a book is often less profitable, word for word and hour for hour, than writing articles. The time expended on the proposal is a major factor in the equation.

Make no mistake: Writing a book can be tremendously profitable from a financial or professional standpoint. But unless you are one of the lucky ones approached by a publisher with a presold idea, undertaking a book requires a leap of faith and considerable effort with no guarantee of a proportionate payback. So be forewarned.

Typically, to sell a nonfiction book, you will need to submit a query letter, a detailed proposal including an outline, and at least one sample chapter. This all must be complete and reviewed—usually over the course of several months, by agents, editors and business managers of the publisher—before the book writing begins in earnest.

For the writer, the proposal process should begin with some solid market research, which can prevent a considerable waste of time and energy. From the agent's or editor's point of view, however, the process starts with the query. That's where this chapter will begin.

> **"Spend as much time researching the market for your book as you would in preparing to sell any product. Remember that publishers are looking for authors who will become their business partners in selling books. Visit a bookstore and try to determine where your book fits into the marketplace. Include any marketing or promotional ideas you have for the work. Do you have viable tour ideas? Will there be special points of sale? Are there unusual marketing opportunities?"**
>
> —Seth Robinson, agent, DHS Literary Inc., Dallas

Query to Agent

Submission Tips

Most authors published by major commercial publishers are represented by agents. Establishing a relationship with an agent is often the first step toward selling your first book. Though you can present a proposal to an agent without a query, it makes more sense to query first. Inability to interest agents in your proposal is a strong sign that you need to rework or scrap your idea.

A query letter to an agent should:

- Make a convincing case for a compelling book concept
- Show why you are the person to write the book
- Outline the market potential for the book, including who the readers will be and what the competition is like.

Sum up your concept in a single paragraph if possible. It may seem impossible, but if you can't do it now, your agent won't be able to do it later. This may be the same hook used by an editor to convince the committee that ultimately decides on your book. Later, it will be used by the publisher's sales rep to get your book into stores. Ultimately, it will be used on the jacket to convince readers to buy it, generating the royalties that make this all a paying venture. So spend considerable time refining this concept.

Equally vital to your query is a brief description of the market for this book, why it's better than the competition, and, essentially, why it will fly off the shelves.

The final leg of the tripod in this query is why you are the perfect person to write this book.

Formatting Specs

- The basic setup for a query to agents is similar to an article query.
- Use a standard font or typeface.
- Use a 1″ margin.
- Single-space the body of the letter; double-space between paragraphs.
- Use letterhead or type your personal information in the top right corner.
- Be polite.
- Try to keep the query to one page, but it's acceptable to go as long as 1½ pages.
- As with an article query, it doesn't hurt to grab the reader's attention with a strong lead making the case for your book.

Other Dos and Don'ts

- Do use a real agent's name, and address that agent. Don't use "To whom it may concern" or other nondescript salutations of its ilk.
- Do the basic research to find out what kinds of books the agent handles.
- Do find out if the agent charges a reading fee. If this is a problem for you, don't bother to query.
- Do summarize any relevant experience you have, especially in publishing books. If you've published before, you're likely to already have an agent, so the query model assumes a first-time book author.
- Do keep your query brief. Agents don't necessarily hold you to the one-page

standard, since this is, after all, an entire book you're pitching. But don't go over two pages, and keep it to one if you can. As noted earlier, your pitch rides on three basic paragraphs.

- Do ask if the agent would like you to submit a full proposal, and indicate whether the proposal is ready now.
- Don't ask for proposal guidelines. Some agents offer these, but express the confidence that you can handle a proposal on your own. After all, you bought this book.
- Don't talk terms of the arrangement at this point. It's premature.

"I don't like to see lots of long overhyping documentation (in a proposal) about how large the market is. If somebody submits a book about swimming and I get twenty-five pages about how many people swim for exercise, I don't want to wade through that. I know that people swim for exercise. Unless it's a really startling, interesting fact that I never would have thought of before, it drives me nuts to have to go through all that. . . . I'm much more interested in what the book is—and is it a book of quality—and secondly if there's a market for it."

—Peter Burford, publisher, Burford Books

QUERY LETTER TO AGENT: NONFICTION BOOK

Roger McCallister
445 W. Fifth St.
Denver, CO 30311
(313) 555-1234
rogerme@aol.com

July 5, 2000

Sabrina Smith
Smith & Smith Literary Agency
222 Forty-ninth St.
New York, NY 10111

Dear Ms. Smith:

When was the last time you tried selling an idea? Probably it was the last time you had a conversation.

In today's economy, regardless of your career, selling ideas is what you really do. And you do it in more directions than ever. Companies sell to customers, but they also sell ideas to suppliers. Employees pitch ideas to their bosses, and vice versa. In the modern team-filled corporation, you may be selling your ideas simultaneously to a wide array of peers, bosses and subordinates. Until now, however, there was no definitive book on how to sell ideas.

That's about to change. I am preparing a book, *Selling Your Ideas: The Career Survival Strategy of the 21st Century*, to fill the void. Hundreds of highly successful books have addressed sales tactics for salespeople, and dozens of highly successful books address persuasion skills for everyone else. But, up to now, no one has addressed a book to cover the one sales job in which everyone in corporate America engages—selling ideas. Unlike other sales and persuasion books, *Selling Your Ideas* addresses everyone in business on a department-by-department, function-by-function basis. Because virtually anyone at any walk of corporate life will see pertinent reflected in this book, the appeal is considerably wider than any previous work of its kind.

Included will be dozens of real-life case studies drawn from my twenty years as a corporate executive, trainer, marketing consultant and columnist for management publications. I am also an adjunct professor in the business department of the University of Denver and a past president of and consultant for the Business Executives Council.

I would be interested in sharing my detailed proposal with you at your convenience.

Sincerely,

Roger McCallister

Encl.: SASE

1 line

Always address a specific agent.

1 line

1 line

The hook

1 line between paragraphs

Single-spaced text

1" margin

Differentiates this book from the competition.

Explains why he should write this book.

A polite offer.

Always include an SASE.

Query to Book Editor

Submission Tips

The goals and strategies for a query to a book editor are essentially the same as with an agent query. Both the agent and editor are looking for a marketable book.

The book editor may play a role in shepherding the book through production—or at least hear about it when there are problems—so he or she may place a somewhat higher priority on the author's writing ability and track record in completing projects. Agents certainly care whether their authors have writing ability, but they're willing to work with or help find ghostwriters for books that are clear winners.

It also pays to be familiar with the publishing house and its imprints and to know of recent titles published and how they've done. When possible, link your idea to a past success without portraying your book as a knockoff of the title you're citing. This not only helps the book editor understand why your book will succeed, but also helps the editor sell the idea internally. Publishers love nothing more than a proven formula for success, frequently shaping new acquisitions along the lines of successful past ones.

If you take this approach, do your homework. Misfiring by making an unsupported comparison or painting as a success a book that really wasn't can hurt you badly. If you're not sure of your facts, you're better to forgo this tactic.

The easiest and most effective way to do the kind of research you need is by using the search engine of an on-line bookseller, such as Amazon.com (www.amazon.com). Not only do the search engines allow you to search by topic and publisher, but they also, in the case of Amazon.com, tell you where the title ranks against all others in sales for that particular bookseller.

Of course, agents are the ones most likely to have the current information on publishing trends and to know the hot buttons of individual book editors, publishing houses and imprints. But, if you think you can handle it on your own, here goes.

Formatting Specs

- Basically, format your letter for a publishing house similar to that for an agent.
- Again, address your letter to a specific editor. Do the research in *Writer's Market* and/or call to find the appropriate editor for your query.
- Show you're familiar with the publisher, possibly by comparing your book with other successful titles from the imprint.
- As with the agent query, build your query on the tripod of a strong, succinct concept, market insight and convincing reason why you're the right person to write the book. Ultimately, "the hook" could be any of those three, or a combination, but you need all three to build your case.

Other Dos and Don'ts

- Do try to keep your letter to one page, but if you need another page to elaborate using some solid information, use a second page.
- Do avoid rambling and wordiness, regardless of length.
- Don't overreach. Build a case for your qualifications based on reality.
- Don't come off as pompous. Even if you do know everything about your topic, don't come off as a know-it-all.

QUERY LETTER TO BOOK EDITOR: NONFICTION

Roger McCallister
445 W. Fifth St.
Denver, CO 30311
(313) 555-1234
rogermc@aol.com

September 28, 2000

Alison Costello
AMACOM Books
500 Avenue of the Americas
New York, NY 10111

Dear Ms. Costello:

When was the last time you tried selling an idea? Probably it was the last time you had a conversation.

In today's economy, regardless of your career, selling ideas is what you really do. And you do it in more directions than ever. Companies sell to customers. Employees pitch ideas to their bosses, and vice versa. In the modern team-filled corporation, you may be selling your ideas simultaneously to a wide array of peers, bosses and subordinates. Until now, however, there was no definitive book on how to sell ideas.

That's about to change. I am preparing a book, *Selling Your Ideas: The Career Survival Strategy of the 21st Century*, to fill the void. No one has addressed a book to cover the one sales job in which everyone in corporate America engages—selling ideas. Unlike other sales and persuasion books, *Selling Your Ideas* addresses everyone in business on a department-by-department, function-by-function basis. Because virtually anyone at any walk of corporate life will see their situations reflected in this book, the appeal is considerably wider than any previous work of its kind.

Included will be dozens of real-life case studies drawn from my twenty years as a corporate executive, trainer, marketing consultant and columnist for management publications. I am also an adjunct professor in the business department of the University of Denver and a past president of and consultant for the Business Executives Council.

I believe *Selling Your Ideas* would build on the winning formulas of two successful AMACOM titles from recent years.

Like *The 2000 Percent Solution*, it will take an often humorous, case study-based approach to the challenging issues of making changes within organizations. But rather than approaching change from an organizational standpoint, *Selling Your Ideas* looks at the more approachable task of becoming a more effective individual agent for change.

Like *The Anatomy of Persuasion*, my book approaches persuasion as an important tool for everyone in business. But *Selling Your Ideas* goes beyond presentation tactics and communications issues to look at a broad range of strategies for selling ideas. I also will analyze strategies for persuading specific people in specific corporate functions, plus look extensively at strategies for selling ideas within corporate teams.

I would be interested in sharing my detailed proposal with you at your earliest convenience.

Sincerely,

Roger McCallister

Encl.: Reply postcard

Always address a specific editor.

1" margin

How his background will help him write *and* sell the book.

Upbeat and polite.

1 line

1 line

1 line

1 line between paragraphs

Single-spaced paragraphs

Shows familiarity with the publisher and the publisher's titles.

Signature

Book Proposals

What You Need to Submit

Like the article query, the book proposal is something of a genre in its own right. The differences are that it takes much more time and can vary considerably in length.

A fully thought-out book proposal should include the following:

- Cover letter
- Cover page
- Overview
- Marketing information or business case
- Competitive analysis
- Author information
- Chapter outline
- Sample chapter(s)
- Attachments that support your case.

Submission Tips

What agents and editors cite as most frequently lacking in book proposals is the marketing information. Authors often don't have a firm vision of who the readers of the book will be and how to reach them, or they don't know what the competition is and how to differentiate their books from existing titles.

Strange that the marketing information is so often missing, because it's really where any author should start. Before you ever set out on the time-consuming, painstaking journey toward a book proposal, you've got to know there's a market for your book. If you can't build a convincing business case for your book, go back to the drawing board.

That's why, even if the marketing and competition information doesn't come first in the proposal lineup, you should prepare these sections first. In fact, you should do your homework on these sections before you query an agent or book editor to submit a proposal.

What follows is a piece-by-piece look at the elements of the proposal.

A book proposal basically needs to include "a description of the book and a compelling reason the book needs to be written, and then the tie to the author. . . . What's most often missing is the author connection, the credential that makes the author the right person to write the book."

—Andrea Pedolsky, Altair Literary Agency, New York

Cover Letter

Submission Tips

Because so much information is included in the rest of the proposal, and because you should have already queried the agent or editor, the cover letter can be fairly brief. Don't use more than one page. This section will be written as if the proposal was being sent to an agent, but follow the same guidelines for submission to book editors.

If you are submitting an unsolicited proposal, the cover letter should incorporate elements of the query letters provided earlier in the chapter, as well as introduce the proposal. The cover letter for a solicited manuscript, which will be modeled on the facing page, simply serves to introduce a proposal and covers the following points:

- An introductory paragraph introducing the proposal.
- An outline of the information included in the proposal.
- A concluding paragraph politely seeking a response.

Formatting Specs

- Use a standard font or typeface for the body of the letter.
- Letterhead is fine, but not required. If you don't use letterhead, put your name, address, phone number, etc. in the top right corner.
- Use a 1″ margin on all sides.
- Address a specific editor.
- Keep it to one page.
- Use block or semiblock letter format.
- Include an SASE or postcard for reply only if the proposal is unsolicited.
- Single-space the body of the letter and double-space between paragraphs.

Other Dos and Don'ts

- Don't start your pitch all over again in the cover letter if you've already queried. Assume if your query made enough of an impression to spark interest that the agent or editor remembers the book idea and who you are.
- Don't ask for advice or criticism regarding your proposal. You'll get it either way, and asking can appear unprofessional. Many agents will offer advice or guidelines for proposals when they ask you to submit one.
- Don't mention copyright information. What you've put down here is indeed copyrighted, and you don't need to imply the agent or editor is out to steal your idea.
- Don't discuss payment or terms. It's still premature.
- Don't staple your cover letter to anything. A butterfly or clamp-style paper clip can hold the proposal elements together, and the cover letter will stand alone in front.
- Don't feel you must have a table of contents for your proposal. It won't hurt to have one, but it's really overkill in a document that's already quite long enough.

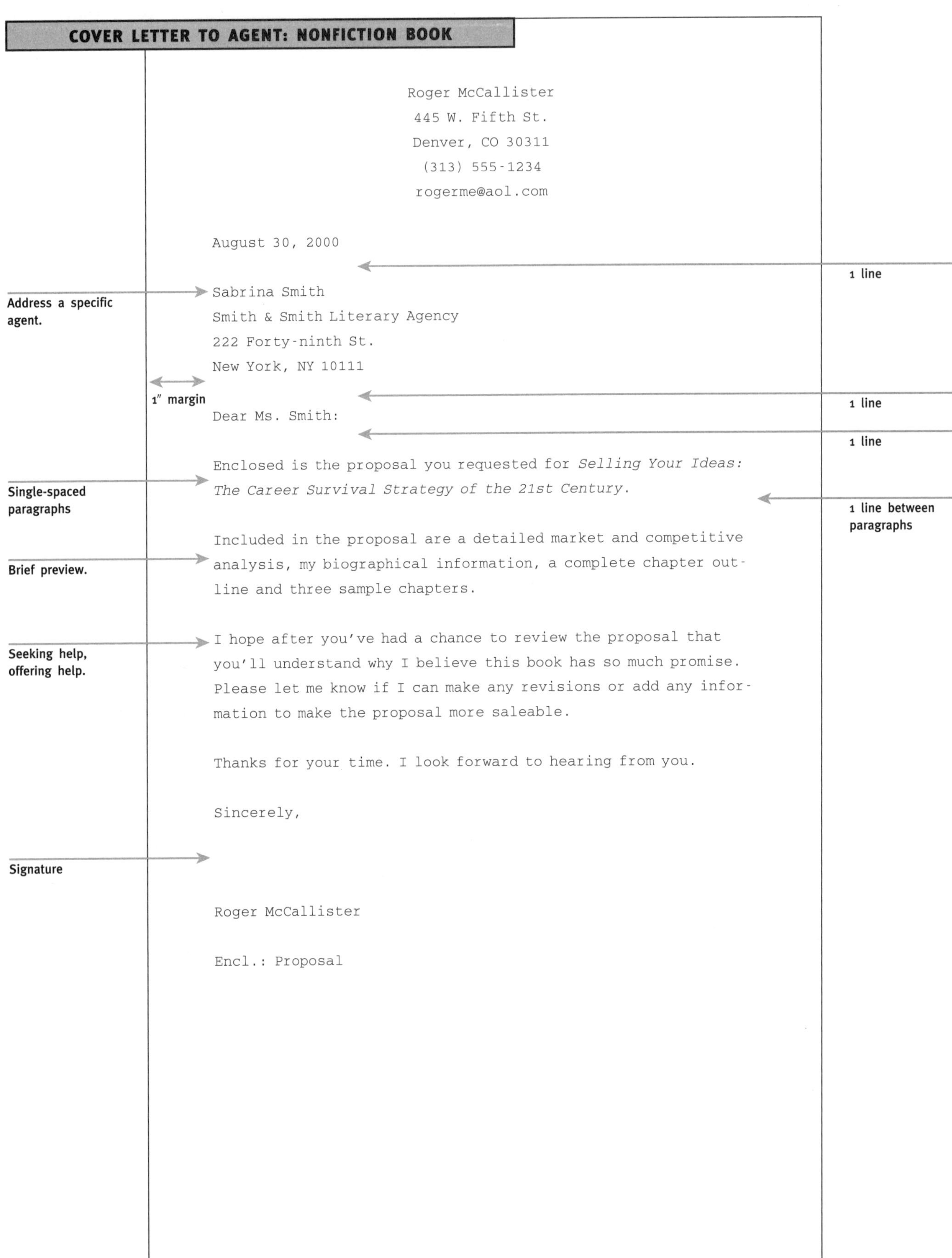
COVER LETTER TO AGENT: NONFICTION BOOK

Roger McCallister
445 W. Fifth St.
Denver, CO 30311
(313) 555-1234
rogerme@aol.com

August 30, 2000

Sabrina Smith
Smith & Smith Literary Agency
222 Forty-ninth St.
New York, NY 10111

Dear Ms. Smith:

Enclosed is the proposal you requested for *Selling Your Ideas: The Career Survival Strategy of the 21st Century*.

Included in the proposal are a detailed market and competitive analysis, my biographical information, a complete chapter outline and three sample chapters.

I hope after you've had a chance to review the proposal that you'll understand why I believe this book has so much promise. Please let me know if I can make any revisions or add any information to make the proposal more saleable.

Thanks for your time. I look forward to hearing from you.

Sincerely,

Roger McCallister

Encl.: Proposal

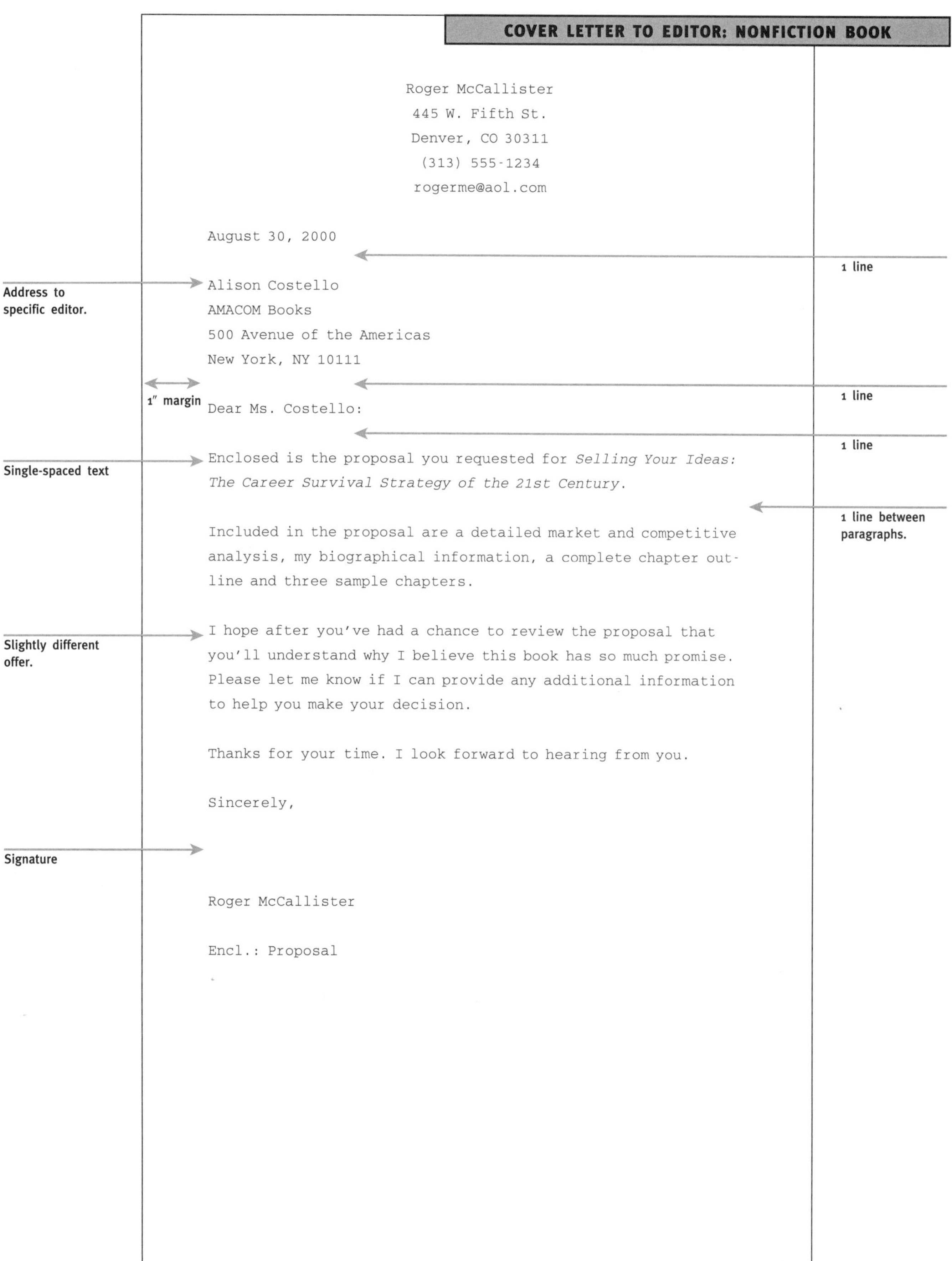

COVER LETTER TO EDITOR: NONFICTION BOOK

Roger McCallister
445 W. Fifth St.
Denver, CO 30311
(313) 555-1234
rogerme@aol.com

August 30, 2000

Alison Costello
AMACOM Books
500 Avenue of the Americas
New York, NY 10111

Dear Ms. Costello:

Enclosed is the proposal you requested for *Selling Your Ideas: The Career Survival Strategy of the 21st Century*.

Included in the proposal are a detailed market and competitive analysis, my biographical information, a complete chapter outline and three sample chapters.

I hope after you've had a chance to review the proposal that you'll understand why I believe this book has so much promise. Please let me know if I can provide any additional information to help you make your decision.

Thanks for your time. I look forward to hearing from you.

Sincerely,

Roger McCallister

Encl.: Proposal

Cover Page

Submission Tips

This is exactly the same as the cover page you'll use with the ultimate manuscript. It includes the title, an estimated word count and either your name and address (if you're submitting direct to an editor) or your agent's name and address (if you're submitting through an agent).

Formatting Specs

- Your name and address go in the top left corner if you're submitting to a book editor.
- If you're using an agent, the agent's name and address go in the bottom right corner, and you don't put your address on the cover.
- Put an estimated word count (for the entire book, not for the proposal) in the top right corner.
- Center the title, subtitle and author's name in the middle of the page.
- Conventionally, the title is in all capital letters and the subtitle is up-and-down. If you want to use boldface for the title and italics for the subtitle, that's fine, too. Your call.

Other Dos and Don'ts

- Don't include both your address and the agent's. Use one or the other, depending on the situation.
- Don't use a header or number the title page.

> **"Too often I think authors put the cart before the horse and assume that editors are only interested in whether there's a market for it [a book] . . . and by extension that if there's a market, it doesn't have to be a book of quality. That's not the case. The book has to do its job, first and foremost."**
>
> —Peter Burford, publisher, Burford Books

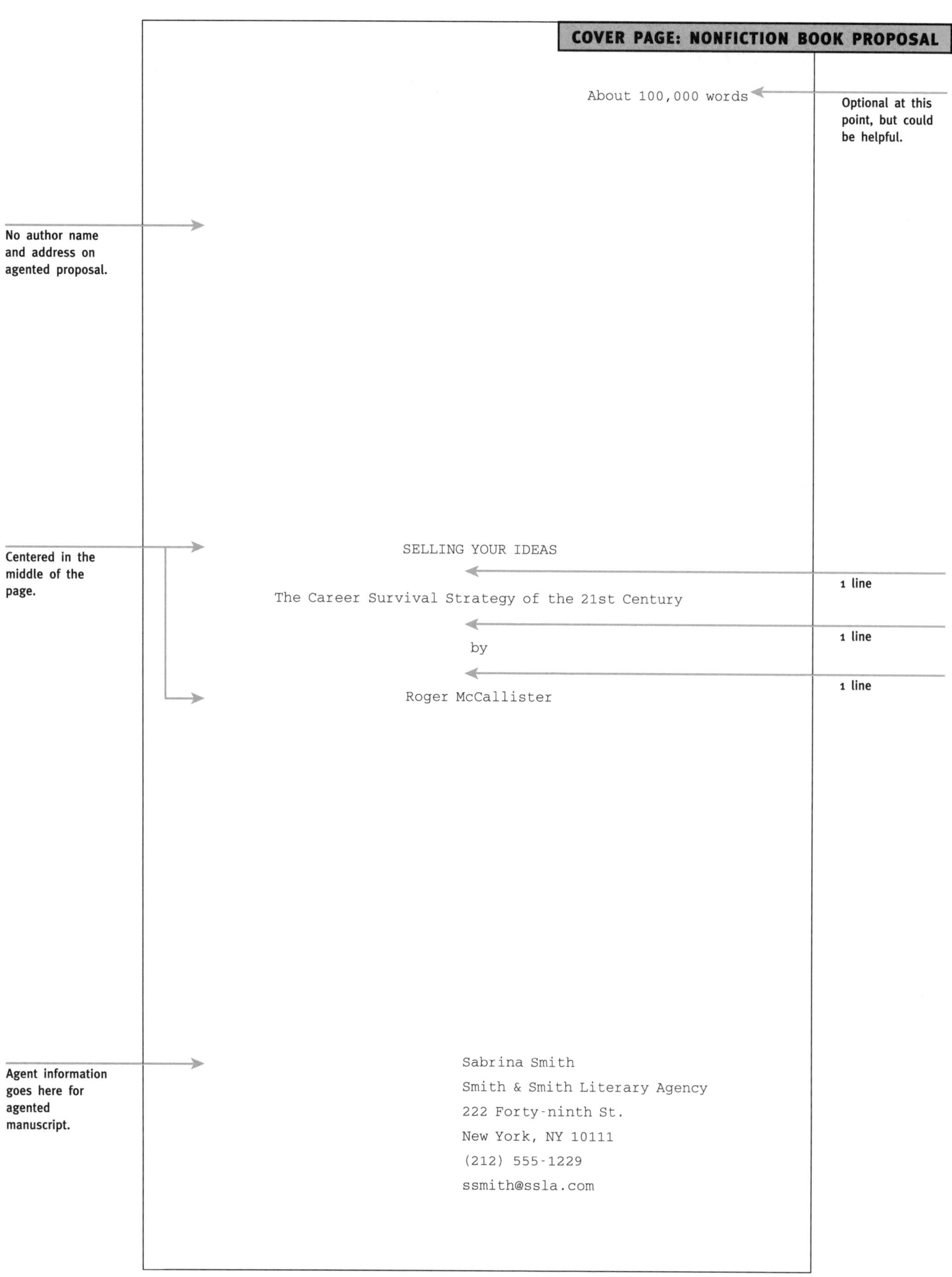
COVER PAGE: NONFICTION BOOK PROPOSAL
About 100,000 words
Optional at this point, but could be helpful.
No author name and address on agented proposal.
Centered in the middle of the page.
SELLING YOUR IDEAS
1 line
The Career Survival Strategy of the 21st Century
1 line
by
1 line
Roger McCallister
Agent information goes here for agented manuscript.
Sabrina Smith
Smith & Smith Literary Agency
222 Forty-ninth St.
New York, NY 10111
(212) 555-1229
ssmith@ssla.com

Overview

Submission Tips

The overview is the place for your thirty-second sound-bite pitch. It incorporates elements of the concept, marketing and competitive analysis, and author information you're about to present and ties them together convincingly, forcefully and coherently.

This is just an overview, so it's only a page. Even though it's a small element of the proposal, it's a powerful one. You may use the same approach you used in the query, but the overview should be even more focused. Try to boil the pitch down to a single sentence, then use a paragraph or two to describe the contents of your book.

Resist the urge to give a blow-by-blow description of the rest of the proposal. No one needs a preview of a proposal. The overview is simply, to borrow from the corporate buzzword lexicon, "the top-line analysis," "the big picture," "the view from ten thousand feet."

You get the picture.

Formatting Specs

- Start numbering your proposal with this page, with numbers in the top right corner.
- Use a slug in the top left corner of the header in this and succeeding pages.
- The slug should read "Proposal: Your Book Title Here."
- Center your heading, "Overview" and underline it.
- Double-space with a 1″ margin from here on out.

Other Dos and Don'ts

- Do make sure the overview conveys a convincing hook, even though it's a freestyle exercise. Think of this as the speech the agent will make to the editor, the editor to the people on the editorial committee, the sales rep to the buyer, the book jacket to the reader.

> **"We provide guidelines (on book proposals) so we know (writers) are covering all the bases. . . . We like the proposal to reflect the author's personality as much as it can. And sometimes you have to break through the box of the guidelines in order to really express what the book is about."**
>
> —Andrea Pedolsky, Altair Literary Agency, New York

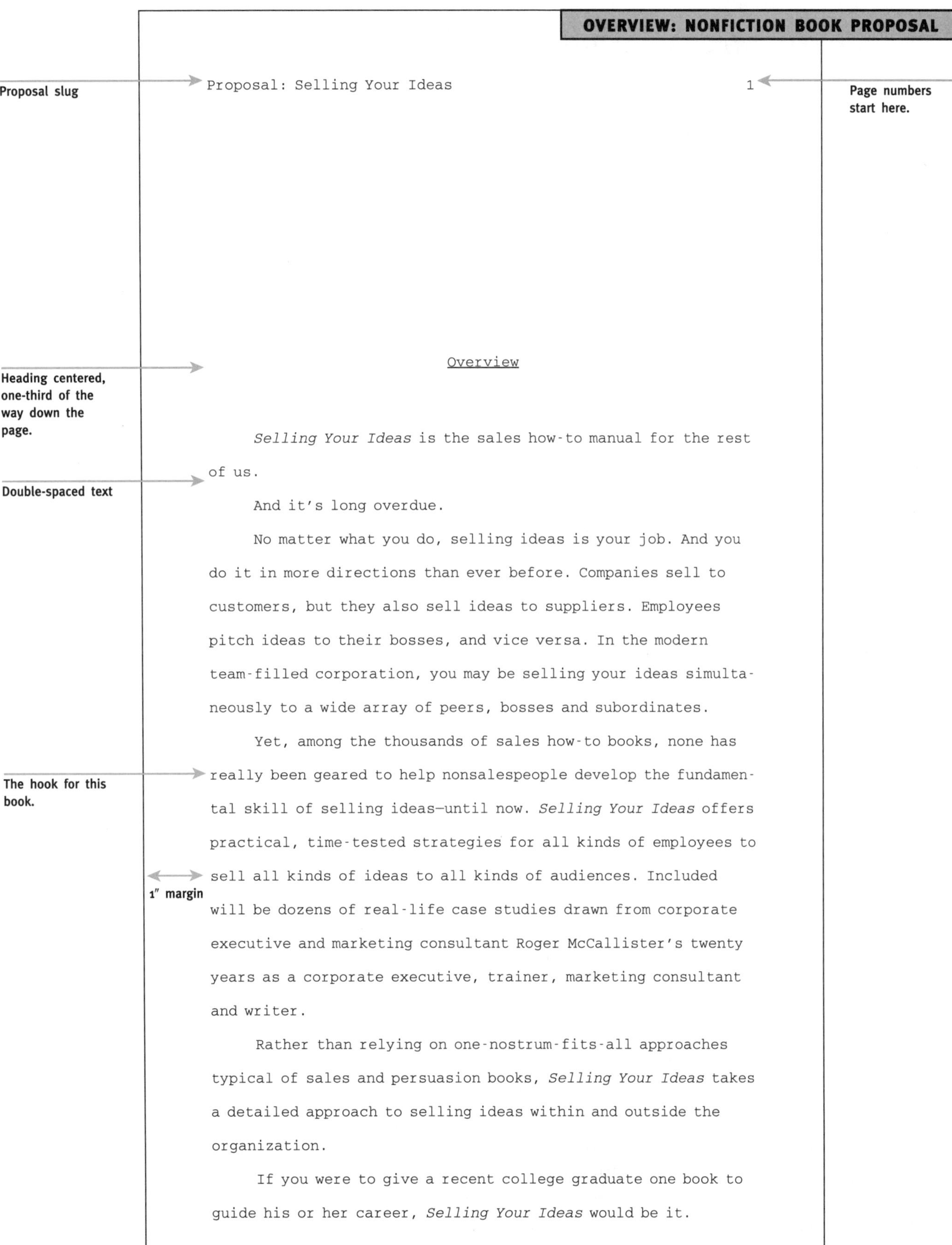

Proposal: Selling Your Ideas 1

Overview

Selling Your Ideas is the sales how-to manual for the rest of us.

And it's long overdue.

No matter what you do, selling ideas is your job. And you do it in more directions than ever before. Companies sell to customers, but they also sell ideas to suppliers. Employees pitch ideas to their bosses, and vice versa. In the modern team-filled corporation, you may be selling your ideas simultaneously to a wide array of peers, bosses and subordinates.

Yet, among the thousands of sales how-to books, none has really been geared to help nonsalespeople develop the fundamental skill of selling ideas—until now. *Selling Your Ideas* offers practical, time-tested strategies for all kinds of employees to sell all kinds of ideas to all kinds of audiences. Included will be dozens of real-life case studies drawn from corporate executive and marketing consultant Roger McCallister's twenty years as a corporate executive, trainer, marketing consultant and writer.

Rather than relying on one-nostrum-fits-all approaches typical of sales and persuasion books, *Selling Your Ideas* takes a detailed approach to selling ideas within and outside the organization.

If you were to give a recent college graduate one book to guide his or her career, *Selling Your Ideas* would be it.

Marketing Analysis

Submission Tips

The marketing information section of your proposal answers that all-important question: Will this book sell? And it should answer the question in as much detail as possible. There are no limits on length here, beyond your ability to research and write. As with any part of your proposal, make this as tight and compelling as you can, but offer any facts or figures you can find to prove your book will be a hit.

This section covers the product—your book—and the consumers—its readers. Among the areas to cover in this section include:

- Who is the audience? Describe them. How big is the potential readership base? Is it growing? What are some important facts about the readership base that a marketer would want to know? What kind of media do they like? What organizations do they belong to? Where do they shop?
- What trends could affect the book? Why would the audience be growing, buying more books or suddenly taking more interest in your book?
- Where, besides bookstores, could this book be sold?
- Are there special events, seasonal approaches or other special channels through which this book can be sold?
- What will the book be like, and how will that appeal to its readers?
- How will you approach the book? Will it have sidebars, callouts, interviews, pictures, charts or other special features to hook the reader?
- What are the sources of information? What will the research be based on?

Closely linked to the marketing analysis is the competitive information that follows it. You may choose, in fact, to combine these into a single section. For the sake of breaking information down into the smallest manageable units, the subjects are handled separately here.

Formatting Specs

Follow the same formatting guidelines as on p. 56-57. Formatting is similar to the rest of the inside of the book proposal.

Other Dos and Don'ts

- Do write concisely.
- Don't be worried about the length. Take as long as you need to present all relevant marketing information.
- Do use charts, tables and graphs here, if you have them.

On the market analysis section of a proposal:
"I don't want to hear the market is two million people. Describe the reader. What kind of magazines do they read? What associations do they belong to? What conferences do they go to? What television shows do they watch? Draw a picture that connects the reader to other areas of the world so that a publisher can find coattails for promoting the book. The author needs to draw a picture of who her reader is and how that reader connects to other aspects of the world."

—Andrea Pedolsky, Altair Literary Agency, New York

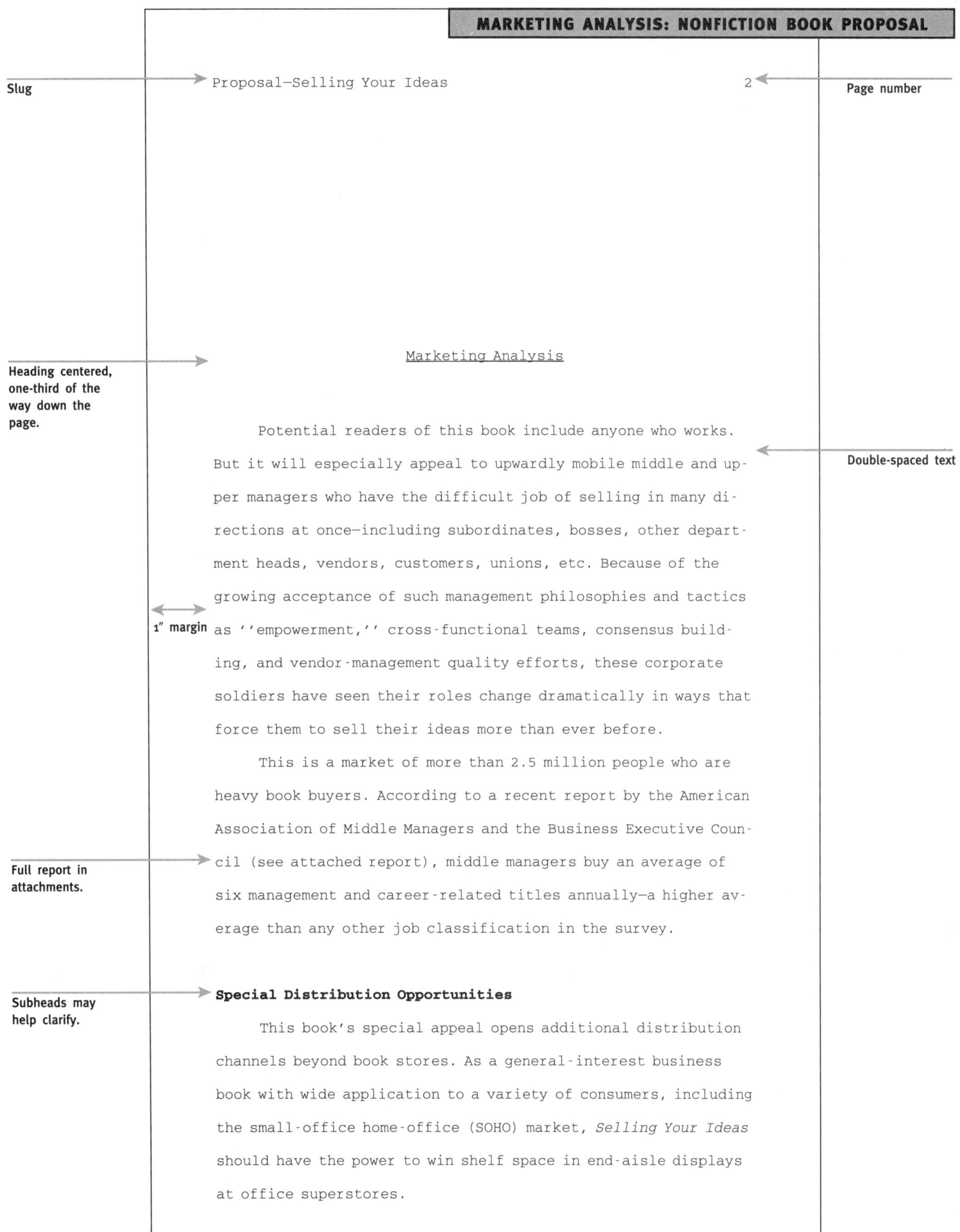
MARKETING ANALYSIS: NONFICTION BOOK PROPOSAL
Slug
Proposal—Selling Your Ideas
2
Page number
Heading centered, one-third of the way down the page.
Marketing Analysis
Potential readers of this book include anyone who works. But it will especially appeal to upwardly mobile middle and upper managers who have the difficult job of selling in many directions at once—including subordinates, bosses, other department heads, vendors, customers, unions, etc. Because of the growing acceptance of such management philosophies and tactics as ''empowerment,'' cross-functional teams, consensus building, and vendor-management quality efforts, these corporate soldiers have seen their roles change dramatically in ways that force them to sell their ideas more than ever before.
Double-spaced text
1" margin
This is a market of more than 2.5 million people who are heavy book buyers. According to a recent report by the American Association of Middle Managers and the Business Executive Council (see attached report), middle managers buy an average of six management and career-related titles annually—a higher average than any other job classification in the survey.
Full report in attachments.
Subheads may help clarify.
Special Distribution Opportunities
This book's special appeal opens additional distribution channels beyond book stores. As a general-interest business book with wide application to a variety of consumers, including the small-office home-office (SOHO) market, Selling Your Ideas should have the power to win shelf space in end-aisle displays at office superstores.

Competitive Analysis

Submission Tips

This section details what books are similar to yours, how they have done in the marketplace, and how your book is different and better than they are.

There's no set format for handling this information, but it helps to begin with an overview of the genre or category into which your book fits, how that category is doing generally, and what the leading competitive titles are.

Then go into an analysis of no more than the top four or five leading competitors, looking at how those books have done and why yours is still needed. Even if the subject already has been covered, it may not have been covered for your audience, or the information may be hopelessly out of date because of changes in social mores or technology.

The traditional, seat-of-the-pants method for gathering this information is to visit a good-size bookstore, look for competing titles, and ask bookstore employees or owners how that title is selling. However, this haphazard approach is unlikely to impress editors.

At the very least, do some research in *Books in Print.* Find the CD-ROM or on-line version, which should be available through large municipal or university libraries.

An easier and potentially more effective desktop approach is to check the search engine at an on-line bookseller, such as Amazon.com (www.amazon.com). Searches here yield a wealth of information beyond the competing titles. You can also see where these titles rank in sales for Amazon.com, get commentaries from readers, and see what other books and authors are also popular buyers of the title. You can't get information on total number of books sold. But, combined with some inside sales information from other authors whose titles are listed at Amazon.com, you might be able to develop a ballpark estimate of how many copies a book has sold based on its Amazon ranking.

Formatting Specs

- Formatting is similar to the rest of the inside of the book proposal.
- Use as much space as you need, but limit the competitive titles you discuss to no more than four or five.
- Bulleted capsule treatment of competitive titles can work here, but isn't absolutely necessary. Do what works best for you.

Other Dos and Don'ts

- Do write concisely.
- Don't trash the competing titles. Point out what shortcomings they have that make room or create demand for your book.
- Don't contend that your book is so unique that it has no competition. Agents and editors will conclude either that you don't know, are fudging big time, or have offered an idea so bizarre or unappealing that no book should be published. You can always find a comparable book if you try hard enough.

> **"If it's a holocaust book by a holocaust survivor, she still needs to differentiate the book from those of other holocaust survivors. The author clearly has to connect with what's out there. You have to move out of your personal realm and into the marketplace. Once you decide you want something published, it's no longer a personal document."**
>
> —Andrea Pedolsky, Altair Literary Agency, New York

COMPETITIVE ANALYSIS: NONFICTION BOOK PROPOSAL

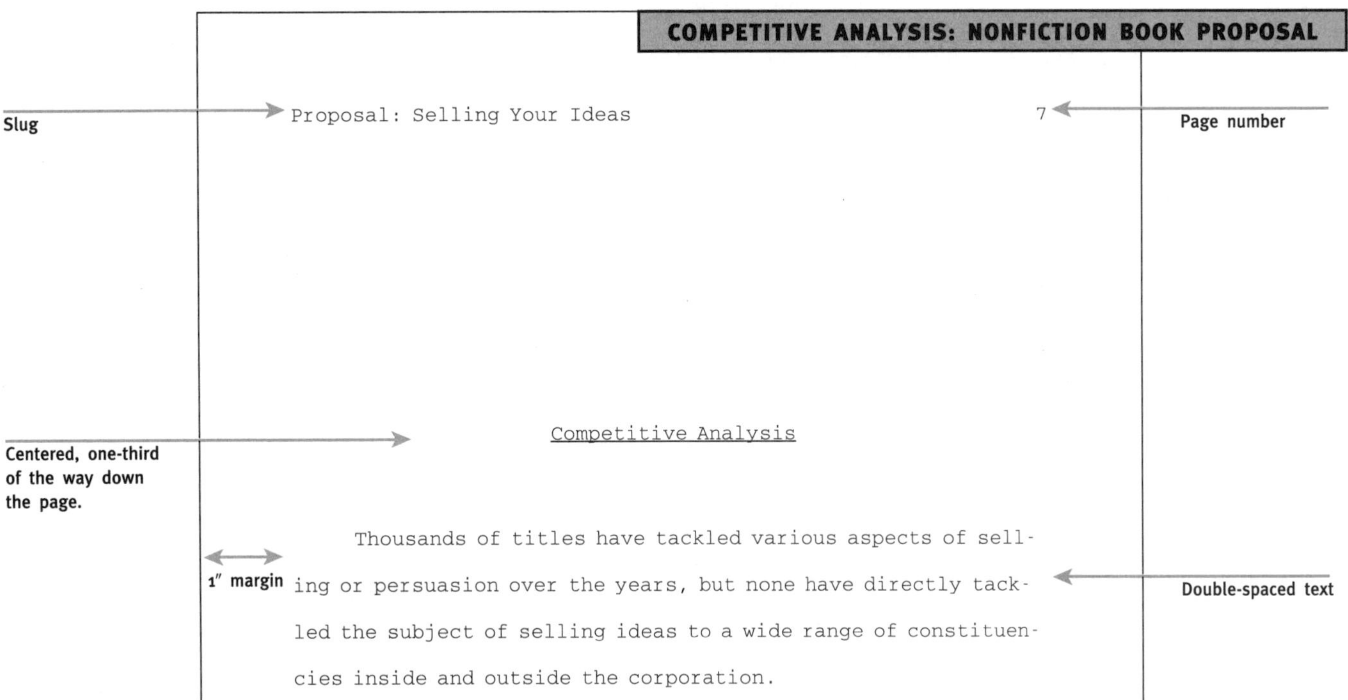

Competitive Analysis

Thousands of titles have tackled various aspects of selling or persuasion over the years, but none have directly tackled the subject of selling ideas to a wide range of constituencies inside and outside the corporation.

Sales and persuasion titles are consistently strong performers. An analysis of titles listed by Amazon.com shows that more than fifty such titles have been published in the past year. They rank between 5 and 64,000 in sales for Amazon.com. In addition, analysis of older titles shows that the top 20 sales and persuasion books have a median ranking of 5,000, compared to 10,000 for the top 20 management theory books and 12,000 for the top 20 time-management books. Backlist sales potential in this category is substantial.

The four recent titles that come closest in subject to *Selling Your Ideas* have an average sales rank of 11,000. Two of those, however, focus narrowly on presentations, the broader books ranking 2,000 and 5,000, respectively.

Below is a detailed analysis of each title.

1) *The Anatomy of Persuasion, How to Persuade Others to Act on Your Ideas, Accept Your Proposals, Buy Your Products or Services, Hire You and Promote You*. This book covers ground similar to *Selling Your Ideas*, but without the department-by-department, case study-based approach. This is primarily a Dale Carnegie-style book that doesn't entirely reflect the forces at play in the modern organization.

Author Information

Submission Tips

This section is about you, but only in the context of what makes you the perfect person to write this book. The section should also highlight any other information that makes you a saleable author. This is not your life story; this is the story of how you will help the publisher sell books.

Good points to include in the author information are:

- Teaching credentials (professors can sell their books to students and other professors).
- Organizational affiliations, groups you head or any special audiences with whom you are connected and which could become channels for marketing the book.
- Previous publishing credits (including books, which show you can do one; articles, which show your expertise; and columns, which show a possible avenue of promotion).
- Any experience you have in other media (radio shows, TV shows, regular radio commentaries—anything that shows you could promote your book effectively in a variety of media).
- Compelling personal history that could help generate publicity and get you booked on talk shows.

This is not a resume. It's a narrative description similar to what might appear on a book jacket.

Don't be crass or belabor the obvious. Editors know if you're founder and president of a group or a professor that you can use these positions to sell books. This section is a little more subtle than the rest. Try to come off as qualified and marketable without sounding like a jerk.

Formatting Specs

- Place the slug in the top left corner. Page number goes in the top right corner. Double-space the text.
- Try to keep this to one page, regardless of how fascinating you are.
- Write this, like the rest of the proposal, in the third person.

Other Dos and Don'ts

- Do write concisely.
- Don't overreach. State your history and qualifications accurately.
- Don't provide information that's irrelevant to the book's marketing, i.e., the story of your life ("He was born in a small log cabin just outside . . ."). Family and other details that may be appropriate in a jacket blurb aren't necessarily helpful here.

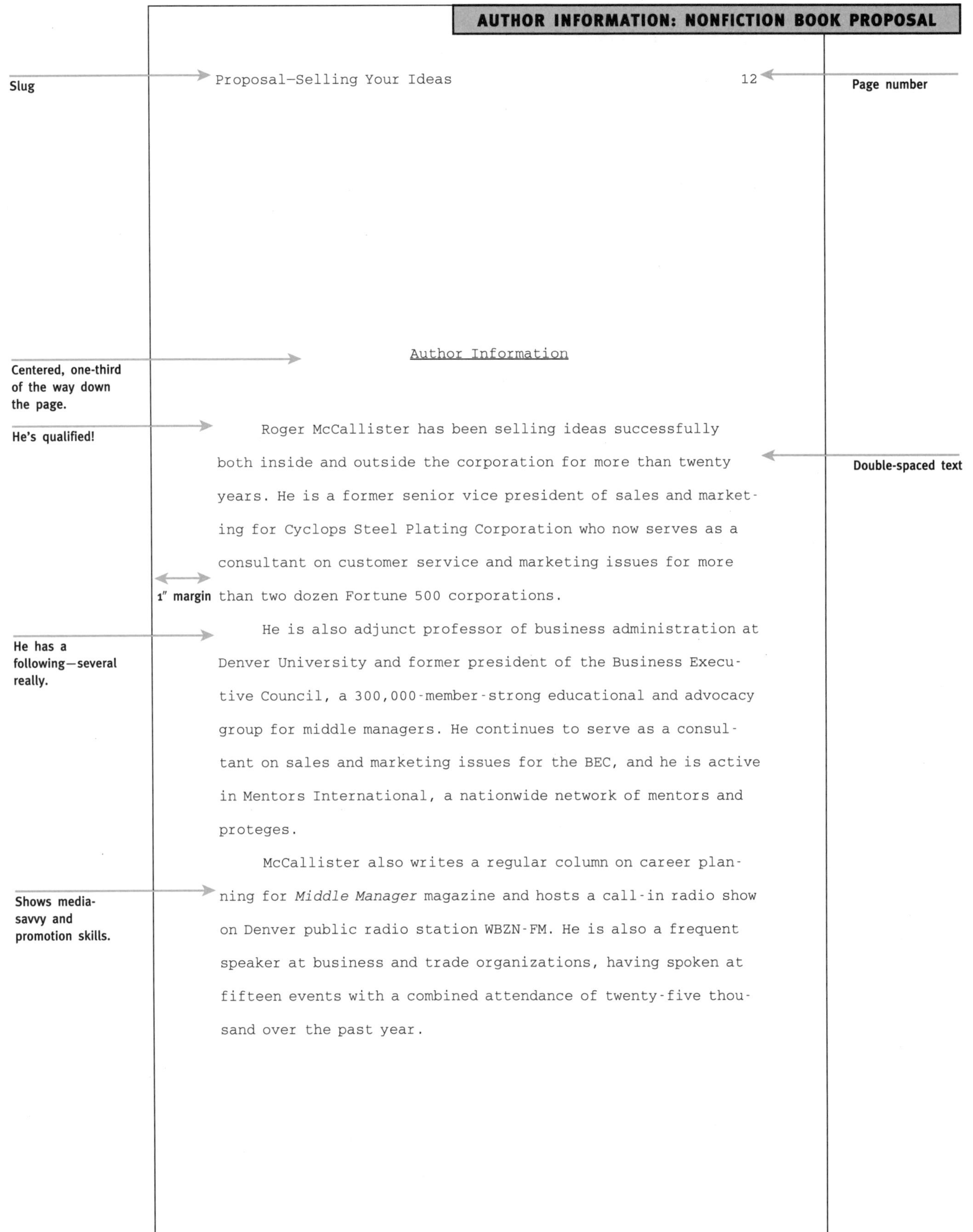

AUTHOR INFORMATION: NONFICTION BOOK PROPOSAL

Proposal—Selling Your Ideas 12

Author Information

Roger McCallister has been selling ideas successfully both inside and outside the corporation for more than twenty years. He is a former senior vice president of sales and marketing for Cyclops Steel Plating Corporation who now serves as a consultant on customer service and marketing issues for more than two dozen Fortune 500 corporations.

He is also adjunct professor of business administration at Denver University and former president of the Business Executive Council, a 300,000-member-strong educational and advocacy group for middle managers. He continues to serve as a consultant on sales and marketing issues for the BEC, and he is active in Mentors International, a nationwide network of mentors and proteges.

McCallister also writes a regular column on career planning for *Middle Manager* magazine and hosts a call-in radio show on Denver public radio station WBZN-FM. He is also a frequent speaker at business and trade organizations, having spoken at fifteen events with a combined attendance of twenty-five thousand over the past year.

Chapter Outline

Submission Tips

The chapter outline provides an extended table of contents for your book. It includes a brief description of each chapter.

This need not, and probably should not, be in the classic outline format you learned in your high school composition class. Such an outline may help you actually write the book, but it's a little dry for the purposes of a proposal, which is meant to sell an editor on the merits of each chapter and show how it fits into the book.

Formatting Specs

- You can put multiple chapters on each page of the outline, but it may be less confusing to describe one chapter per page.
- Number pages of the outline, continuing with the last number of the author information section.
- Use the same header you use with the rest of the proposal.
- If the book is divided into parts as well as chapters, first list the part and part heading, then the chapter and chapter heading.
- Indent paragraphs and otherwise follow the same format as the rest of the proposal.

Other Dos and Don'ts

- Don't insert a new title page and start numbering all over again with the outline. The proposal is a single entity.
- Do describe how the chapter will unfold, including any sidebars, tables, charts, photos or other illustrations that will be included.
- Don't tell how many pages or photos you'll have in each chapter. Assuming you haven't actually written the book yet, it's impossible to know, and the information isn't likely to sway an editor.

On manuscript formatting:
"The best thing is to keep it really simple. You get a manuscript in the conventional printed form and edit on that, because it's easier to edit on that. Once all that's cleaned up, you have a hard-copy printout you turn over to a designer or typesetter. That person will style the heads. If the author has gone nuts with trying to style his or her own manuscript with a lot of italics or boldfacing or whatever, this creates a lot of extra work for the editor or typesetter. Keep it as simple as possible and as consistent as you can without trying to desktop publish the manuscript. The designer ultimately just clicks and undoes all that stuff."

—Peter Burford, publisher, Burford Books

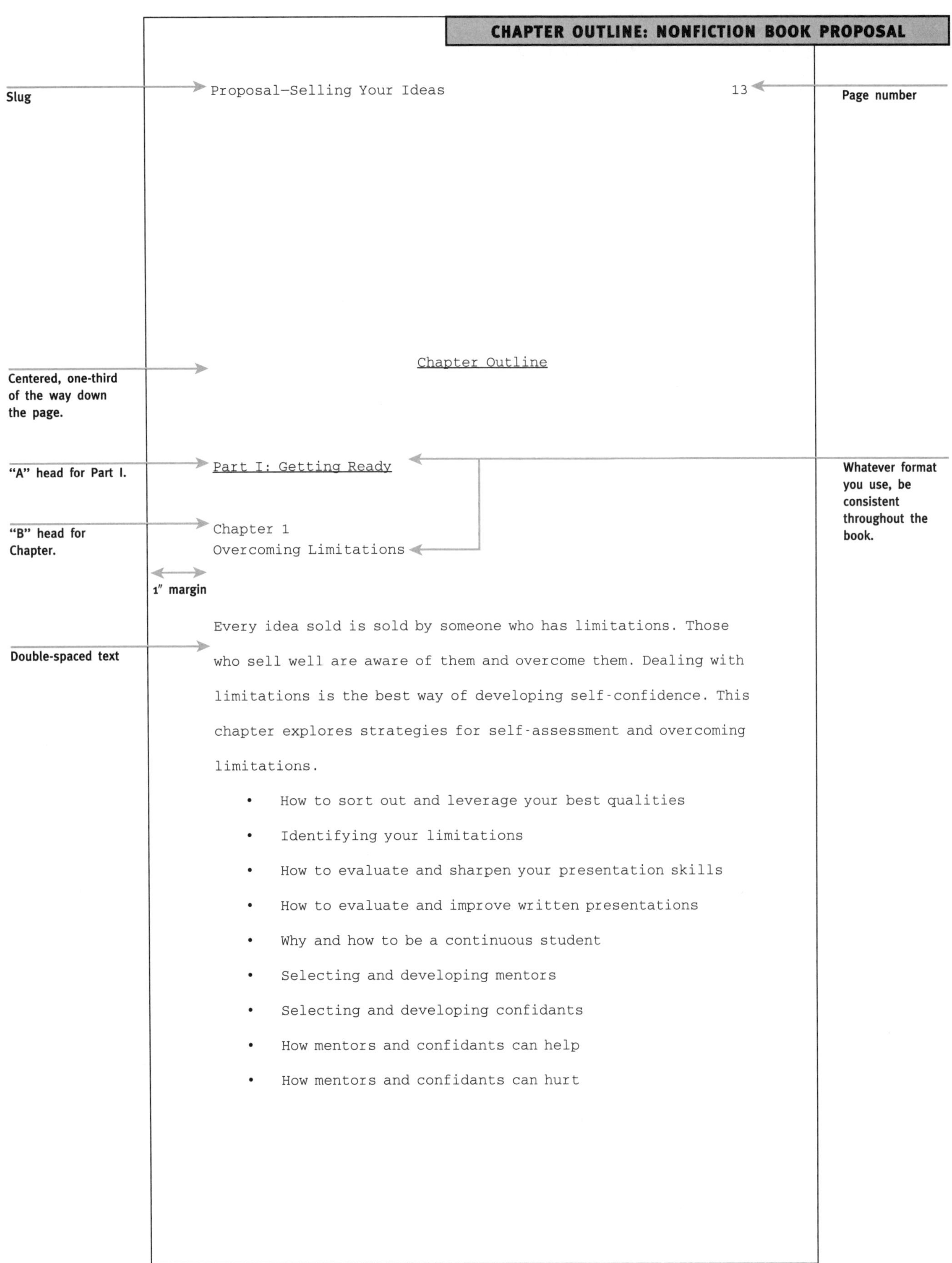
CHAPTER OUTLINE: NONFICTION BOOK PROPOSAL
Slug
Proposal—Selling Your Ideas
13
Page number
Chapter Outline
Centered, one-third of the way down the page.
Part I: Getting Ready
"A" head for Part I.
Whatever format you use, be consistent throughout the book.
Chapter 1
Overcoming Limitations
"B" head for Chapter.
1″ margin
Every idea sold is sold by someone who has limitations. Those who sell well are aware of them and overcome them. Dealing with limitations is the best way of developing self-confidence. This chapter explores strategies for self-assessment and overcoming limitations.
Double-spaced text
• How to sort out and leverage your best qualities
• Identifying your limitations
• How to evaluate and sharpen your presentation skills
• How to evaluate and improve written presentations
• Why and how to be a continuous student
• Selecting and developing mentors
• Selecting and developing confidants
• How mentors and confidants can help
• How mentors and confidants can hurt

Sample Chapter(s)

Submission Tips

Agents and editors almost always want to see at least one sample chapter, even from established authors. If you've already written a book in the same subject area, you might get by without a sample chapter. Even then, however, some editors insist.

The author's natural inclination is to send Chapter 1, but some agents recommend against this. If Chapter 1 seems too complete, they argue, it might be hard to make a case for the rest of the book.

Ultimately, the number of sample chapters and which ones to send is your judgment call. Look at the chapter outline. Which chapters are most intriguing, most needed to make a case for the book, or most likely to make editors wonder if you can actually deliver on the promise made in the chapter outline? These are the chapters you should include.

Formatting Specs

- Continue with the same slug and pagination as in the rest of the proposal.
- After the first page of the sample chapter, continue using the header and page number. You need not indicate the chapter number or title in subsequent pages.
- Use a 1″ margin on all sides.
- Double-space the text.
- Use a 10- or 12-point plain font such as Times New Roman, Arial or Courier.

"What I'm looking for in the sample chapter is evidence that the author can write well and that the style is appropriate for what the book is trying to accomplish."

—Peter Burford, publisher, Burford Books

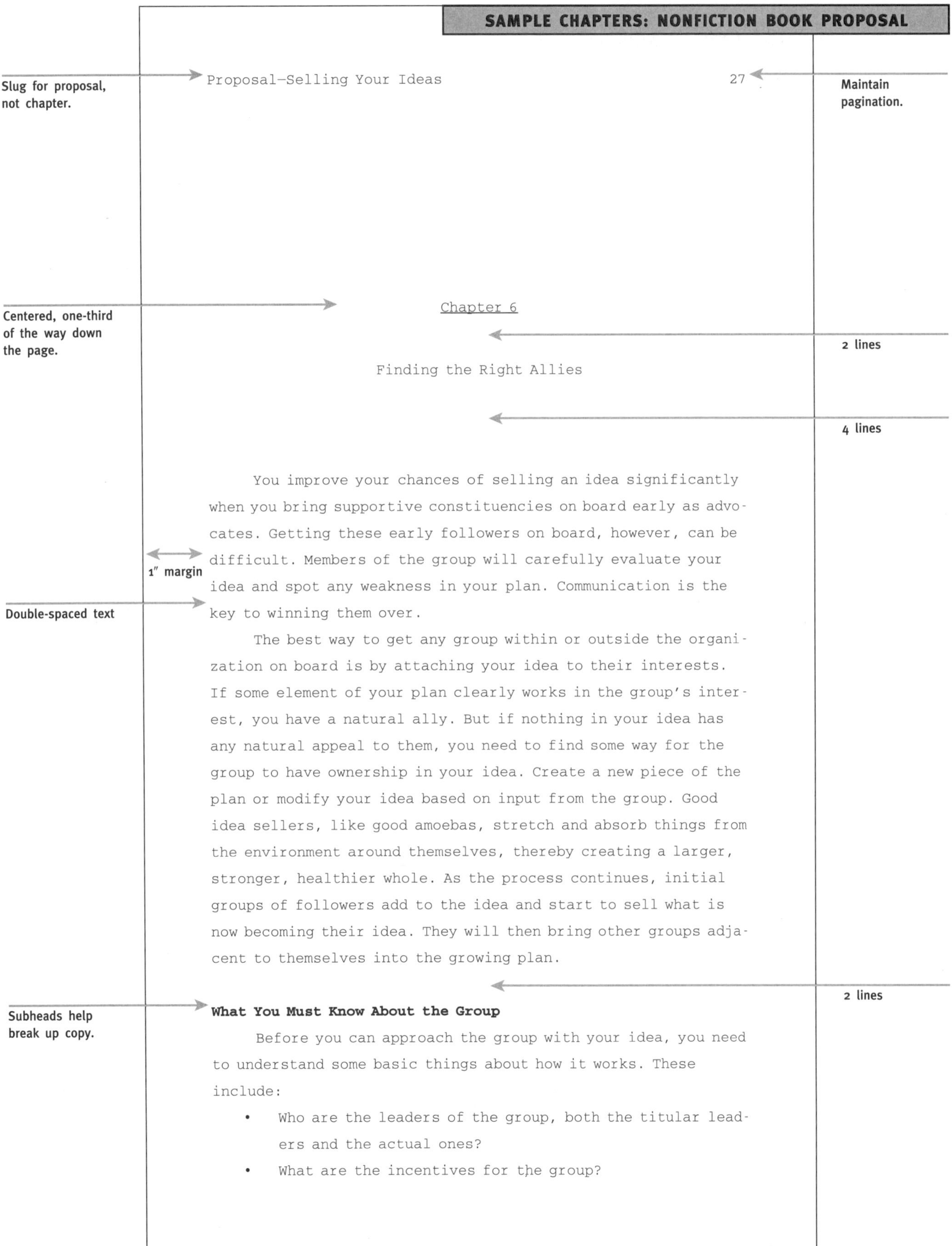
SAMPLE CHAPTERS: NONFICTION BOOK PROPOSAL
Slug for proposal, not chapter.
Proposal—Selling Your Ideas
27
Maintain pagination.
Centered, one-third of the way down the page.
Chapter 6
2 lines
Finding the Right Allies
4 lines
You improve your chances of selling an idea significantly when you bring supportive constituencies on board early as advocates. Getting these early followers on board, however, can be difficult. Members of the group will carefully evaluate your idea and spot any weakness in your plan. Communication is the key to winning them over.
1" margin
Double-spaced text
The best way to get any group within or outside the organization on board is by attaching your idea to their interests. If some element of your plan clearly works in the group's interest, you have a natural ally. But if nothing in your idea has any natural appeal to them, you need to find some way for the group to have ownership in your idea. Create a new piece of the plan or modify your idea based on input from the group. Good idea sellers, like good amoebas, stretch and absorb things from the environment around themselves, thereby creating a larger, stronger, healthier whole. As the process continues, initial groups of followers add to the idea and start to sell what is now becoming their idea. They will then bring other groups adjacent to themselves into the growing plan.
2 lines
Subheads help break up copy.
What You Must Know About the Group
Before you can approach the group with your idea, you need to understand some basic things about how it works. These include:
• Who are the leaders of the group, both the titular leaders and the actual ones?
• What are the incentives for the group?

Attachments

Submission Tips

If you have supporting materials for your proposal, attach them at the end, preceded by a page that serves as a brief table of contents for them.

Articles from magazines or newspapers that support comments made in your proposal, and articles and columns you have published on the subject are good examples of the types of material that should be attached.

Formatting Specs

- Use a single page with the heading "Attachments" or "Supporting Documents," followed by lines describing the documents.
- Number the Attachments introduction, but not the pages of the documents attached.

Other Dos and Don'ts

- Do attach copies of any articles or documents you reference in the proposal, other than information in the actual sample chapter.
- Do use endnotes if you have material from the sample chapter that needs to be referenced. For a discussion of endnotes, see the section on back matter later in this chapter.
- Don't attach material just to make your proposal look more impressive. Size does not matter.

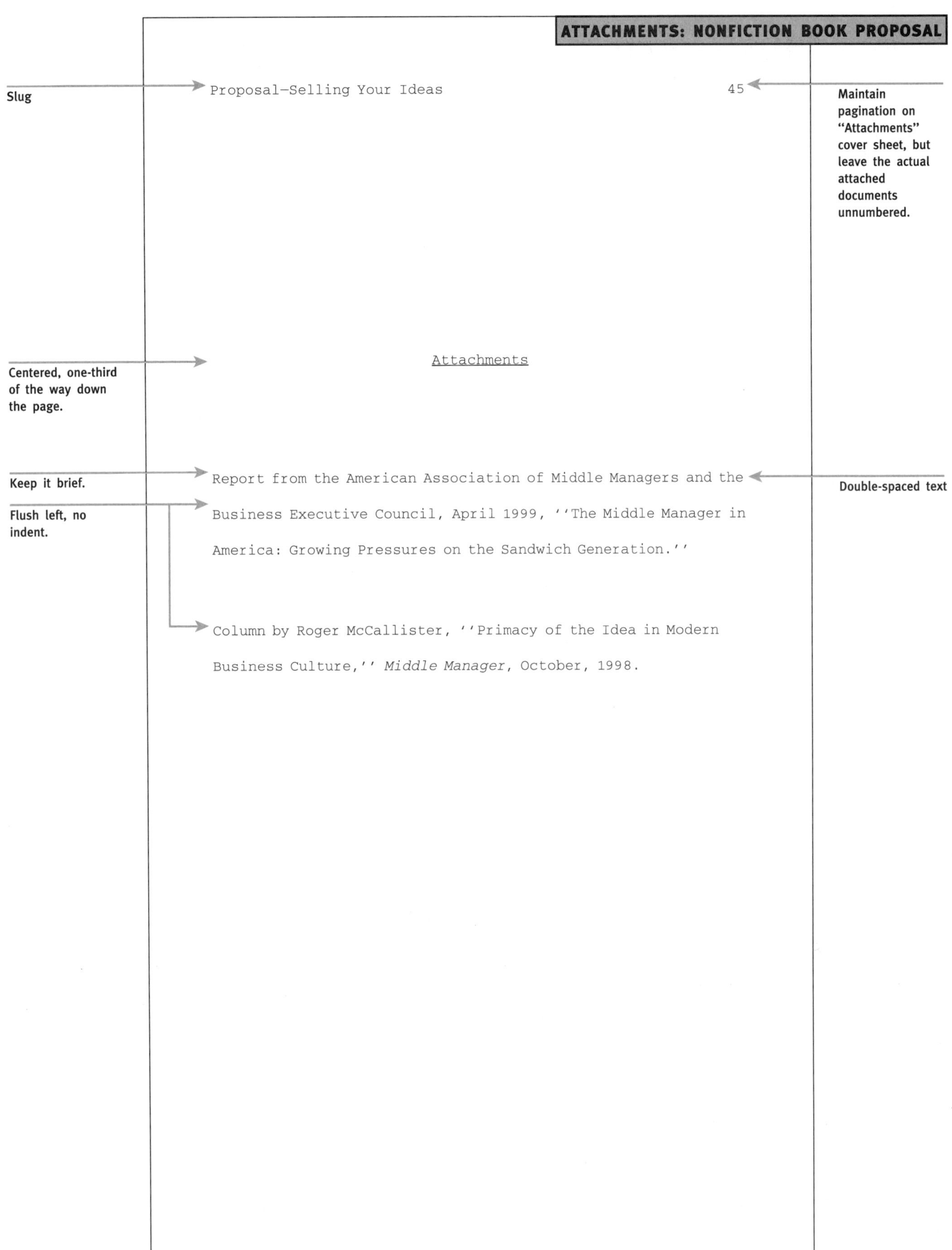

ATTACHMENTS: NONFICTION BOOK PROPOSAL

Slug

Proposal–Selling Your Ideas 45

Maintain pagination on "Attachments" cover sheet, but leave the actual attached documents unnumbered.

Centered, one-third of the way down the page.

Attachments

Keep it brief.

Flush left, no indent.

Double-spaced text

Report from the American Association of Middle Managers and the Business Executive Council, April 1999, ''The Middle Manager in America: Growing Pressures on the Sandwich Generation.''

Column by Roger McCallister, ''Primacy of the Idea in Modern Business Culture,'' *Middle Manager*, October, 1998.

Book Manuscript

Submission Tips

The book manuscript is similar in most respects to the proposal format. This section begins with the basics of the body of the manuscript, then looks at the specific requirements for various elements of the front matter and back matter.

You may well end up submitting the manuscript in two or three stages to the publisher rather than in one installment, and you won't necessarily do this in sequential order. Regardless of that, maintain the same pagination system. Your word processing system will allow you to start with any page number you want in the header. Keep track of the first and last page numbers of each chapter to avoid confusion.

Books, like newspapers and magazines, have become increasingly varied in design in recent years. Sidebars, callout quotes, subheads and short pieces within chapters abound. No universal guidelines exist for handling these formats within books, so confer with your editor early on for guidelines.

Formatting Specs

- Use a 1″ margin on all sides.
- Use a title page.
- Don't number the title page. Begin numbering with the first page of the text of the book, which usually will be the introduction or chapter one.
- Use a slug, usually either your last name or title of the book.
- Double-space the entire text of the book.
- Use a 10- or 12-point plain font such as Times New Roman, Arial or Courier.
- Generally, put sidebars, captions and other elements that fall outside the flow of the main chapter at the end of the chapter rather than where you think they should fall. Design and space constraints will dictate their placement, and it's easier for editors and designers to have the elements in a single, easy-to-find location.

Other Dos and Don'ts

- Do not staple anything.
- Do not punch holes in the pages or submit it in a three-ring binder.
- Do submit the manuscript loose-leaf in an envelope—that's why the slug and page numbers are there. If the editor wants to put it in a binder, he will do so.
- Do keep an original copy for yourself both on your computer hard drive and on a separate storage medium kept in a secure place, such as a fireproof safe.
- Don't justify text or align the right margin.
- Don't put any copyright information on the manuscript. It's copyrighted when you write it, and the editor knows this.

Electronic Submissions

Most publishing houses accept manuscripts on disk these days, but get guidelines or discuss specifications with your editor. You likely won't submit a disk until content editing is complete since the publishing house is not interested in printing out your entire book.

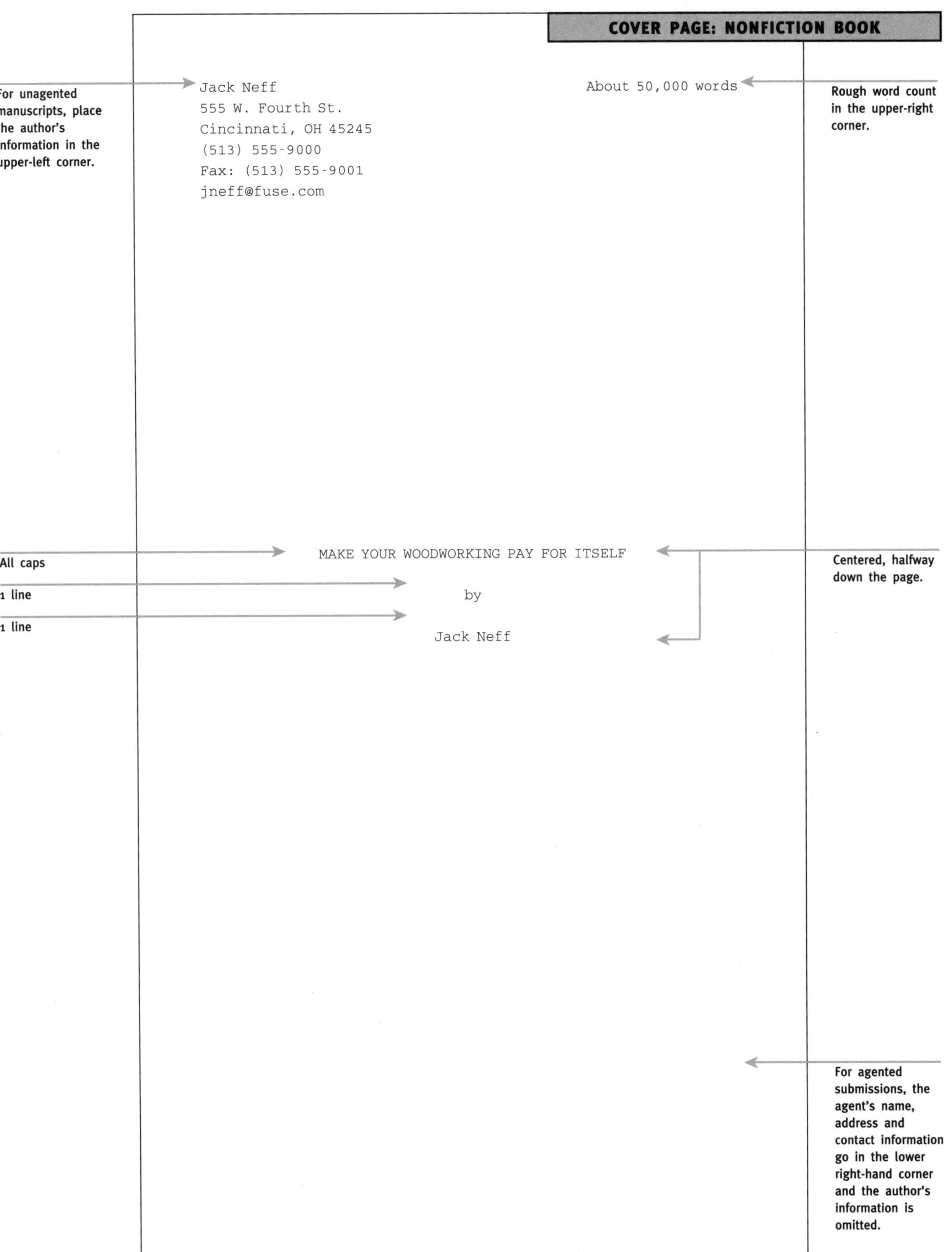
COVER PAGE: NONFICTION BOOK
For unagented manuscripts, place the author's information in the upper-left corner.
Jack Neff
555 W. Fourth St.
Cincinnati, OH 45245
(513) 555-9000
Fax: (513) 555-9001
jneff@fuse.com
About 50,000 words
Rough word count in the upper-right corner.
All caps
MAKE YOUR WOODWORKING PAY FOR ITSELF
1 line
by
1 line
Jack Neff
Centered, halfway down the page.
For agented submissions, the agent's name, address and contact information go in the lower right-hand corner and the author's information is omitted.

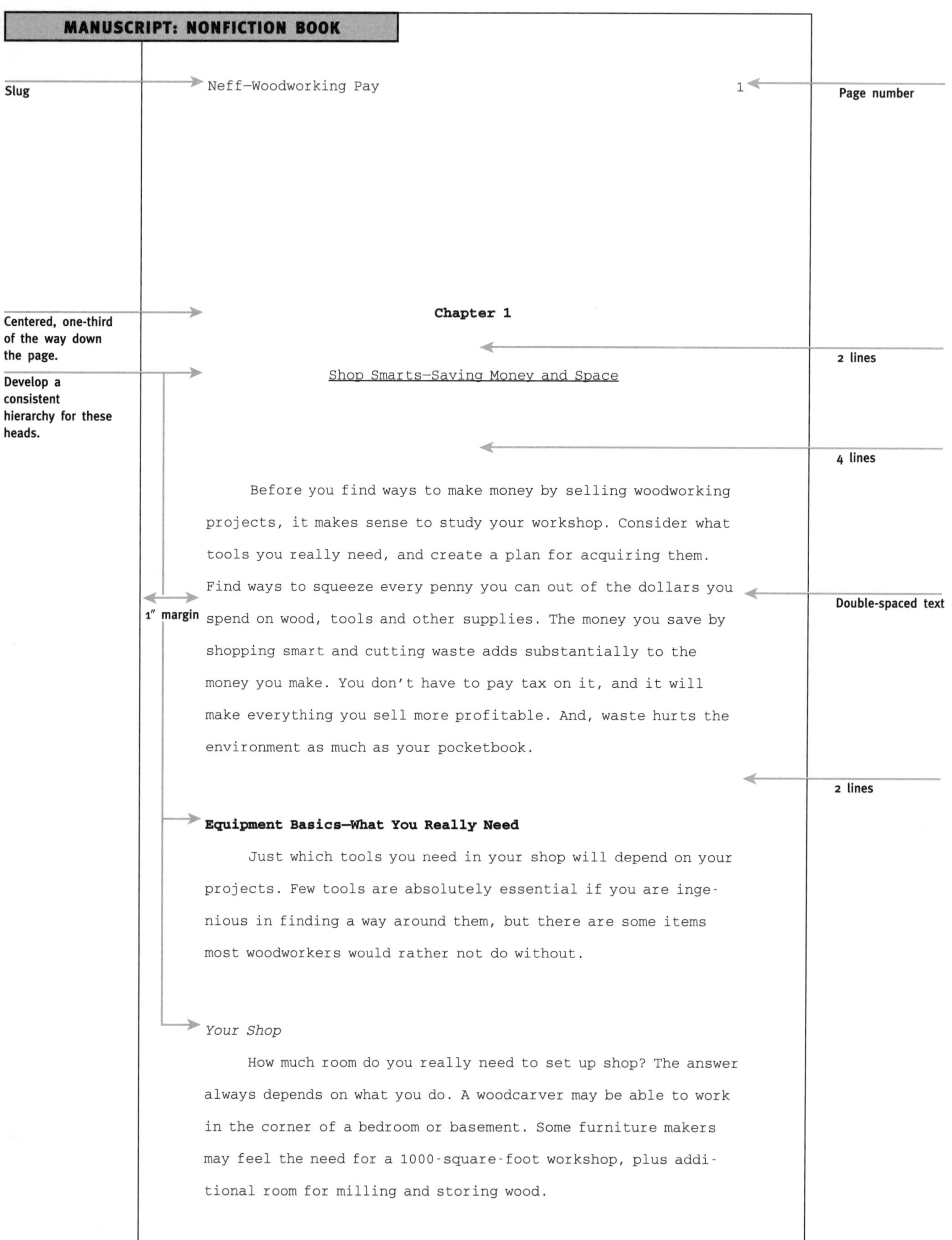
MANUSCRIPT: NONFICTION BOOK
Slug
Page number
Centered, one-third of the way down the page.
Develop a consistent hierarchy for these heads.
2 lines
4 lines
1″ margin
Double-spaced text
2 lines
Neff–Woodworking Pay
1
Chapter 1
Shop Smarts–Saving Money and Space
Before you find ways to make money by selling woodworking projects, it makes sense to study your workshop. Consider what tools you really need, and create a plan for acquiring them. Find ways to squeeze every penny you can out of the dollars you spend on wood, tools and other supplies. The money you save by shopping smart and cutting waste adds substantially to the money you make. You don't have to pay tax on it, and it will make everything you sell more profitable. And, waste hurts the environment as much as your pocketbook.
Equipment Basics–What You Really Need
Just which tools you need in your shop will depend on your projects. Few tools are absolutely essential if you are ingenious in finding a way around them, but there are some items most woodworkers would rather not do without.
Your Shop
How much room do you really need to set up shop? The answer always depends on what you do. A woodcarver may be able to work in the corner of a bedroom or basement. Some furniture makers may feel the need for a 1000-square-foot workshop, plus additional room for milling and storing wood.

SIDEBAR, PAGE 1: NONFICTION BOOK

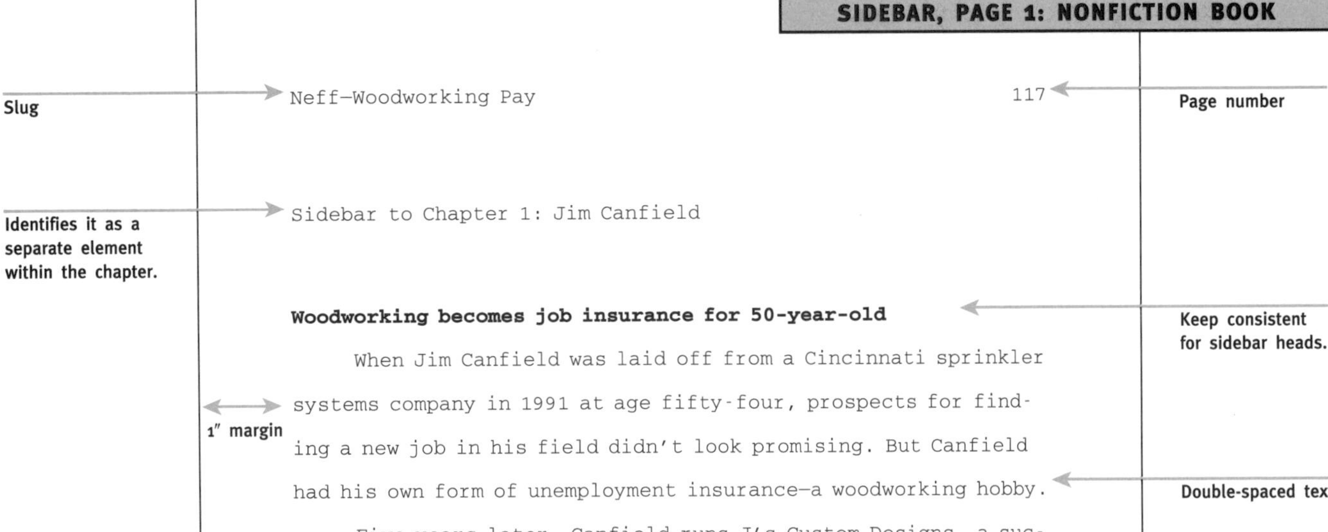

Neff—Woodworking Pay 117

Sidebar to Chapter 1: Jim Canfield

Woodworking becomes job insurance for 50-year-old

When Jim Canfield was laid off from a Cincinnati sprinkler systems company in 1991 at age fifty-four, prospects for finding a new job in his field didn't look promising. But Canfield had his own form of unemployment insurance—a woodworking hobby.

Five years later, Canfield runs J's Custom Designs, a successful custom cabinetmaking business in Milford, Ohio. Having overcome the hurdles of developing a reputation in a new business, he now feels better off than when he lost his job.

''The majority of us working for the company had in the back of our minds that we were going to retire there,'' Canfield says. ''But I think you've got to get something to fall back on, because I don't think there are any jobs you can call secure today.''

Canfield already had some experience selling wood crafts as a sideline occupation. He had made a potato bed for his wife after she had threatened to pay thirty-five dollars for one if he didn't do it. After he made the first one, he used it as a pattern to make 250 more. He also made rocking dinosaurs, modeled on rocking horses, for kids, and sold those through craft fairs.

But he hadn't thought too seriously about turning his sideline into a new business. Years earlier, Canfield had considered starting his own woodworking business but rejected the idea as too risky at a time he had five children at home. Though he had spent twenty-five years with his old employer, Canfield wasn't planning to retire yet or embark on a new career. But when he was laid off, he figured he had little to lose.

''When you're out of a job, you've got to do something,'' he says. ''I didn't want to relocate, and I didn't want to get back into fire protection.''

SIDEBAR, PAGE 2: NONFICTION BOOK

Continue with the same slug.

Neff–Woodworking Pay 118

Maintain pagination.

Canfield minimized the risk of his new venture several ways. He was able to rely on his wife's health insurance, removing one worry in starting his business. He started with the tools he already owned–a table saw, scroll saw, band saw, drill press, shaper, a few routers and assorted hand tools. His severance pay wasn't enough to buy more tools, and he didn't want risk going into debt.

He used some savings to rent a shop space in Blue Ash that helped him attract some walk-in customers. But he says the hardest part of the business for him initially was getting his name around.

''All of my contacts were in an entirely different field,'' he says. ''But the quality of my work helped get the name around. We tried other forms of advertising, but it really didn't work for what we do, which is custom furniture.''

J's Custom Designs now generates gross revenues of more than $100,000 a year. That's enough to allow Canfield to employ one of his sons. And it makes for a career Canfield prefers to his old one.

''It's enjoyable work. It's creative work. And every once in a while, you get a customer who pretty much gives you free hand in what you want to do–and that's even better.''

Keep with the element illustrated by photos—since the photos illustrate the sidebar text, they're placed here.

Captions

Photo A:

Use codes if you have more than one.

Jim Canfield sprays glue on a section of an entertainment center.

Photo B:

Jim Canfield tightens clamps on a section of an entertainment center.

Front Matter

Submission Tips

The term "front matter" refers to a wide variety of items that fall between the cover and the body of the finished product. These include:

- Table of contents
- Dedication
- Epigraph or Inscription
- Foreword
- Preface
- Prologue
- Acknowledgments

As books have become increasingly graphic, publishers largely have done away with such genteel niceties as lists of illustrations, photos or tables, which could become books unto themselves and take up space without conveying much useful information.

Tables of contents, on the other hand, have grown to become more detailed and complex, as publishers push for more page breaks, sidebars and other nontraditional points of entry to appease readers with increasingly short attention spans.

One thing all front matter has in common is that it is not numbered as part of your manuscript. In some cases, publishers number these elements separately with Roman numerals in the actual book. Generally, you don't need to worry about this unless you have a lot of front matter, or individual elements begin to span more than two pages. If your front matter is lengthy, number it using Roman numerals, or Arabic numerals and an altered slug that indicates the pages belong to the front matter.

Formatting Specs

- Generally, front-matter pages are not numbered.
- Front-matter pages get slugs in the header.
- Heads for each element are centered.

Other Dos and Don'ts

- Don't get carried away with most of these elements. Readers routinely skip over them, and they take up space that should be devoted to the text of the book. A book overladen with front matter is as annoying as a speaker who repeatedly clears his throat before speaking or opens with a long, pointless anecdote.
- Do have a good reason for including any of these elements. They are not requirements. You will not be penalized for skipping them, except for the table of contents and the acknowledgments.

> **"In the front matter, people need to know how to spell the word *foreword*."**
>
> —Leslie Towle, editorial supervisor, Heritage Books Inc.

Table of Contents

Submission Tips

This is what it's all about. Tables of contents are one of the first places a potential consumer goes to evaluate a nonfiction book. Somewhere along the line, publishers got wise to this fact. Now, editors look for the table of contents to be more complete, descriptive and compelling than ever.

Nonfiction tables of contents are as varied as the books they describe, so prescribing a slapdash formula for them is pointless. Many remain bare bones, merely listing the chapter titles and page numbers. Increasingly, however, the table of contents for many books looks like the chapter outline in the book proposal—no-holds-barred hucksterism aimed at doing the same sales job on the reader as the author and/or agent did on the editor. So, keep that book proposal handy as you prepare the table of contents.

Formatting Specs

- Center the heading "Table of Contents" or "Contents" one-third of the way down the page.
- Provide extra-wide margins, at least 1½″.
- Don't number pages as part of the manuscript.
- Use a slug in the same place as the header in the rest of the manuscript.
- At the very least, include the chapter titles.
- Include such front-matter elements as prefaces, forewords and prologues.
- Include back matter, such as the appendix or glossary.
- Don't include acknowledgments, dedications and other short bits of front matter.
- Page numbers are the numbers as they occur in your manuscript. The numbers in the book will be different, of course, and impossible for you to predict.

Other Dos and Don'ts

- Do get a sense from the editor of what direction she wants from the table of contents. This should dictate how much you present and how you present it.

On front matter:

"We usually do the front matter ourselves because it's so changeable with the ultimate page count of the book. If you end up with a book that's 162 pages and you have to cut two pages to make it an even signature, you go to the front matter and figure out how to do that. Front matter is such a very minor editorial chore that I think the author should just (stick with the) obvious."

—Peter Burford, publisher, Burford Books

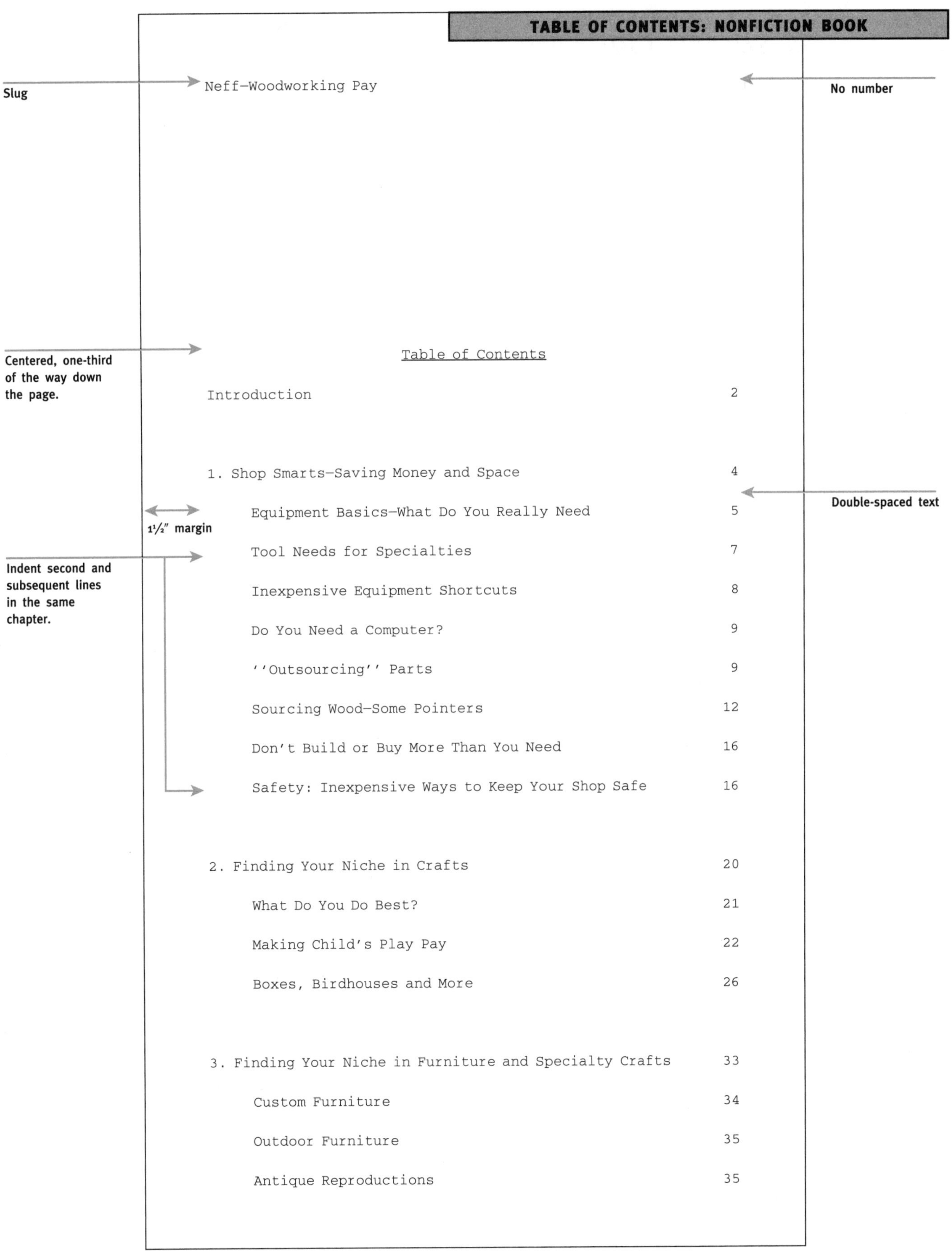
TABLE OF CONTENTS: NONFICTION BOOK
Slug
Neff–Woodworking Pay
No number
Centered, one-third of the way down the page.
Table of Contents
Introduction 2
1. Shop Smarts–Saving Money and Space 4
Double-spaced text
Equipment Basics–What Do You Really Need 5
1½" margin
Tool Needs for Specialties 7
Indent second and subsequent lines in the same chapter.
Inexpensive Equipment Shortcuts 8
Do You Need a Computer? 9
''Outsourcing'' Parts 9
Sourcing Wood–Some Pointers 12
Don't Build or Buy More Than You Need 16
Safety: Inexpensive Ways to Keep Your Shop Safe 16
2. Finding Your Niche in Crafts 20
What Do You Do Best? 21
Making Child's Play Pay 22
Boxes, Birdhouses and More 26
3. Finding Your Niche in Furniture and Specialty Crafts 33
Custom Furniture 34
Outdoor Furniture 35
Antique Reproductions 35

Dedications, Epigraphs and Inscriptions

Submission Tips

These short pieces are all handled similarly from a format standpoint. A dedication is a short statement dedicating the book to a person or persons, often in combination with some expression of affection. An epigraph or inscription is a quote that sums up, signifies or sets the tone for the book.

Formatting Specs

- Dedications and epigraphs are centered about a third of the way down the page.
- Don't number the page.
- Use the slug in the header.
- Keep them to two or three short lines.
- Don't put a heading above these to label them (e.g., "Dedication").

Foreword

Submission Tips

A foreword is a commentary or review of the book written by an expert in the field or someone familiar with the story of the book's creation. If the name and the review do not add something to the appeal of the book, they serve no function.

Formatting Specs

- Like the rest of the front matter, the foreword has a slug but no page numbers.
- Use a heading, starting about a third of the way down the first page.
- The name of the foreword's author goes flush right at the end of the text, followed by title and affiliation.
- Optional: Flush left after the text may go the city and year where and when the foreword was written.

Other Dos and Don'ts

- Don't confuse the foreword with the preface or introduction. The foreword is written by someone other than the author.

> **"It's got to be the wave of the future to do submissions electronically. It sure doesn't bother me, and I think it saves a lot of time and desk space, to send proposals by E-mail or on disk. More and more authors are sending ideas by E-mail, and I think that's a very healthy direction, because you can enclose quite a bit more on an E-mail more conveniently and it's a lot less paper involved. Paper is the enemy of all editors."**
>
> —Peter Burford, publisher, Burford Books

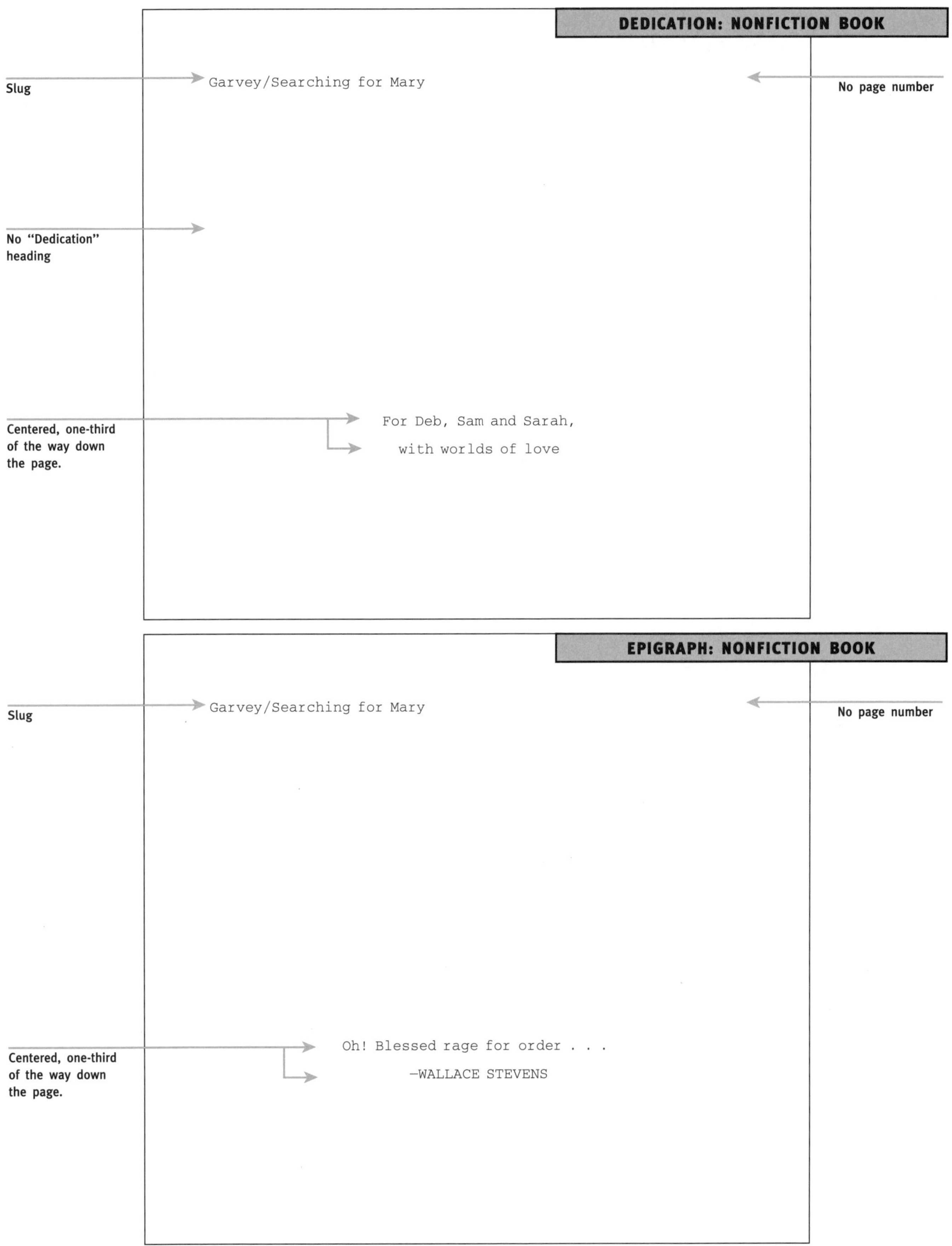
DEDICATION: NONFICTION BOOK
Slug
Garvey/Searching for Mary
No page number
No "Dedication" heading
Centered, one-third of the way down the page.
For Deb, Sam and Sarah,
with worlds of love
EPIGRAPH: NONFICTION BOOK
Slug
Garvey/Searching for Mary
No page number
Centered, one-third of the way down the page.
Oh! Blessed rage for order . . .
—WALLACE STEVENS

FOREWORD: NONFICTION BOOK
One way to keep front matter organized is by providing a slug for the section. Whatever information you include in your slug, make sure it's consistent throughout the manuscript.
Foreword: Selling Your Ideas
No number
Foreword
Centered heading, one-third of the way down the page.
4 lines
I was there when Roger McCallister had his first big idea in business. He was a twenty-two-year-old sales representative for Cyclops Steel just out of college when he returned from a sales call very excited, clutching a handful of napkins covered with notes, scribbles and diagrams. After he calmed down a bit, I soon discovered that he had landed on a concept that would radically change the steel industry forever.
I never did quite understand how a sales rep fresh out of college came up with what would be known as the continuous casting process, but I quickly realized the power of his proposal. Unfortunately, the guys in engineering weren't used to taking cues from downy-faced salesmen just out of college. I knew we had a tough selling job ahead of us internally.
Good thing Roger already had an instinct for how to work the system. He had enlisted the help of his boss—me—and given me ownership of the idea at an early stage. Soon, I was using my contacts with junior-level executives in the engineering department to find out if this idea truly had legs. By the time we made a formal presentation to the engineering department, we already had the support of key people in that organization.
I watched Roger's career skyrocket after that day, and was witness to plenty more good ideas where the first came from. But more than just having good ideas, Roger learned quickly how to get other people to embrace them as their own.
When he came into my office twenty-three years later with the idea for this book, I knew he had a winner. If there was one person I would want selling my idea up and down the organization chart, Roger is the man. I know readers will come away armed with insights into how the system works and how ideas go from napkins to blueprints.
Double-spaced text
1" margin
2 lines
Flush left.
Pittsburgh, 1999
Herman Oreschmelter
CEO, CycleX Corp.
Flush right.

Preface, Prologue and Acknowledgments

Submission Tips

Formatting for each of these front-matter elements is very similar, though each serves a different purpose. We've chosen to show you a sample acknowledgments page (opposite), but the same formatting applies to all front-matter elements discussed on this page.

A preface explains the story behind the book—the reason why it was written, the background, the unusual stories that were part of its creation. In other cases, a preface may serve as another pitch for the book, explaining why it's needed and how to use it—at least that's the theory. A preface sometimes gets muddled in with the purposes of an introduction or a prologue.

A prologue explains events or history that provide a context for the rest of the book. If you're writing a book that chronicles an event, for instance, the prologue might describe the events or forces that led up to that event.

Acknowledgments are the place where you thank the folks who helped you put the book together. Though the preface and prologue are purely optional, the acknowledgments are not. It's virtually impossible to write a nonfiction book without someone's help, and it's just plain impolite not to thank them. Though this is front matter, it's among the last things you'll write.

Publishers and editors generally consider the introduction part of the body of the book. But in some cases, the book's introduction is treated as front matter, too, and handled the same way as these other elements.

Formatting Specs

- As with other front-matter elements, these are not numbered as part of the rest of the manuscript. They do, however, get slugs.
- If you have only one page for these elements, stick with the regular manuscript slug.
- If you have two or more pages in these elements, use a specialized slug for each element (e.g., Acknowledgments: Selling Your Idea), or use the regular manuscript slug and number the entire front-matter section separately using Roman numerals. Your call, depending on how much you enjoy Roman numerals.
- For each element, drop about a third of the way down the page and use a centered heading.
- Then, drop an extra line, indent and get started.

Other Dos and Don'ts

- Do include these elements if they truly add something to the book.
- Don't include prefaces or prologues just to appear impressive. This is truly the mark of an amateur.
- Don't forget anyone who helped in preparation of the book when you write the acknowledgments, unless they don't want to be mentioned. It can pay to keep a running file of names and ways that people helped so you don't have to scramble for this information at the end.

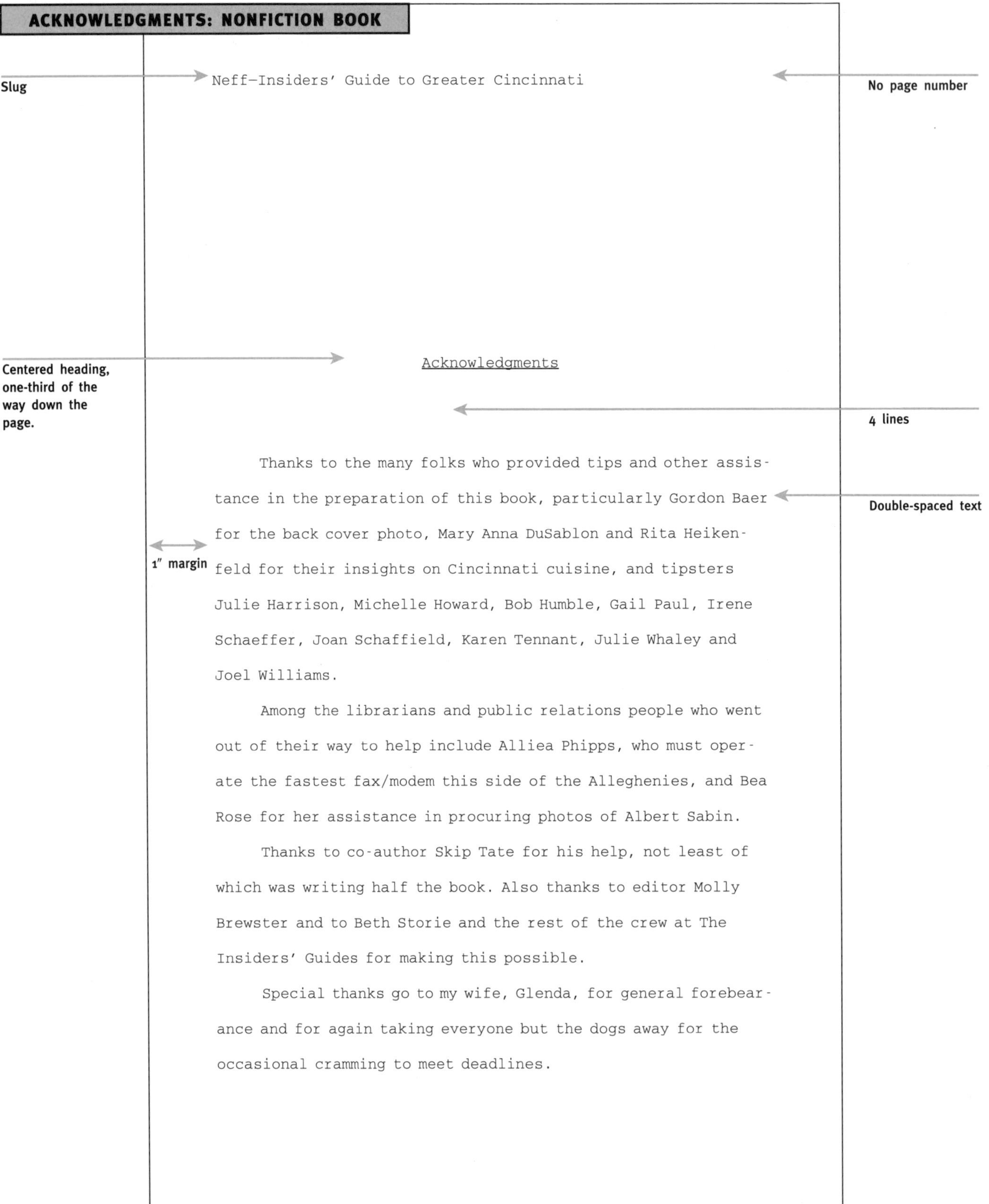

Neff–Insiders' Guide to Greater Cincinnati

Acknowledgments

Thanks to the many folks who provided tips and other assistance in the preparation of this book, particularly Gordon Baer for the back cover photo, Mary Anna DuSablon and Rita Heikenfeld for their insights on Cincinnati cuisine, and tipsters Julie Harrison, Michelle Howard, Bob Humble, Gail Paul, Irene Schaeffer, Joan Schaffield, Karen Tennant, Julie Whaley and Joel Williams.

Among the librarians and public relations people who went out of their way to help include Alliea Phipps, who must operate the fastest fax/modem this side of the Alleghenies, and Bea Rose for her assistance in procuring photos of Albert Sabin.

Thanks to co-author Skip Tate for his help, not least of which was writing half the book. Also thanks to editor Molly Brewster and to Beth Storie and the rest of the crew at The Insiders' Guides for making this possible.

Special thanks go to my wife, Glenda, for general forebearance and for again taking everyone but the dogs away for the occasional cramming to meet deadlines.

Back Matter

Submission Tips

It's a dirty job, but somebody has to do it—that would be you.

Back matter is that mostly unglamorous but necessary part of any nonfiction book that includes the endnotes, appendix, glossary, bibliography, epilogue and index. Here's information on what they are and how to handle them:

- **Endnotes** are used mainly for scholarly manuscripts and business proposals but are sometimes included in other nonfiction books based on significant documentary research. They can be handy in eliminating the need to pepper the manuscript with attributions, allowing instead a quick reference to the endnote for anyone seeking the source of information. Endnotes may also be included in more scholarly articles. *The Chicago Manual of Style* is the definitive source on handling these and other back-matter issues.
- The **appendix** is used for material that supports information or arguments in the book but which is too lengthy to include or would hamper the natural flow of the book. It's similar to the attachments found on a book proposal.
- A **glossary** lists and defines special terminology used in the book, such as technical phrases, foreign words and phrases or any other specialized lexicon or patois.
- The **bibliography** is a list of books cited in the manuscript, used in researching the manuscript or otherwise useful as further reading. A bibliography with a brief commentary or review of significant titles and why they're helpful adds some value to an otherwise fairly dry formality. The bibliography may also be called "Recommended Reading" or incorporated into a section on "Resources" that includes information on Web sites of interest, events or where to buy products related to the book's subject.
- The **epilogue** provides a final thought from the author, perhaps summing up the work's impact on the author or, in a revised edition, detailing changes that have occurred since or because of the book.
- The **index** is a more or less detailed listing of all the people, places, things and concepts cited in the book. Generally, indexes are prepared by professional indexers who are paid a relatively nominal fee out of the author's royalties. Unless you have a special love for this kind of work, you're best off leaving it this way. This book won't cover how to do the index, but several specialized books are available if you're interested.

Formatting Specs

- Unlike front matter, back matter is numbered as part of your manuscript.
- Back-matter pages take the same slug as the rest of the manuscript.
- All elements of the back matter start with a centered heading about a third of the way down the page and are double-spaced, like the rest of the manuscript.
- Because the details of these listings are far easier to grasp by seeing than reading about them, check the models that follow for additional details.
- The format for the appendix and epilogue are the same as for front-matter elements, except that they are numbered as part of the manuscript. See the front-matter section on page 75 for details.

Other Dos and Don'ts

- Do only include these elements if you have a good reason. As with front matter, you don't get any extra credit for having a well-rounded assortment of back matter. Except for the index, and at times the bibliography, none of these elements are indispensable.

ENDNOTES: NONFICTION BOOK

Slug

Simopoulos—The Omega Plan 332

Page number

Centered heading, one-third of the way down the page.

Comments and Endnotes

4 lines

1" margin

Chapter 1: Found: The Missing Ingredients for Optimal Health

2 lines

Indent each endnote.

1. The chart has been adapted from a chart that appeared in reference 10 above. It compares the number of patients who were free from cardiac death and nonfatal heart attacks.

Double-spaced text

Authors

Title

2. De Longeril, M., P. Salen, and J. Delaye. ''Effect of a Mediterranean Type of Diet on the Rate of Cardiovasular Complications in Patients With Coronary Artery Disease.'' *J Amer Coll Cardiology*, 1996; 28(5):1103-8.

Journal title/year/volume/number.

Page numbers

3. Grady, D. ''Unusual Molecule Could Be Key to Cancer Patients' Weight Loss,'' in *The New York Times*. Jan. 4, 1996, p. B10.

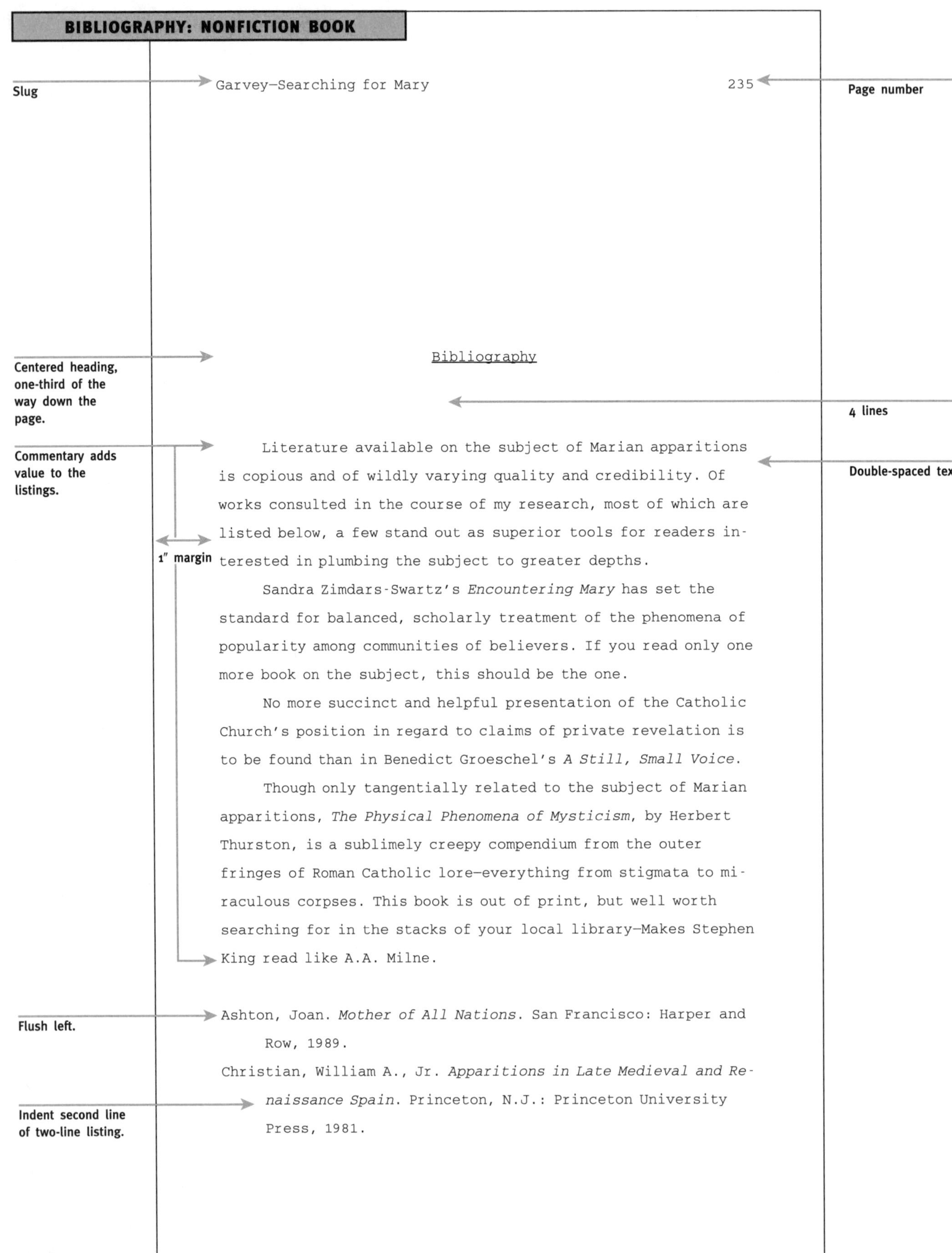

Garvey—Searching for Mary 235

Bibliography

Literature available on the subject of Marian apparitions is copious and of wildly varying quality and credibility. Of works consulted in the course of my research, most of which are listed below, a few stand out as superior tools for readers interested in plumbing the subject to greater depths.

Sandra Zimdars-Swartz's *Encountering Mary* has set the standard for balanced, scholarly treatment of the phenomena of popularity among communities of believers. If you read only one more book on the subject, this should be the one.

No more succinct and helpful presentation of the Catholic Church's position in regard to claims of private revelation is to be found than in Benedict Groeschel's *A Still, Small Voice*.

Though only tangentially related to the subject of Marian apparitions, *The Physical Phenomena of Mysticism*, by Herbert Thurston, is a sublimely creepy compendium from the outer fringes of Roman Catholic lore—everything from stigmata to miraculous corpses. This book is out of print, but well worth searching for in the stacks of your local library—Makes Stephen King read like A.A. Milne.

Ashton, Joan. *Mother of All Nations*. San Francisco: Harper and Row, 1989.

Christian, William A., Jr. *Apparitions in Late Medieval and Renaissance Spain*. Princeton, N.J.: Princeton University Press, 1981.

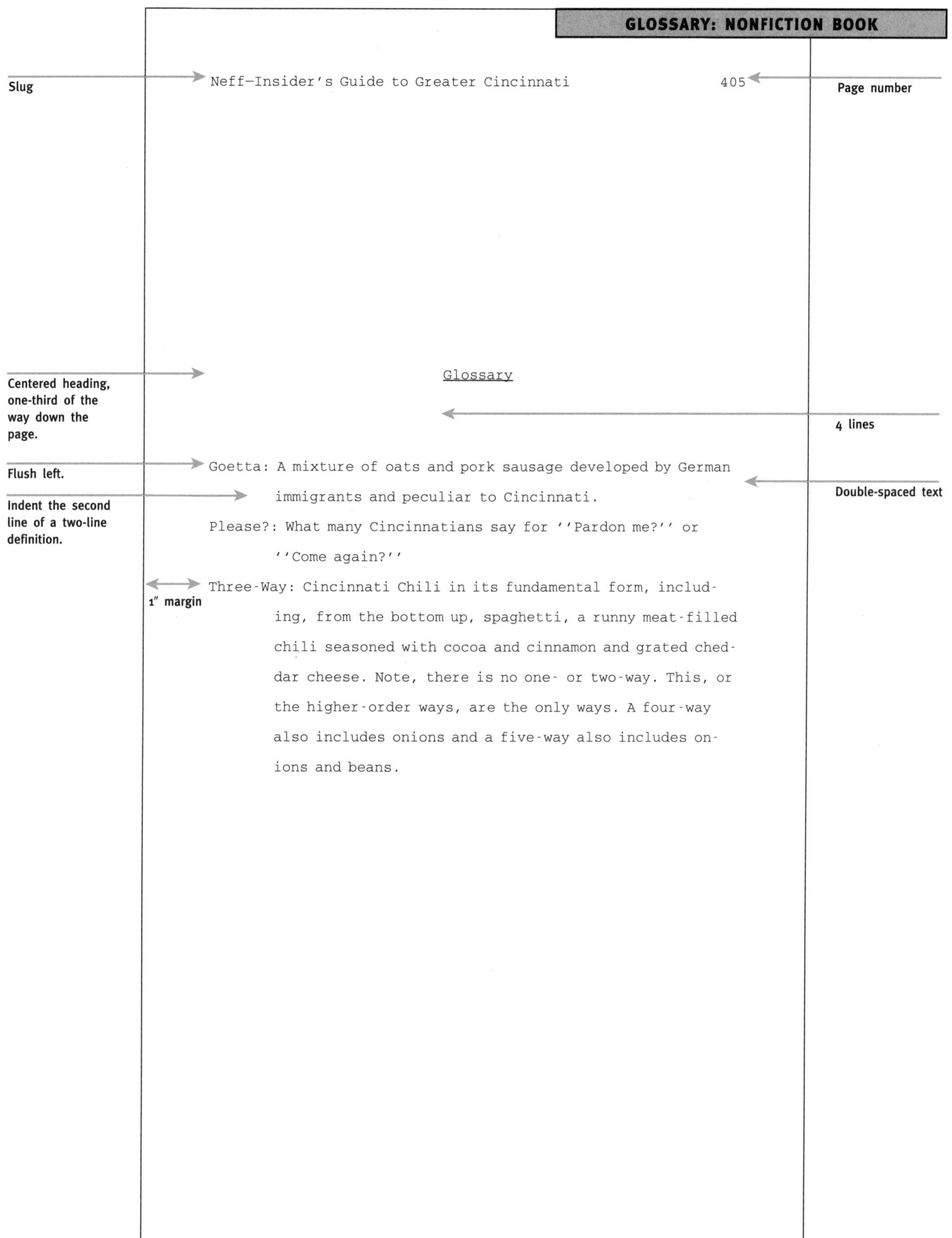
GLOSSARY: NONFICTION BOOK
Slug
Neff—Insider's Guide to Greater Cincinnati
405
Page number
Centered heading, one-third of the way down the page.
Glossary
4 lines
Flush left.
Goetta: A mixture of oats and pork sausage developed by German
Indent the second line of a two-line definition.
immigrants and peculiar to Cincinnati.
Double-spaced text
Please?: What many Cincinnatians say for ''Pardon me?'' or
''Come again?''
1" margin
Three-Way: Cincinnati Chili in its fundamental form, includ-
ing, from the bottom up, spaghetti, a runny meat-filled
chili seasoned with cocoa and cinnamon and grated ched-
dar cheese. Note, there is no one- or two-way. This, or
the higher-order ways, are the only ways. A four-way
also includes onions and a five-way also includes onions and beans.

CHAPTER THREE

SHORT AND SPECIALIZED PIECES

Fillers/Anecdotes

Submission Tips

Submission of other short forms generally follows the guidelines for articles, with a few exceptions. Since these are short pieces, it would be pointless to query editors on them. Simply submit these items with a brief cover letter noting what's enclosed, provide a brief paragraph on your background and politely request a response.

These items usually take up a page or less. When they take more, follow the same guidelines for pagination and headers as you would with articles. It's OK to leave less white space above the item to make it fit on one page.

Formatting Specs

- Use a 1″ margin on all sides.
- Don't number the first page.
- If you need a second page, put a slug, or one- to two-word name at the top left corner of the header. Also put a page number at the top right-hand corner of the second page.
- Include rights offered or negotiated and a word count in the top right corner of the first page.
- Include name, address and phone number (include fax and E-mail, when applicable) in the top left corner of the first page.
- When appropriate, put the working title in all caps or boldface and the subtitle underlined or in italic centered, about one-third of the way down the page from the top margin.
- Don't include a byline. Such short items rarely get them. Occasionally, an editor will give the writer credit in a tag line, but you don't need to include your name with the manuscript.
- Drop four lines, indent and begin the item.
- Double-space the entire text of the item.
- Keep type size 10-12 points.
- To submit articles by fax, use the same guidelines. Simply use the fax cover sheet to replace the mail cover sheet version. And consider using a sans serif font and 12-point type to make the manuscript more legible.

Other Dos and Don'ts

- Don't use a notation of any kind at the end of the item.
- Don't staple the manuscript to the cover letter; insert them loose-leaf.
- Don't use a separate cover page.
- Do put one item per page when making multiple submissions.
- Don't insult the editor's intelligence or intentions by putting a copyright notice on the manuscript. It's copyrighted as soon as you write it.
- Don't use unusual fonts. A simple Times Roman will do fine.

Electronic Submissions

These short items are ideally suited for electronic submissions. Generally, you'll send unformatted text files as attachments or in the body of the E-mail. But don't go clicking away until you've ascertained the electronic submission policies of the publication or syndicate to which you're sending material. Writer's guidelines (see Request for Guidelines Letter on page 23) should spell out the electronic guidelines.

FILLER/ANECDOTE

Jon Newberry
444 W. Eighteenth St.
Cincinnati, OH 45226
(513) 555-3334
newberr@fuse.net

First North American Rights
About 225 words

Rights offered.

Word count.

Title in all caps, centered, one-third of the way down the page.

CONFESSIONS OF A USED-CAR SALESMAN

No byline.

4 lines

On my first day as a used car salesman for a dealership owned by Marge Schott (former owner of the Cincinnati Reds known for dismissing managers and front office staff on, shall we say, whimsical grounds), she fired the guy who had hired me. Another salesman said: ''Don't worry. I've been here for two years, and that's the twentieth sales manager I've worked for.''

Double-spaced text

Actually, the highlight of my career was my first job at Toyota of Cincinnati, then part of what's now the Performance chain. They rewrote and refined the book on high-pressure sales techniques. First day there, my manager (still the best salesman I've ever seen in action—probably a millionaire by now) was showing me the ropes. He talked some poor girl into putting down a fifty-dollar deposit to hold a car so that we couldn't sell it before she brought her husband back to see it that night. I kept calling them to see when they were gonna come back and at least pick up their deposit, and they said we could keep it. They knew if they set foot back on the lot, they'd own a car when they left. She was terrified.

1″ margin

That summer we finally toppled Jake Sweeney from the top of the list as the number one used-car lot in the city.

Columns and Op-Eds

Submission Tips

Columns, be they how-to, business or op-ed pieces, are all styled similarly and generally follow the article format described earlier. The only difference is a brief (usually one-sentence) biographical paragraph appended to the end of the column.

Clearly, you do need to query before landing a regular column assignment with a publication, preferably with three or more ideas (see the Column Query on p. 93). A query isn't necessary for an op-ed submission, though it can certainly help to write ahead for writer's guidelines (especially with magazines) before making a submission.

A brief cover letter introducing either assigned or speculative submissions is in order. Mention the enclosure and provide any other information that may help in editing the piece, including the best times to reach you at the phone number(s) you provide. Especially with newspapers, editors' hours can vary widely, so give both a daytime and evening phone number. Also provide any information or contact phone numbers that could help in fact checking.

Formatting Specs

- Use a 1″ margin on all sides.
- Use the upper-left corner for your name, address, phone number and other particulars (single-spaced).
- Include rights offered (First North American Rights are generally assumed) and a rough word count (single-spaced) in the upper-right corner.
- Put suggested title or headline in all caps or boldface centered, starting about a third of the way down the page.
- Drop a line and put "by" in lowercase, centered.
- Drop a line and type your name, centered.
- Double-space the rest of the column or op-ed.
- Indent paragraphs, except for your bio at the end of the piece.
- On the second page, use a slug (generally your last name) in the top left corner, and number pages in the top right corner.
- At the end of the column, type a return and then, with no indentation, write your bio. This can be in italic, if you want, but it doesn't need to be. Keep your bio to one sentence, mentioning your name, what you do and any other fact that may be of relevance to readers of the column or op-ed. Only in the most compelling of circumstances add another sentence.

Other Dos and Don'ts

- Do include daytime and evening phone numbers for submissions to newspapers.
- Do research your column or op-ed as thoroughly as you would anything else you write. Just because it's an opinion doesn't mean you don't need facts. Indeed, the need to verify facts is, if anything, even more pronounced in an opinion piece.
- Do use your real name in an op-ed submission. No worthwhile publication accepts opinion pieces from anonymous contributors.
- Do be brief. About 700 words is generally the top end for opinion pieces. Generally, the shorter the piece, the better its chance of being published, though anything under 250 words is generally letter-to-the-editor material rather than an op-ed piece.

Electronic Submissions

Usually your first-time submission will be on paper, unless you make other arrangements in advance. Many newspapers do have electronic submission guidelines that can be found on their editorial or op-ed pages. Magazines with regular opinion features, such as *Newsweek*, provide writer's guidelines on paper (see Request for Guidelines Letter on page 23).

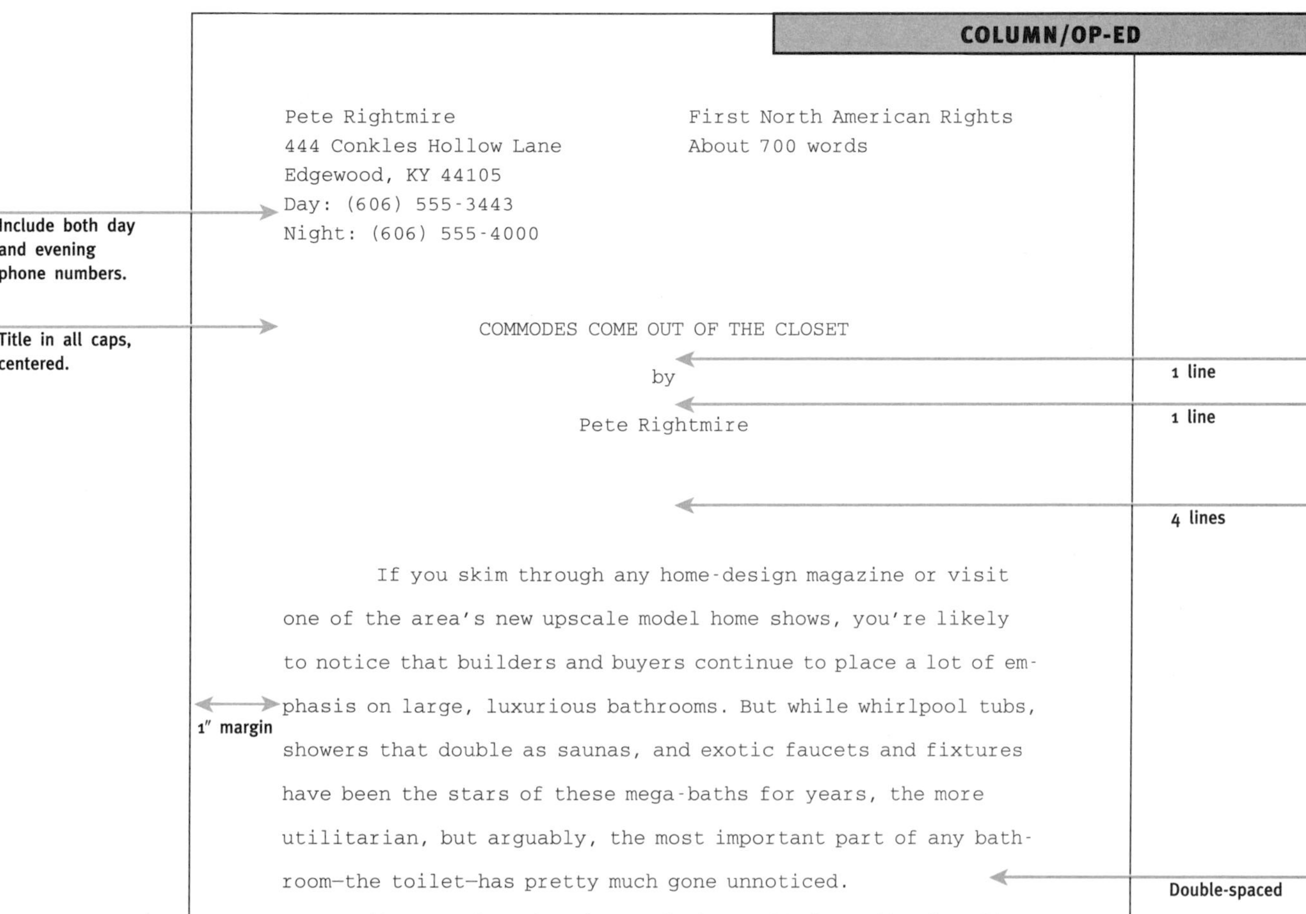

Pete Rightmire
444 Conkles Hollow Lane
Edgewood, KY 44105
Day: (606) 555-3443
Night: (606) 555-4000

First North American Rights
About 700 words

COMMODES COME OUT OF THE CLOSET

by

Pete Rightmire

If you skim through any home-design magazine or visit one of the area's new upscale model home shows, you're likely to notice that builders and buyers continue to place a lot of emphasis on large, luxurious bathrooms. But while whirlpool tubs, showers that double as saunas, and exotic faucets and fixtures have been the stars of these mega-baths for years, the more utilitarian, but arguably, the most important part of any bathroom—the toilet—has pretty much gone unnoticed.

1″ margin

Double-spaced

Until recently, that is. It looks as if the toilet has finally come into its own. Last year the National Park Service built a two-stall facility in a Pennsylvania recreational area at a cost of $391,000. That's almost $196,000 a head.

And while no one's as efficient as the federal government at flushing money down the drain, New York City recently took the plunge, building $200,000-plus comfort stations in its city parks. But with four stalls and one urinal each, the total construction cost, per toilet, came to only $45,000, a fraction of what the Park Service spent.

If you're one of those folks who thinks nothing's too good for your pet, you can cough up $215 for the Litter Maid, an electric litter box that cleans itself after every use. This is just for cats, because, as one pet shop owner put it, ''A cat's insulted going to a box that's not scooped.'' Dogs, on the other hand, aren't anywhere near as picky about where they take care of business. Pretty much like most men.

Bio line is flush left, italic (optional) and one sentence.

Pete Rightmire is a freelance writer who lives in Edgewood, KY.

Radio and TV Commentaries

Submission Tips

Because many radio and TV commentaries come from people who don't write for a living, and some are submitted in the form of demo tapes rather than manuscripts, the style here is fairly informal. It's best to contact the station directly, find out who deals with commentary submissions and discuss with them what form they prefer.

Generally, the manuscript should indicate how long it will take you to deliver the piece and provide a brief bio and a suggested lead-in for the announcer. Otherwise, commentaries work like other articles and short forms.

Formatting Specs

- Use a 1″ margin on all sides.
- Use the top left corner for a title for your piece, your name, address, phone number and other particulars (single-spaced).
- At the top right corner, include a word count and estimated air time.
- Put suggested title in all caps or boldface centered, starting about a third of the way down the page.
- Drop a line and put "by" in lowercase, centered.
- Drop a line and type your name, centered.
- If possible, include a brief, one- or two-sentence lead-in that can be used by an announcer to introduce your piece.
- Double-space the rest of the column or op-ed.
- Indent paragraphs, except for your bio at the end of the piece.
- On the second page use a slug (generally your last name) in the top left corner, and number pages in the top right corner.
- At the end of the column, with no indentation, write your bio. This can be in italic, if you want, but it doesn't need to be. Generally, keep your bio to one sentence, mentioning your name, what you do and any other relevant fact.

Other Dos and Don'ts

- Do include daytime and evening phone numbers.
- Do research your column or op-ed as thoroughly as you would anything else you write. Just because it's an opinion doesn't mean you don't need facts. Indeed, the need to verify facts is, if anything, even more pronounced in an opinion piece.
- Do use your real name.

Electronic Submissions

Some stations may accept electronic submissions. Check with the contact person at the station for guidelines.

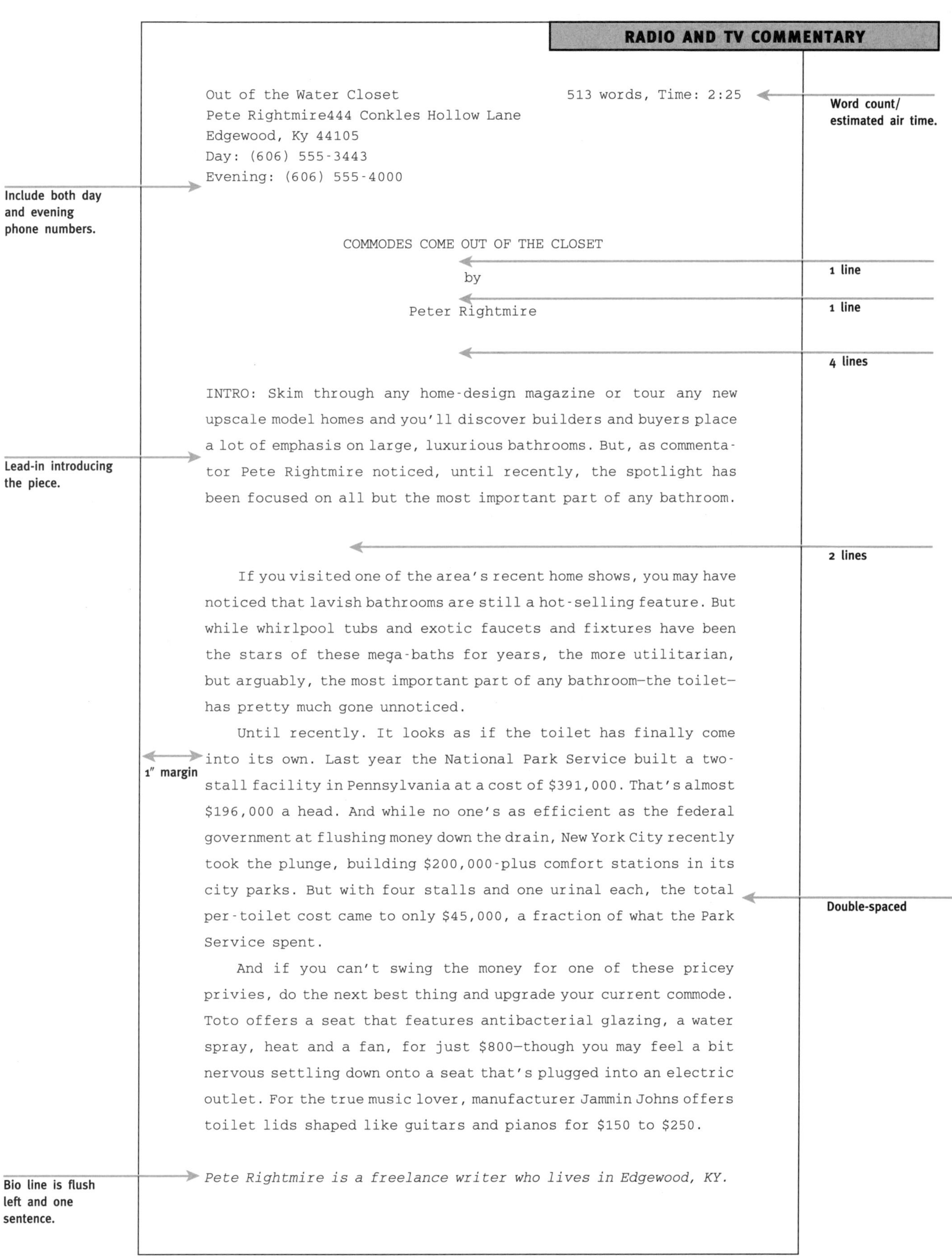
RADIO AND TV COMMENTARY

Out of the Water Closet 513 words, Time: 2:25
Pete Rightmire444 Conkles Hollow Lane
Edgewood, Ky 44105
Day: (606) 555-3443
Evening: (606) 555-4000

COMMODES COME OUT OF THE CLOSET

by

Peter Rightmire

INTRO: Skim through any home-design magazine or tour any new upscale model homes and you'll discover builders and buyers place a lot of emphasis on large, luxurious bathrooms. But, as commentator Pete Rightmire noticed, until recently, the spotlight has been focused on all but the most important part of any bathroom.

If you visited one of the area's recent home shows, you may have noticed that lavish bathrooms are still a hot-selling feature. But while whirlpool tubs and exotic faucets and fixtures have been the stars of these mega-baths for years, the more utilitarian, but arguably, the most important part of any bathroom—the toilet—has pretty much gone unnoticed.

Until recently. It looks as if the toilet has finally come into its own. Last year the National Park Service built a two-stall facility in Pennsylvania at a cost of $391,000. That's almost $196,000 a head. And while no one's as efficient as the federal government at flushing money down the drain, New York City recently took the plunge, building $200,000-plus comfort stations in its city parks. But with four stalls and one urinal each, the total per-toilet cost came to only $45,000, a fraction of what the Park Service spent.

And if you can't swing the money for one of these pricey privies, do the next best thing and upgrade your current commode. Toto offers a seat that features antibacterial glazing, a water spray, heat and a fan, for just $800—though you may feel a bit nervous settling down onto a seat that's plugged into an electric outlet. For the true music lover, manufacturer Jammin Johns offers toilet lids shaped like guitars and pianos for $150 to $250.

Pete Rightmire is a freelance writer who lives in Edgewood, KY.

Part Two
FICTION

CHAPTER FOUR

SHORT STORIES

What You Need to Submit

Submitting short stories is quite simple. Unlike with novels (where you typically need to submit a query letter as well as a few sample chapters, an outline and a synopsis), with a short story you only need to send a cover letter and the story (in its entirety). But before you actually submit your story, obtain a copy of the magazine's writer's guidelines. To save time, first try to locate the magazine's Web site to obtain the guidelines. A search engine such as www.yahoo.com can help locate a magazine's Web site. If you can't find the Web site, then proceed to write to the magazine.

Request for Guidelines Letter

Submission Tips

Just send a brief letter stating that you'd like to receive the writer's guidelines. It's also a good idea to ask whether the magazine offers the guidelines on its Web site (if there is one).

Formatting Specs

- Address it to the correct editor.
- Use a 1″ margin on all sides.
- Use block or semiblock format.
- Keep it to one paragraph.
- Include your name, address and phone number (include E-mail and fax, if applicable).
- Enclose an SASE.

Other Dos and Don'ts

- Don't mention anything about your story at this point—all you want are the guidelines.
- Don't mention anything about yourself.
- Don't use "Dear Sir," "Dear Madame," etc. in your salutation.
- Don't address it Mr., Ms., Mrs. or Miss unless you're certain of the person's gender and marital status. If unsure, write, "Dear Pat Smith."
- Do keep the letter brief and to the point.

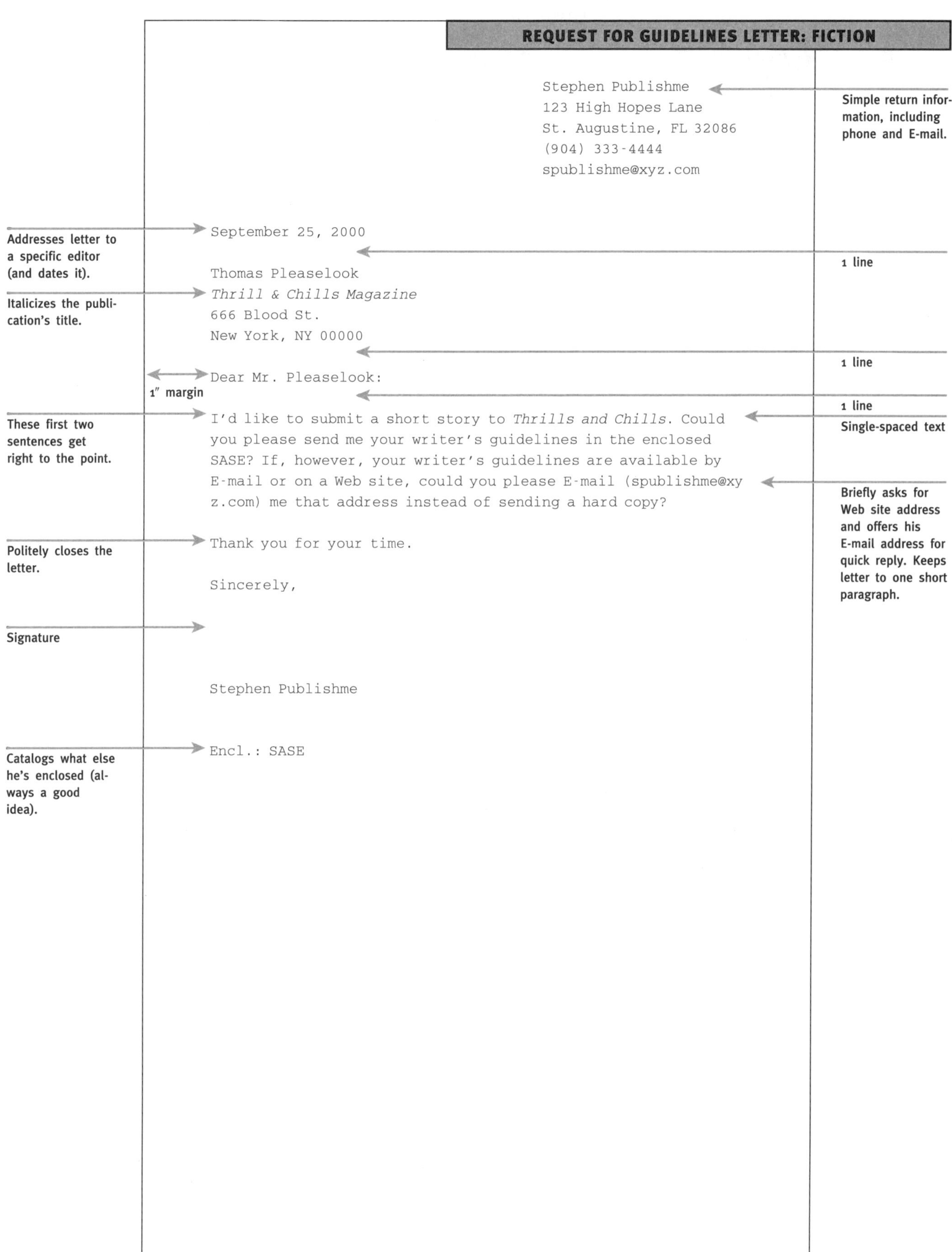

REQUEST FOR GUIDELINES LETTER: FICTION

Stephen Publishme
123 High Hopes Lane
St. Augustine, FL 32086
(904) 333-4444
spublishme@xyz.com

September 25, 2000

Thomas Pleaselook
Thrill & Chills Magazine
666 Blood St.
New York, NY 00000

Dear Mr. Pleaselook:

I'd like to submit a short story to *Thrills and Chills*. Could you please send me your writer's guidelines in the enclosed SASE? If, however, your writer's guidelines are available by E-mail or on a Web site, could you please E-mail (spublishme@xyz.com) me that address instead of sending a hard copy?

Thank you for your time.

Sincerely,

Stephen Publishme

Encl.: SASE

Simple return information, including phone and E-mail.
Addresses letter to a specific editor (and dates it).
1 line
Italicizes the publication's title.
1 line
1" margin
1 line
These first two sentences get right to the point.
Single-spaced text
Briefly asks for Web site address and offers his E-mail address for quick reply. Keeps letter to one short paragraph.
Politely closes the letter.
Signature
Catalogs what else he's enclosed (always a good idea).

Cover Letter

Submission Tips

Your cover letter is important for two reasons: It lets the editor know who you are and how you write. The best cover letters contain three short paragraphs, in the following order:

- The **introductory** paragraph (state the story's title, then hook the editor with a brief description of your story).
- The **biographical** paragraph (in one or two sentences, explain a bit about yourself that's pertinent to the story, such as previous publishing credits, why you're sending it to this particular magazine or how a personal experience influenced your story).
- The **concluding** paragraph (politely close the letter).

While publication will hinge on the story itself, a strong cover letter will ensure your story will at least get a close read. Remember to keep it brief and to the point.

Formatting Specs

- Use a standard font or typeface (avoid bold, script or italics, except for publication titles).
- Put your name, address and phone number (include E-mail and fax) in the top right-hand corner or on your letterhead.
- Use a 1″ margin on all sides.
- Address it to a specific editor (call and get the appropriate editor's name, and make sure you know the gender).
- Keep it to one page.
- Use block or semiblock letter format (no indentations, extra space between paragraphs).
- Include an SASE or postcard for reply, and state in the letter that you have done so. (The postcard is cheaper and easier for everyone involved. You can have them printed in bulk.)
- Single-space the body of the letter; double-space between paragraphs.
- Give the story's exact word count.
- Thank the editor for considering your story.
- Optional: Mention whether you're soliciting other magazines.
- Optional: Mention how long you'll wait for a response.
- Optional: Mention that your manuscript is disposable and does not need to be returned (this is often just assumed).
- Optional: State that you're able to send your story on disk or via E-mail (this doesn't come up until the editor actually wants to publish your story).

Other Dos and Don'ts

- Do mention if your story has been—or will be—published in another publication.
- Do indicate familiarity with the publication. Make a brief positive comment about the publication, but keep it to a sentence, be sincere and don't go overboard.
- Don't use "Dear Sir," "Dear Madame," etc. in your salutation. Don't use Mr.,

Ms., Mrs. or Miss unless you're certain of the person's gender and marital status. If unsure, write, "Dear Pat Smith."

- Don't state that some other publication has rejected your story.
- Don't ask for advice or criticism—that's not the editor's job at this stage in the game.
- Don't mention anything about yourself not pertinent to the story: you're a first-time writer, that you've never been published, or how much time you've spent on the story. Your story must stand on its own.
- Don't bring up payment for the story. It's premature.
- Don't mention copyright information.
- Don't include your social security number.
- Don't staple your cover letter to your story (a paper clip is OK).

"A truly terrible cover letter would include any in which the writer (1) compares himself to a great literary figure, (2) details the personal trauma that motivated his story, (3) writes more than a paragraph about the story, (4) includes pages of credits that have no relevance to fiction writing, (5) encloses a beefcake photo—may predispose editors/readers to take this writer less seriously than they otherwise would.

What we like to see? A letter which preferably spells the name of the magazine correctly and succinctly gives us the following information: relevant publication credits and relevant educational information. If a writer does not have these weapons in his arsenal, a little humor is always welcome, as are comments that demonstrate the writer has read our magazine."

—Adrienne Brodeur, editor in chief, *Zoetrope*

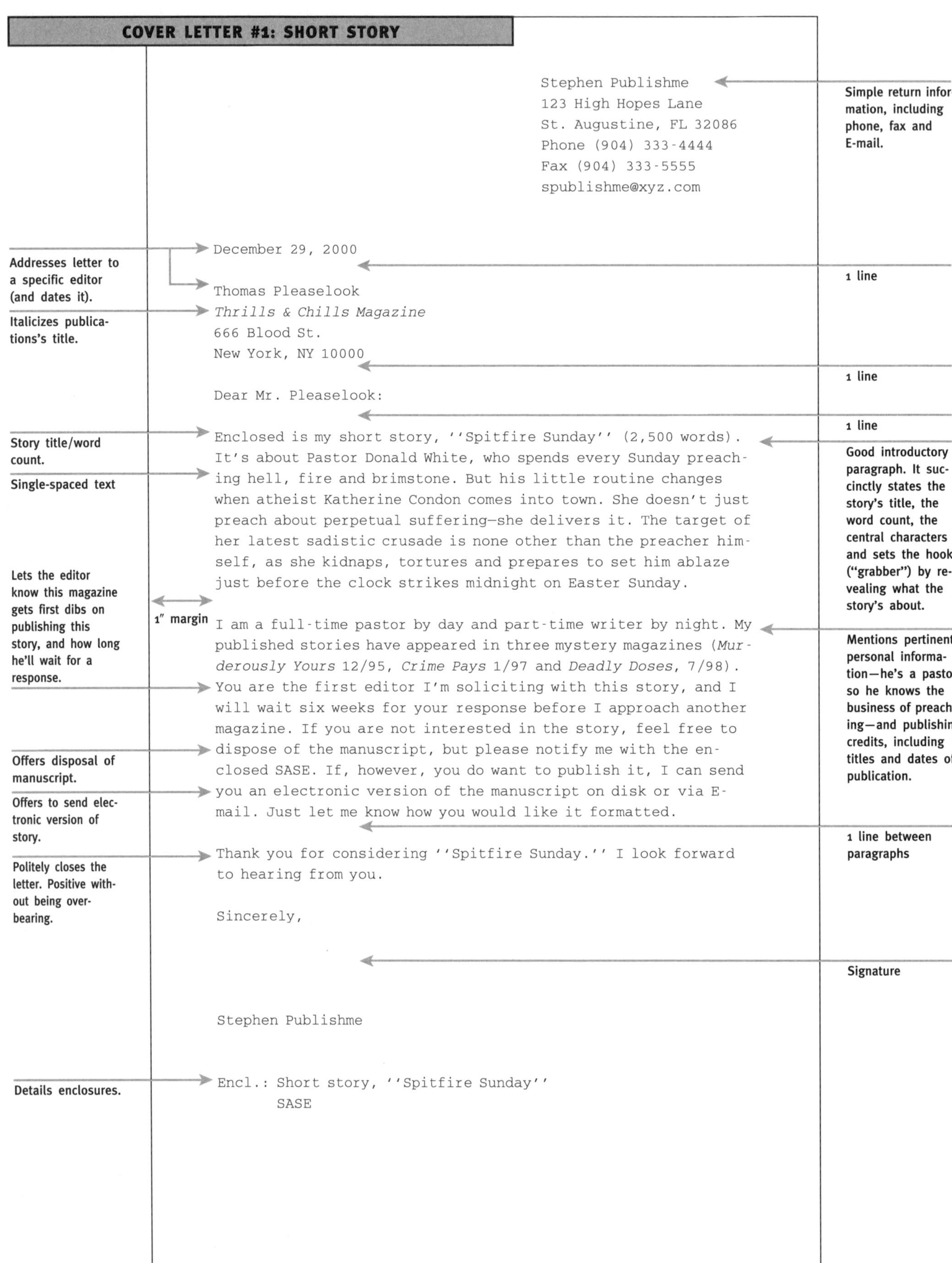

COVER LETTER #1: SHORT STORY

Stephen Publishme
123 High Hopes Lane
St. Augustine, FL 32086
Phone (904) 333-4444
Fax (904) 333-5555
spublishme@xyz.com

December 29, 2000

Thomas Pleaselook
Thrills & Chills Magazine
666 Blood St.
New York, NY 10000

Dear Mr. Pleaselook:

Enclosed is my short story, ''Spitfire Sunday'' (2,500 words). It's about Pastor Donald White, who spends every Sunday preaching hell, fire and brimstone. But his little routine changes when atheist Katherine Condon comes into town. She doesn't just preach about perpetual suffering—she delivers it. The target of her latest sadistic crusade is none other than the preacher himself, as she kidnaps, tortures and prepares to set him ablaze just before the clock strikes midnight on Easter Sunday.

I am a full-time pastor by day and part-time writer by night. My published stories have appeared in three mystery magazines (*Murderously Yours* 12/95, *Crime Pays* 1/97 and *Deadly Doses*, 7/98). You are the first editor I'm soliciting with this story, and I will wait six weeks for your response before I approach another magazine. If you are not interested in the story, feel free to dispose of the manuscript, but please notify me with the enclosed SASE. If, however, you do want to publish it, I can send you an electronic version of the manuscript on disk or via E-mail. Just let me know how you would like it formatted.

Thank you for considering ''Spitfire Sunday.'' I look forward to hearing from you.

Sincerely,

Stephen Publishme

Encl.: Short story, ''Spitfire Sunday''
SASE

Simple return information, including phone, fax and E-mail.
Addresses letter to a specific editor (and dates it).
1 line
Italicizes publications's title.
1 line
1 line
Story title/word count.
Good introductory paragraph. It succinctly states the story's title, the word count, the central characters and sets the hook ("grabber") by revealing what the story's about.
Single-spaced text
Lets the editor know this magazine gets first dibs on publishing this story, and how long he'll wait for a response.
1" margin
Mentions pertinent personal information—he's a pastor so he knows the business of preaching—and publishing credits, including titles and dates of publication.
Offers disposal of manuscript.
Offers to send electronic version of story.
1 line between paragraphs
Politely closes the letter. Positive without being overbearing.
Signature
Details enclosures.

COVER LETTER #2: SHORT STORY

Stephen Publishme
123 High Hopes Lane
St. Augustine, FL 32086
Phone (904) 333-4444
Fax (904) 333-5555
spublishme@xyz.com

Simple return information, including phone, fax and E-mail.

Addresses letter to a specific editor (and dates it).

December 29, 2000

1 line

Thomas Pleaselook
Thrills & Chills Magazine
666 Blood St.
New York, NY 10000

Italicizes publications's title.

1 line

Dear Mr. Pleaselook,

1 line

Enclosed is my short story, ''Spitfire Sunday'' (2,500 words). It's about Pastor Donald White, who spends every Sunday preaching hell, fire and brimstone. But his little routine changes when atheist Katherine Condon comes into town. She doesn't just preach about perpetual suffering—she delivers it.

1" margin

Single-spaced text

Really brief introductory paragraph. It includes the story's title, the word count and the central characters, but doesn't say much about the story itself.

1 line between paragraphs

I have published three previous stories. You are the first editor I'm soliciting with this story. I will wait six weeks for your response before I approach another magazine.

Only mentions that he's a published writer—no mention of specific publishing credits.

Lets the editor know this magazine gets first dibs on publishing this story, and how long he'll wait for a response.

Thank you for considering ''Spitfire Sunday.''

Politely closes the letter.

Sincerely,

Signature

Stephen Publishme

Encl.: Short story, ''Spitfire Sunday''
SASE

Catalogs every item being sent (including SASE).

QUERY MISTAKES TO AVOID

Stephen Publishme
123 High Hopes Lane
St. Augustine, FL 32086

No telephone number or E-mail.

December 29, 2000

Thomas Pleaselook
Thrills & Chills Magazine
666 Blood St.
New York, NY 10000

Salutation is far too informal.

Dear Tom,

Every sentence in this paragraph begins with "I".

Should begin with information about the story, not himself.

Tells the editor he's never been published by a professional publication.

Spends too much time trying to impress the editor.

Who cares—what qualifies them to give a valued opinion?

I have been a man of the pulpit for the last twenty-two years and I know about faith and evil and sin and redemption. I am also a published poet and fiction writer. I've had numerous poems published in our local paper and I write weekly stories for the church bulletin. I get lots of praise from my congregation for my stories, and other people in the community have made glowing remarks about my poetry.

Too colloquial.

Always a bad idea to tell the editor how much time you've spent on the story—irrelevant.

Should be "who" not "that."

Of course he'd like the magazine to publish it—doesn't need to be stated.

Doesn't tell enough about the story, but does reveal the ending! Where's the story's hook? Sounds stupid, obsequious and manipulative—fails to let the story stand on its own.

Anyhow, I've been working on this one short story for about five months now that I'd like your magazine to publish. It's about a minister who gets caught on fire and burned to death by a new woman in town that doesn't agree with his preaching practices. I'm sure you'll appreciate this story as it is based on some real people I have known and therefore it is based in reality but I made a lot of it up too. It'll scare the heck out of your readers.

Never ask for advice or criticism—that's not the editor's job at this stage in the game.

If for some reason you do not wish to publish this story, I would appreciate your wise and professional opinion about how to make it better.

Thank you for your time.

Sincerely,

Stephen Publishme

No mention of the story in the enclosures.

Encl.: SASE

Nowhere on this page does the writer mention the word count, the story's title or the main characters. This letter is way too self-congratulatory, informal, laden with errors and altogether unappealing. Even if the enclosed story is spectacular, the editor will be skeptical when reading it (if he bothers reading it after wading through this poor cover letter).

Reply Postcards

If you're a bit paranoid about whether your story actually makes it to the publication, you may send a reply postcard along with your story. Having it signed by the editor (or someone on the staff) and sent back to you will alleviate any worries that the package didn't make it to its destination. Two caveats: 1) Not all editors are gracious enough to send your reply postcards back—but most do; 2) Just because you receive a postcard reply from a publication, you cannot assume your story has been read or will be read in the next few days or even weeks. Your reply postcard's only function is to let you know your submission has been received.

Your best bet to ensure an editor will return your reply postcard is to make it neat and simple to use. That means typing your postcard and not asking the editor to do anything other than note your submission has been received. Although it's okay to leave a small space for "Comments," keep the space very small and never expect it to be filled in—most editors simply don't have the time or a reason to write anything in it. You'll turn off an editor if you ask him to do too much.

Creating a suitable and functional reply postcard is easy. If you create a reply postcard similar to the one below you'll be just fine. Above all, remember to keep things short and sweet—and, of course, always be sure the postcard has a stamp in the top right corner on the side with your address.

REPLY POSTCARD

Stephen Publishme
123 High Hopes Lane
St. Augustine, FL 32086

Your story was received on____________________

We need more time to consider your story and will be in touch. ☐

Yes, we are interested in your idea. An editor will be in touch soon. ☐

No, we are not interested in your story at this time. ☐

Comments: ____________________

Short Story Manuscript

Submission Tips

Establish yourself as a professional by following the correct short story format. A separate cover/title page is not necessary; it marks you as an amateur.

Formatting Specs

- Use a 1″ margin on all sides.
- Do not number the first page.
- Include the word count and rights offered in the top right corner of the first page.
- Include name, address and phone number (fax and E-mail, if possible) in the top left corner of the first page.
- Put the story's title, centered in all caps, about one-third of the way down the page from the top margin.
- Skip a line and write "by" in lowercase, then skip another line and put your name in all caps. (If using a pseudonym, put that name in all caps, and then on the next line put your real name in parentheses.)
- Drop four lines, indent and begin your story.
- Double-space the entire text of the story.
- Put a slug or one- to two-word name in the top right corner of every ensuing page (your last name and the page number or the story's title and the page number).
- Optional: Typing "THE END" in all caps when the story is finished. (Some editors like this because it closes the story; other editors prefer the story just end and consider it an insult for you to tell them it's the end. Your call.)

Other Dos and Don'ts

- Do paper clip pages together in the top left corner (butterfly clamps work well for stories longer than ten pages).
- Do keep an original copy of the story for yourself.
- Don't put your social security number on the manuscript.
- Don't use a separate cover/title page.
- Don't justify the text or align the right margin. Ragged right is fine.
- Don't insult the editor's intelligence or intentions by putting a copyright notice on the manuscript. It's copyrighted as soon as you write it.
- Don't include or submit a disk version of your story unless the editor asks for it.
- Don't use unusual fonts. A simple Times Roman, Arial or Courier is fine.

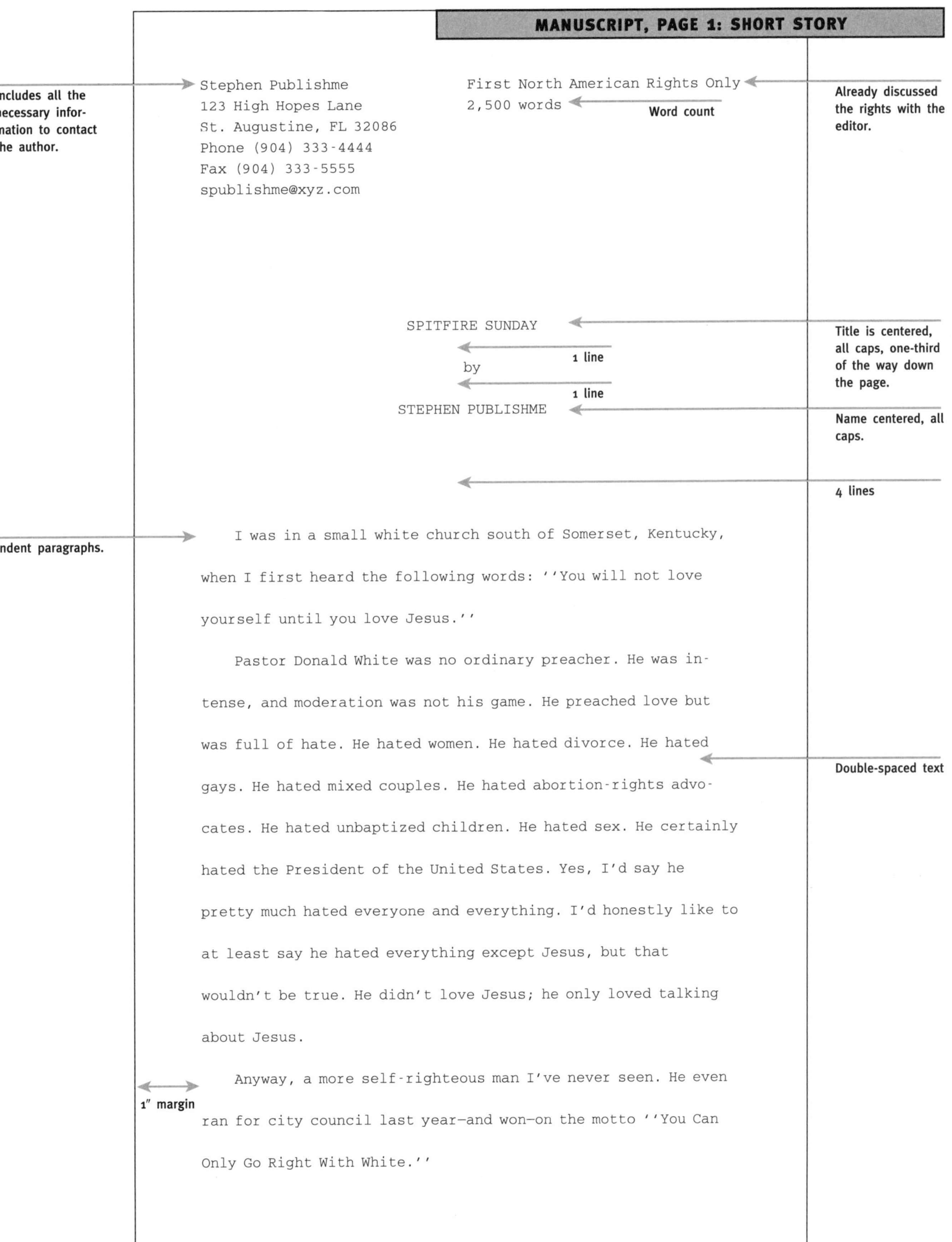
MANUSCRIPT, PAGE 1: SHORT STORY
Includes all the necessary information to contact the author.
Stephen Publishme
123 High Hopes Lane
St. Augustine, FL 32086
Phone (904) 333-4444
Fax (904) 333-5555
spublishme@xyz.com
First North American Rights Only
2,500 words
Word count
Already discussed the rights with the editor.
SPITFIRE SUNDAY
1 line
by
1 line
STEPHEN PUBLISHME
Title is centered, all caps, one-third of the way down the page.
Name centered, all caps.
4 lines
Indent paragraphs.
I was in a small white church south of Somerset, Kentucky, when I first heard the following words: ''You will not love yourself until you love Jesus.''
Pastor Donald White was no ordinary preacher. He was intense, and moderation was not his game. He preached love but was full of hate. He hated women. He hated divorce. He hated gays. He hated mixed couples. He hated abortion-rights advocates. He hated unbaptized children. He hated sex. He certainly hated the President of the United States. Yes, I'd say he pretty much hated everyone and everything. I'd honestly like to at least say he hated everything except Jesus, but that wouldn't be true. He didn't love Jesus; he only loved talking about Jesus.
Double-spaced text
Anyway, a more self-righteous man I've never seen. He even ran for city council last year—and won—on the motto ''You Can Only Go Right With White.''
1" margin

MANUSCRIPT LAST PAGE: SHORT STORY

Upper-left corner is blank; the manuscript is often held together with a paperclip in the upper-left corner.

Publishme 15

Slug is in upper-right corner for short stories.

As she poked and prodded him with that scalding hot brand-ing iron, he danced amidst the flames, cursing and wailing at her. ''You shall not be torn between loving yourself and loving Jesus,'' he said. ''For Jesus is life, and if you do not love Je-sus you cannot love your own life. You can hate me and torture me all you want. I know you're only doing it because you don't love Jesus. You don't love yourself!''

Katherine couldn't bear to hear one more word. She took the branding iron and pressed it to his mouth. He could not speak; he could barely scream. A look of horror fell over his face as he collapsed in the ring of fire. Then she pointed the gun at him. I thought she was finally going to shoot him, to put an end to this poor man's suffering. But she didn't. She dropped the gun, watched him burn, and smiled. Once his screaming stopped, Katherine picked up the pistol as if to finish the act, to make sure he'd be dead.

To my surprise, she put the pistol in her mouth and fired.

Optional, but perfectly placed if used.

THE END

CHAPTER FIVE

NOVELS

The Novel Proposal

What You Need to Submit

There are a few ways to submit your novel proposal to an agent or publisher, depending on the individual agent's or publisher's submission guidelines. Some want only the query letter, others request a query letter and the complete manuscript, others demand the query letter plus three sample chapters and a synopsis, and still others request that you submit a query letter as well as a few sample chapters, an outline and a synopsis. All want an SASE (self-addressed stamped envelope) with adequate postage.

To determine what you need to submit, consult the current edition of *Novel and Short Story Writer's Market* or *Writer's Market* if you plan on submitting to a publisher, or go to *Guide to Literary Agents* if you plan on soliciting an agent. All three books have submission specifications that come straight from the editors and agents telling you just what to send, when to expect a response and other information unique to the agent or editor you will be soliciting.

Expect to send at least a query letter, a synopsis and three consecutive sample chapters. These are the most important—and most requested—parts of your novel proposal. However, some agents and editors might request an outline, as well as an author biography and an endorsements page. If you don't know whom you'll be soliciting and what they demand, try to have the following prepared before you start sending out submissions:

- A darn good query or cover letter
- A synopsis
- At least three consecutive sample chapters
- A chapter-by-chapter outline
- An author biography
- Endorsements

We will explore each of these six components in detail throughout the ensuing pages (the sample chapters are in The Novel Manuscript section on page 132), including specific submission tips, formatting specs, other dos and don'ts and samples for each. Know that your novel proposal will probably mix and match several of these six components. Rarely will you need to send them all in the same submission package, since each agent and editor has his or her own preferences. But you probably will need to use each of them at one time or another, so try to prepare everything before you actually start submitting your novel. Finally, include a Novel Proposal Contents Page (see page 121) with your novel proposal, just to keep things organized. This is especially helpful when submitting two or more proposal items, particularly when one is a chapter-by-chapter outline (so it doesn't get confused with the sample chapters). And, of course, always include an SASE.

Query Letter to Agent or Publisher

Submission Tips

A query letter is your letter of inquiry. It serves two functions: to tell the agent or editor what you have to offer, and to ask if they're interested in seeing it.

Though you can send the query letter attached to a novel proposal, many agents and editors prefer you send the query letter either by itself or with a synopsis and a few sample pages from your novel (not more than twenty). This is called a blind query or a preproposal query, because you're sending it without having been asked to send it. No matter what you call it, it's your three-minute chance to hook the agent or editor on your novel. If she likes your query, she'll call and ask for either specific parts of your novel proposal (a synopsis and three sample chapters, for example) or the entire manuscript. Then she'll make her decision.

Some agents and editors, however, prefer you accompany your initial query letter with other parts of your novel proposal. If that's the case, include the required materials (a synopsis, sample chapters, outline, etc.) specified by the particular agent or publisher (in the listing in *Novel & Short Story Writer's Market*, *Writer's Market* and *Guide to Literary Agents*). When you accompany your query with your novel proposal, the query also becomes your cover letter.

Whether you submit the query by itself or accompanying other material, it is vital. You must make it compelling, interesting, even funny—*anything* to make it outstanding to the reader (the agent or editor you're soliciting). But limit it to a page or a page and one-half.

Although every winning query works its own magic, all good queries should contain the following:

- A "grabber" or hook sentence that makes the reader want to get his hands on the actual novel.
- One to three paragraphs about your novel.
- A short paragraph about you and your publishing credentials (if you have any).
- A good reason why you're soliciting the person you're soliciting. (Why this agent or publisher instead of another?)
- The length of the novel.
- A sentence or two about the intended audience.
- An indication that an SASE is enclosed.

Arguably the most important aspect of any query is the grabber, the hook that lures the reader into wanting to see—and, of course, read—your novel. Your grabber should be part of the paragraphs you devote to telling about the novel. Another good idea is to point out why your novel is different from all the others. Then spend a few sentences telling about yourself, in which you list your publishing credentials (if you have any) or toss in a personal anecdote that's pertinent to the novel (explain that you spent two years in the Peace Corps in Somalia if that's where your story takes place). In another paragraph, mention why you're sending your query to this particular agent or editor. Feel free to allude to an author the publisher publishes (or the agent represents) whose work is similar to yours. Doing this is not just name-dropping, but proof you've done your research. Finally, always include an SASE.

Formatting Specs

- The basic setup for a query to an agent or publisher is similar to a short story or article query.
- Use a standard font or typeface.
- Use a 1″ margin on all sides.
- Use block or semiblock letter format.
- Use letterhead or put your name, address and phone number (include E-mail and fax, if applicable) in the top right corner.
- Address your query to a specific agent or editor (call to get the appropriate name).
- Try to keep the query to one page, but it's acceptable to go as long as 1½ pages.
- Single-space the body of the letter; double-space between paragraphs.
- Catalog every item you're sending in your enclosures.

Other Dos and Don'ts

- Do state any previous publishing credits.
- Do mention if your novel isn't finished, and state the date your manuscript will be complete.
- Do tell if you're sending simultaneous submissions to other agents and editors.
- Do address your letter to a specific agent or editor.
- Don't mention that you're a first-time writer or that you've never been published.
- Don't spend much time trying to sell yourself. Your manuscript will stand on its own.
- Don't state that some other agent or editor has rejected your novel.
- Don't ask for advice or criticism—that's not the agent's or editor's job at this stage in the game.
- Do summarize any relevant experience you have.
- Don't mention anything about yourself not pertinent to the novel.
- Don't bring up payment expectations (advances, royalties, etc.).
- Don't mention copyright information.
- Don't staple your query letter to your manuscript.
- Don't go over two pages.

"I prefer to receive concise, one-page query letters (with SASEs) that tell me a bit about the kind of book it is—i.e., what genre it falls in, other titles that the author might compare it to—and something brief about its plot or distinguishing hook. I also like such letters to include basic information about the author; I especially want to know if the author has ever been published or represented before (if so, when, where and by whom), and any other distinguishing information relevant (even in a quirky way) to his or her profile as an author."

—Theresa Park, agent, Sanford J. Greenburger Associates

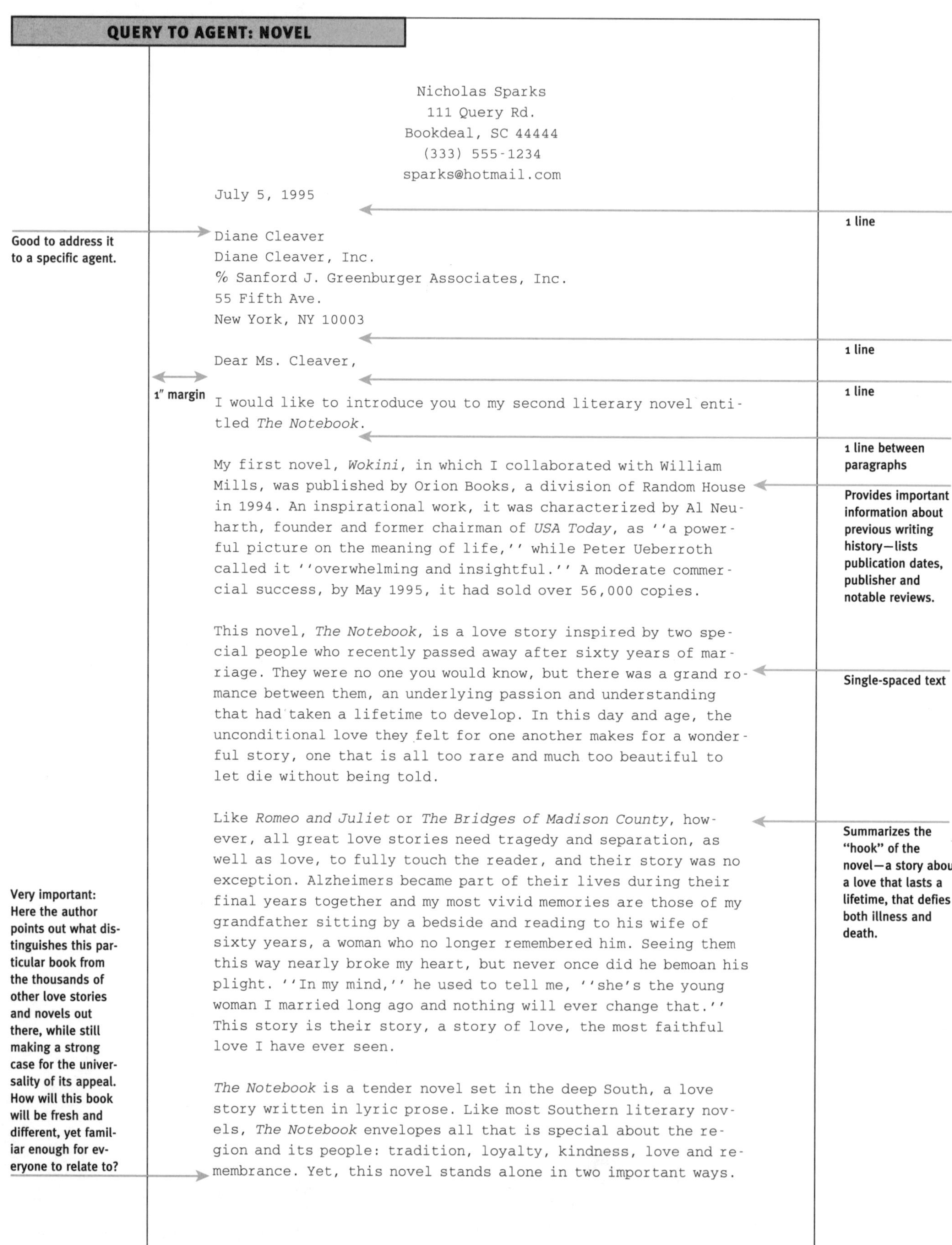

QUERY TO AGENT: NOVEL

Nicholas Sparks
111 Query Rd.
Bookdeal, SC 44444
(333) 555-1234
sparks@hotmail.com

July 5, 1995

Diane Cleaver
Diane Cleaver, Inc.
% Sanford J. Greenburger Associates, Inc.
55 Fifth Ave.
New York, NY 10003

Dear Ms. Cleaver,

I would like to introduce you to my second literary novel entitled *The Notebook*.

My first novel, *Wokini*, in which I collaborated with William Mills, was published by Orion Books, a division of Random House in 1994. An inspirational work, it was characterized by Al Neuharth, founder and former chairman of *USA Today*, as ''a powerful picture on the meaning of life,'' while Peter Ueberroth called it ''overwhelming and insightful.'' A moderate commercial success, by May 1995, it had sold over 56,000 copies.

This novel, *The Notebook*, is a love story inspired by two special people who recently passed away after sixty years of marriage. They were no one you would know, but there was a grand romance between them, an underlying passion and understanding that had taken a lifetime to develop. In this day and age, the unconditional love they felt for one another makes for a wonderful story, one that is all too rare and much too beautiful to let die without being told.

Like *Romeo and Juliet* or *The Bridges of Madison County*, however, all great love stories need tragedy and separation, as well as love, to fully touch the reader, and their story was no exception. Alzheimers became part of their lives during their final years together and my most vivid memories are those of my grandfather sitting by a bedside and reading to his wife of sixty years, a woman who no longer remembered him. Seeing them this way nearly broke my heart, but never once did he bemoan his plight. ''In my mind,'' he used to tell me, ''she's the young woman I married long ago and nothing will ever change that.'' This story is their story, a story of love, the most faithful love I have ever seen.

The Notebook is a tender novel set in the deep South, a love story written in lyric prose. Like most Southern literary novels, *The Notebook* envelopes all that is special about the region and its people: tradition, loyalty, kindness, love and remembrance. Yet, this novel stands alone in two important ways.

Good to address it to a specific agent.
1" margin
Very important: Here the author points out what distinguishes this particular book from the thousands of other love stories and novels out there, while still making a strong case for the universality of its appeal. How will this book be fresh and different, yet familiar enough for everyone to relate to?
1 line
1 line
1 line
1 line between paragraphs
Provides important information about previous writing history—lists publication dates, publisher and notable reviews.
Single-spaced text
Summarizes the "hook" of the novel—a story about a love that lasts a lifetime, that defies both illness and death.

First, it is one of the few passionate love stories written about the elderly, and it reveals a rare but dignified portrait of a couple struggling with the ultimate reality that their lives will be ending soon. Even more importantly, however, *The Notebook* is the first novel that describes the heart-wrenching effects of Alzheimers disease on two people who had loved each other all their lives. The result is a moving eulogy to old age itself—a story of love and grief which pretty much sums up the notable context of most lives.

As a young writer in South Carolina, I am looking for an experienced agent based in New York and your reputation is impeccable. Your varied experiences as an editor at Doubleday, Straight Arrow, Scribner's and Simon & Schuster are impressive, and it would be an honor to work with you on this novel.

The author has done significant research on the agent and had chosen her for specific reasons. He is a professional who had spent some time thinking about the kind of agent he thought would be most appropriate for his work.

I have included a short biography for your review. The novel is 52,000 words and fully complete. May I send you a copy of the manuscript? I look forward to hearing from you soon.

Including a brief biography is always a good idea—educational background, publications (if any), anything else relevant to your profile as an author.

Sincerely,

Signature

Nicholas Sparks

P.S. Because 22 percent of the people in this country (40+ million) are over 52 years old and 4.5 million people suffer from Alzheimers, this book is unique and marketable to a wide audience. In addition, at 52,000 words, it is short enough not to be cost-prohibitive to most publishing houses.

An extremely important postscript—here the author tells me who the potential market for this book is, and why it might be particularly attractive to a publisher, from a marketing perspective.

This letter was initially addressed to Diane Cleaver, an agent at Sanford J. Greenburger Associates, without the knowledge that Diane had passed away three months earlier. The letter was passed on to Theresa Park of Sanford J. Greenburger Associates who provided these comments.

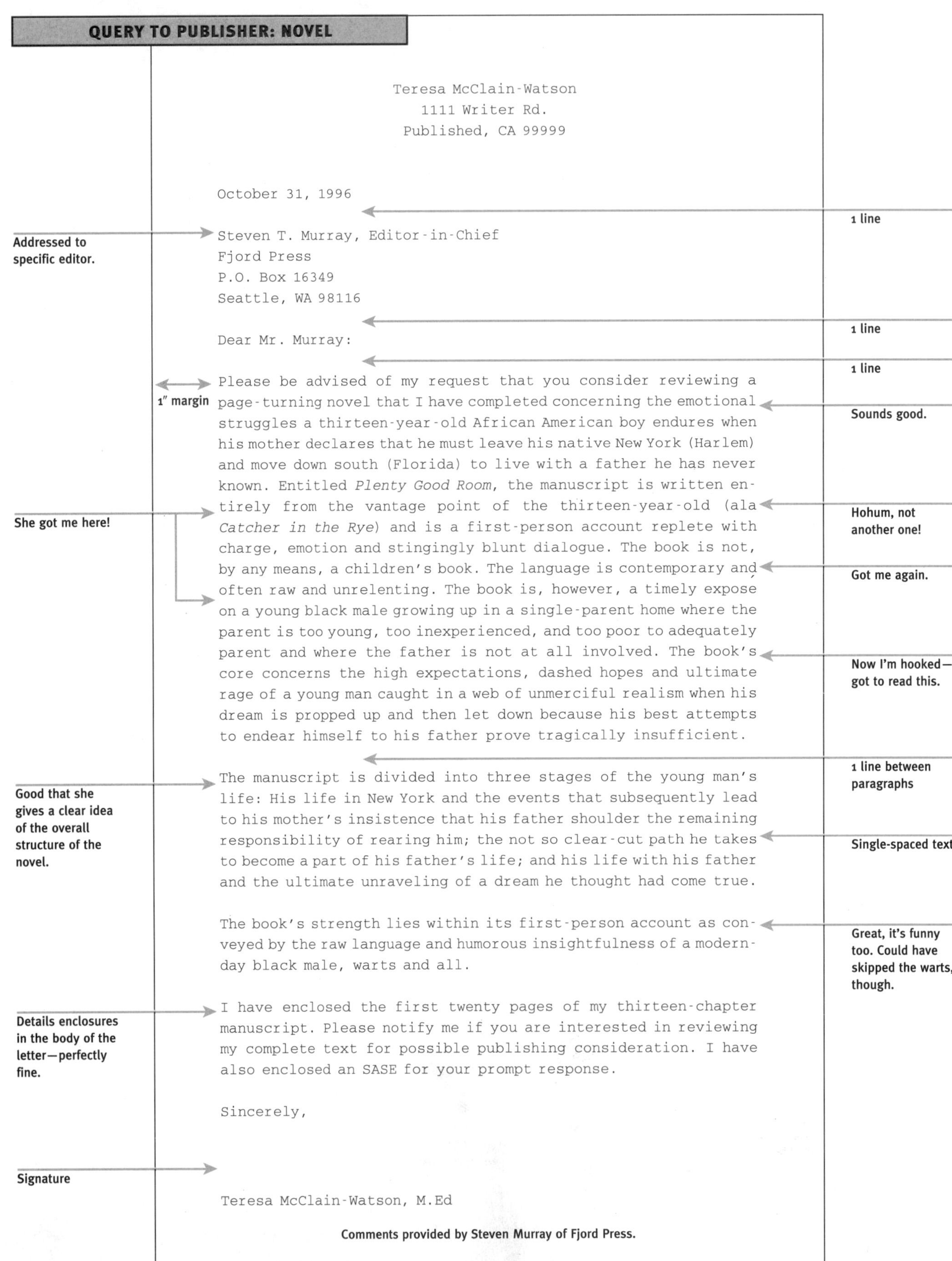

QUERY TO PUBLISHER: NOVEL

Teresa McClain-Watson
1111 Writer Rd.
Published, CA 99999

October 31, 1996

Steven T. Murray, Editor-in-Chief
Fjord Press
P.O. Box 16349
Seattle, WA 98116

Dear Mr. Murray:

Please be advised of my request that you consider reviewing a page-turning novel that I have completed concerning the emotional struggles a thirteen-year-old African American boy endures when his mother declares that he must leave his native New York (Harlem) and move down south (Florida) to live with a father he has never known. Entitled *Plenty Good Room*, the manuscript is written entirely from the vantage point of the thirteen-year-old (ala *Catcher in the Rye*) and is a first-person account replete with charge, emotion and stingingly blunt dialogue. The book is not, by any means, a children's book. The language is contemporary and often raw and unrelenting. The book is, however, a timely expose on a young black male growing up in a single-parent home where the parent is too young, too inexperienced, and too poor to adequately parent and where the father is not at all involved. The book's core concerns the high expectations, dashed hopes and ultimate rage of a young man caught in a web of unmerciful realism when his dream is propped up and then let down because his best attempts to endear himself to his father prove tragically insufficient.

The manuscript is divided into three stages of the young man's life: His life in New York and the events that subsequently lead to his mother's insistence that his father shoulder the remaining responsibility of rearing him; the not so clear-cut path he takes to become a part of his father's life; and his life with his father and the ultimate unraveling of a dream he thought had come true.

The book's strength lies within its first-person account as conveyed by the raw language and humorous insightfulness of a modern-day black male, warts and all.

I have enclosed the first twenty pages of my thirteen-chapter manuscript. Please notify me if you are interested in reviewing my complete text for possible publishing consideration. I have also enclosed an SASE for your prompt response.

Sincerely,

Teresa McClain-Watson, M.Ed

Addressed to specific editor.
1″ margin
She got me here!
Good that she gives a clear idea of the overall structure of the novel.
Details enclosures in the body of the letter—perfectly fine.
Signature
1 line
1 line
1 line
Sounds good.
Hohum, not another one!
Got me again.
Now I'm hooked—got to read this.
1 line between paragraphs
Single-spaced text
Great, it's funny too. Could have skipped the warts, though.

Comments provided by Steven Murray of Fjord Press.

Cover Letter

Submission Tips

A cover letter accompanying a novel proposal is a tightened version of a query letter. Like the query letter, your cover letter lets the editor know who you are *and* what you have to offer. But, because so much information is included in the rest of the proposal, and because you should have already queried the agent or editor, the cover letter can be fairly brief—no more than 1-1½ pages.

With a cover letter, you don't need to spend as much time explaining why what you have to offer is worthwhile; you just need to introduce the material. Why spend a lot of space synopsizing your novel and telling about yourself when you've included a synopsis, three sample chapters and an author bio? Of course, you still want to hook the editor or agent into believing your novel is worth considering, but you don't need to go into as much detail as you would in a blind query letter.

A good rule of thumb is to keep your cover letter to three or four short paragraphs and organize it in the following order:

- The introductory paragraph (state the novel's title, then hook the editor with a brief description of your novel).
- The biographical paragraph (in one or two sentences explain a bit about yourself that's pertinent to the novel, such as previous publishing credits, or why you're sending it to this particular agency or publisher).
- The concluding paragraph (politely close the letter).

Formatting Specs

- Use a standard font or typeface (no bold, script or italic).
- Place your name, address and phone number (include E-mail and fax) in the top right corner.
- Use a 1″ margin on all sides.
- Address it to a specific editor (call and get the appropriate editor's name).
- Keep it to one page.
- Use block or semiblock letter format.
- Single-space the body of the letter; double-space between paragraphs.
- Catalog every item you're sending in your enclosures (three chapters, synopsis, SASE).

> **"At Harlequin/Silhouette, when we request authors to send a query letter, we'd like to see a one-page cover letter with a two-page, single-spaced synopsis of the story along with a self-addressed stamped envelope."**
>
> —Isabel Swift, editor, Harlequin Books

Other Dos and Don'ts

- Do thank the editor.
- Do give the novel's exact word count.
- Do mention whether you're soliciting other agents or editors.
- Do include an SASE or postcard for reply, and state in the letter that you have done so.
- Don't mention that you're a first-time writer, or that you've never been published, or that someone else has rejected your novel.
- Don't start your pitch all over again in the cover letter. If your query made enough of an impression to spark the editor or agent's interest, alluding to their request to see the proposal is enough. Your novel will stand on its own.
- Don't ask for advice or criticism—that's not the agent's or editor's job at this stage in the game.
- Don't mention anything about yourself not pertinent to the novel.
- Don't bring up payment (advances, royalties, etc.); it's premature.
- Don't mention copyright information. What you've written is already copyrighted, and you don't need to imply the editor or agent is out to steal your idea.
- Don't include your social security number.
- Don't staple your cover letter to your novel proposal. A butterfly or clamp-style paperclip can hold the proposal elements together, and the cover letter stands alone in front.
- Don't put a page number on the cover letter.

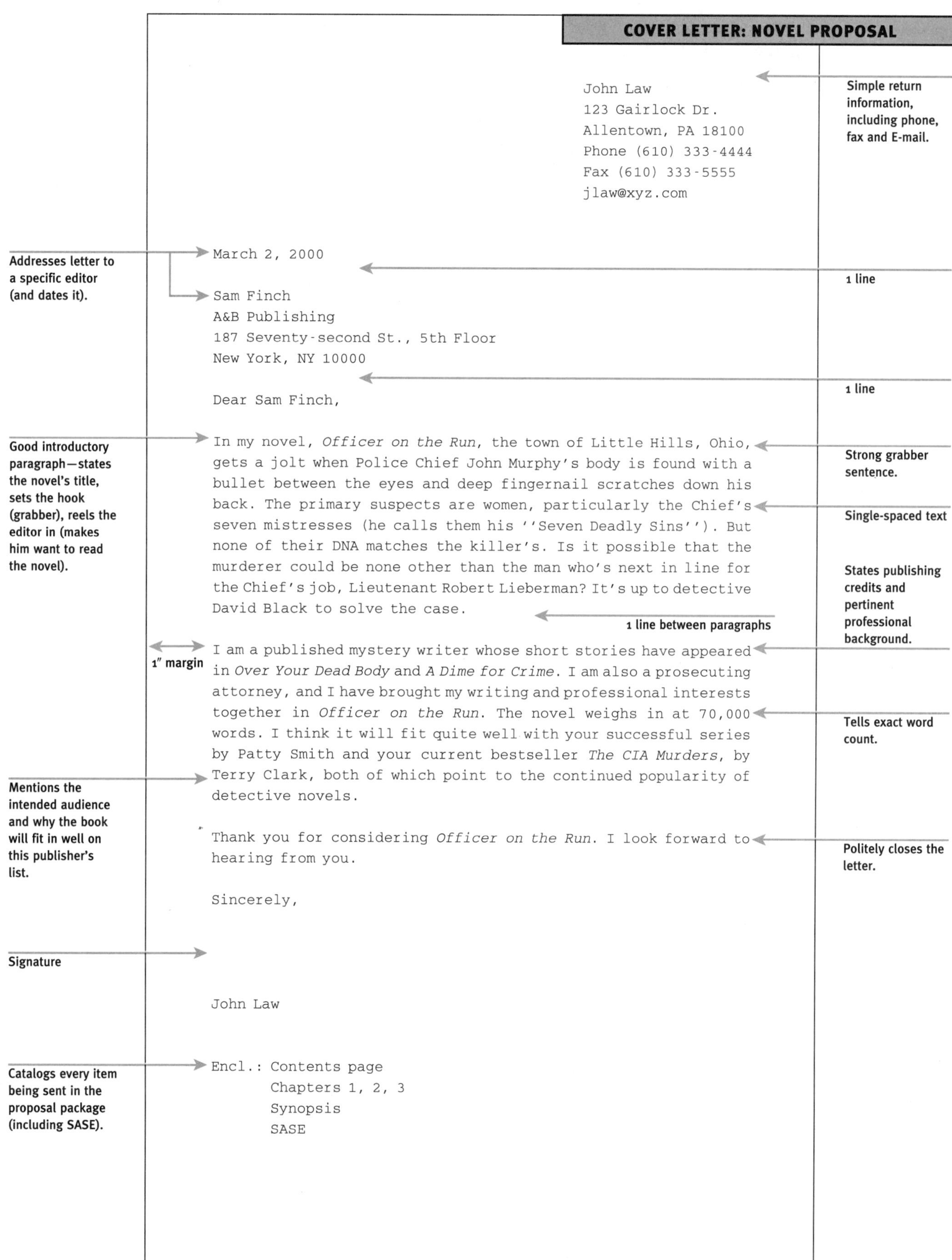

COVER LETTER: NOVEL PROPOSAL

John Law
123 Gairlock Dr.
Allentown, PA 18100
Phone (610) 333-4444
Fax (610) 333-5555
jlaw@xyz.com

March 2, 2000

Sam Finch
A&B Publishing
187 Seventy-second St., 5th Floor
New York, NY 10000

Dear Sam Finch,

In my novel, *Officer on the Run*, the town of Little Hills, Ohio, gets a jolt when Police Chief John Murphy's body is found with a bullet between the eyes and deep fingernail scratches down his back. The primary suspects are women, particularly the Chief's seven mistresses (he calls them his ''Seven Deadly Sins''). But none of their DNA matches the killer's. Is it possible that the murderer could be none other than the man who's next in line for the Chief's job, Lieutenant Robert Lieberman? It's up to detective David Black to solve the case.

I am a published mystery writer whose short stories have appeared in *Over Your Dead Body* and *A Dime for Crime*. I am also a prosecuting attorney, and I have brought my writing and professional interests together in *Officer on the Run*. The novel weighs in at 70,000 words. I think it will fit quite well with your successful series by Patty Smith and your current bestseller *The CIA Murders*, by Terry Clark, both of which point to the continued popularity of detective novels.

Thank you for considering *Officer on the Run*. I look forward to hearing from you.

Sincerely,

John Law

Encl.: Contents page
Chapters 1, 2, 3
Synopsis
SASE

Simple return information, including phone, fax and E-mail.
Addresses letter to a specific editor (and dates it).
1 line
1 line
Good introductory paragraph—states the novel's title, sets the hook (grabber), reels the editor in (makes him want to read the novel).
Strong grabber sentence.
Single-spaced text
States publishing credits and pertinent professional background.
1 line between paragraphs
1" margin
Tells exact word count.
Mentions the intended audience and why the book will fit in well on this publisher's list.
Politely closes the letter.
Signature
Catalogs every item being sent in the proposal package (including SASE).

Cover Page

Submission Tips

This is exactly the same as the cover page you'll use with the ultimate manuscript. It includes the title, an estimated word count and either your name and address (if you're submitting direct to an editor) or your agent's name and address (if you're submitting through an agent).

Formatting Specs

- Put your name and address in the top left corner if you're submitting to a book editor.
- If you're using an agent, put the agent's name and address in the bottom right corner and don't put your name and address on the cover.
- Put an estimated word count (for the entire book, not for the proposal) in the top right corner.
- Center the title, subtitle and author's name in the middle of the page.
- Conventionally, the title is in all capital letters and the subtitle is up-and-down. If you want to use boldface for the title and italics for the subtitle, that's fine, too. Your call.

Other Dos and Don'ts

- Don't include both your name and address and the agent's. Use one or the other, depending on the situation.
- Don't use a header or number the title page.

"I like full proposals, not just query letters. I can't make a judgment about a work from a one-page letter. By a full proposal, I mean a brief cover letter, the first three consecutive chapters (or about fifty pages of text), and a three- to five-page synopsis. That's sufficient material for me to make a reasonable decision. I like the synopsis to give me the crux of the story—the highlights—from beginning to end. I certainly hate when someone fails to mention the ending. Tell the entire story. Don't play footsie with your editor."

—Melissa Ann Singer, senior editor, Tor Books

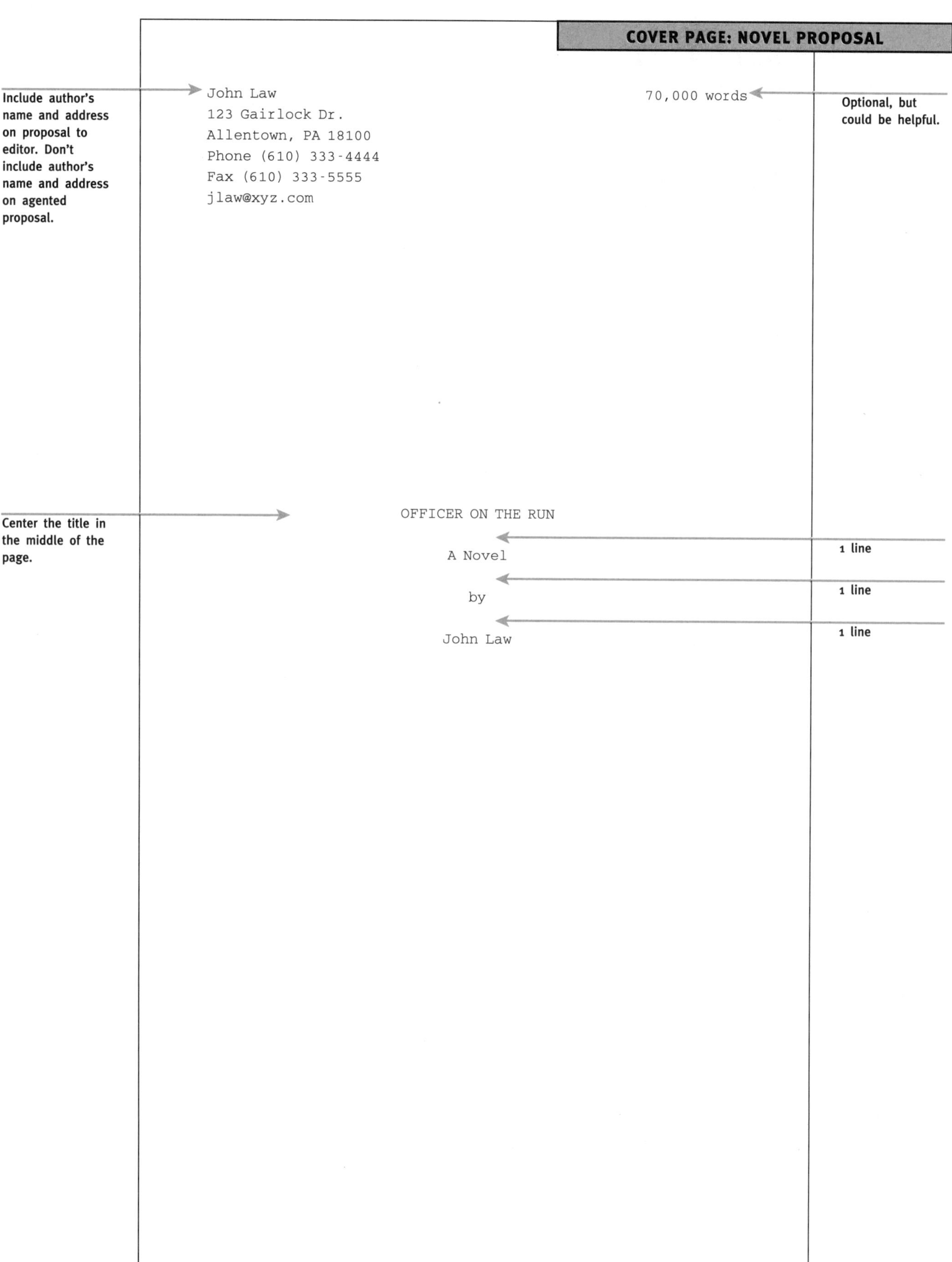
COVER PAGE: NOVEL PROPOSAL
Include author's name and address on proposal to editor. Don't include author's name and address on agented proposal.
John Law
123 Gairlock Dr.
Allentown, PA 18100
Phone (610) 333-4444
Fax (610) 333-5555
jlaw@xyz.com
70,000 words
Optional, but could be helpful.
Center the title in the middle of the page.
OFFICER ON THE RUN
1 line
A Novel
1 line
by
1 line
John Law

Table of Contents

Your novel proposal's contents page should let the editor know precisely what's in your proposal package. The first thing you want to do is use a slugline in the top left margin. It should contain your last name, a slash, your novel's title in all capital letters, another slash, and the word Contents. It should look like this: Law/OFFICER ON THE RUN/ Contents. Next drop about six lines and put the heading "Proposal Contents" or "Contents," flush with the left margin in bold (and in a large font, if you wish). Then list all the contents. Be sure to catalog every item you're sending in your proposal (synopsis, sample chapters, chapter-by-chapter outline, about the author, endorsements) and the corresponding page numbers as they appear in your proposal. Make your contents page neat and easy on the eyes, which means organizing it according to sections (see sample) and double-spacing. Finally, do not number the page.

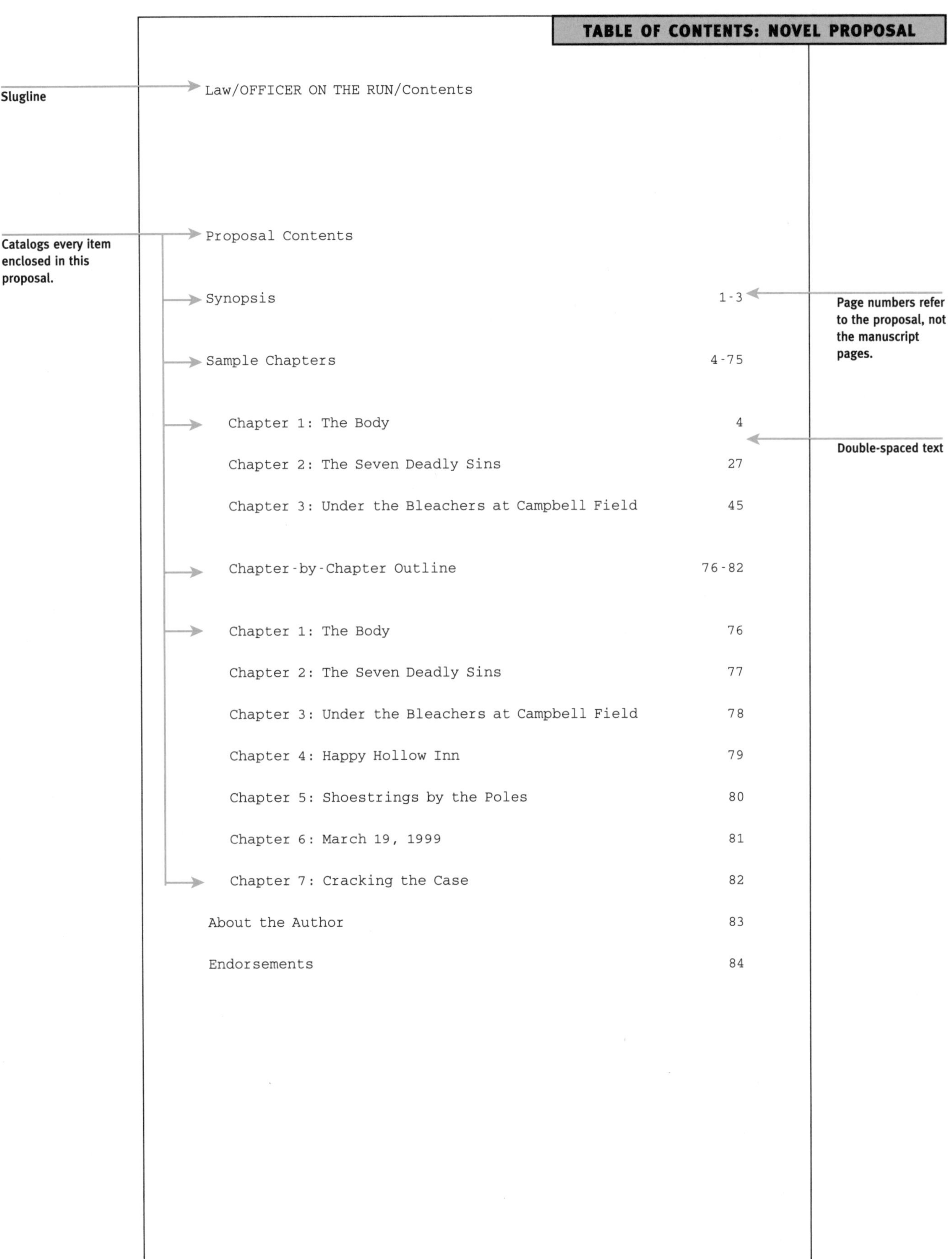
TABLE OF CONTENTS: NOVEL PROPOSAL
Slugline
Law/OFFICER ON THE RUN/Contents
Catalogs every item enclosed in this proposal.
Proposal Contents
Synopsis 1-3
Page numbers refer to the proposal, not the manuscript pages.
Sample Chapters 4-75
Chapter 1: The Body 4
Double-spaced text
Chapter 2: The Seven Deadly Sins 27
Chapter 3: Under the Bleachers at Campbell Field 45
Chapter-by-Chapter Outline 76-82
Chapter 1: The Body 76
Chapter 2: The Seven Deadly Sins 77
Chapter 3: Under the Bleachers at Campbell Field 78
Chapter 4: Happy Hollow Inn 79
Chapter 5: Shoestrings by the Poles 80
Chapter 6: March 19, 1999 81
Chapter 7: Cracking the Case 82
About the Author 83
Endorsements 84

Synopsis

Submission Tips

The synopsis supplies key information about your novel (plot, theme, characterization, setting), while also showing how all these coalesce to form the big picture (your novel). You want to quickly tell what your novel is about without making the editor or agent read the novel in its entirety.

There are no hard and fast rules about the synopsis. Some editors and agents look at it as a one-page sales pitch, while others expect it to be a comprehensive summary of the entire novel. Not surprisingly, there's conflicting advice about the typical length of a synopsis. We've contacted numerous editors and agents to get their take on just how long it should be. Nearly all prefer a short synopsis that runs from one to two single-spaced pages, or three to five double-spaced pages. Every one of them said the same thing: "The shorter, the better."

On the other hand, some plot-heavy fiction, such as thrillers and mysteries, might need more space and can run from ten to twenty-five double-spaced pages, depending on the length of the manuscript and the number of plot shifts. If you opt for a longer synopsis, aim for one synopsis page to every twenty-five manuscript pages (a 250-page manuscript should get a 10-page synopsis), but try to keep it as short as possible.

Your best bet on knowing how long to make your synopsis is to follow the guidelines in the agency's or publisher's listing (for agents, consult *Guide to Literary Agents*; for publishers, consult *Novel & Short Story Writer's Market* or *Writer's Market*). If the listing provides no specific information about the length of the synopsis and you're still unsure, call and ask. You might have to compose a few versions of your synopsis to meet the demands of various agents and editors.

Even if your novel is written in the third person, write your synopsis in the first person. Another good idea is to write the synopsis in the present tense, a narrative account of the novel. Write it as if you're telling the story to a friend. Focus on the essential parts of your story, and try not to include sections of dialogue unless you think they are absolutely necessary (it is OK to inject a few strong quotes from your characters, but keep them brief). Finally, even though the synopsis is but a condensed version of your novel, it must seem complete. Keep events in the same order as they happen in the novel (but don't break them down into individual chapters). Remember that your synopsis should have a beginning, a middle and an ending (yes, you must tell how the novel ends to round out your synopsis).

That's what's required of a synopsis: You need to be concise, compelling and complete at the same time.

Formatting Specs

- Use a 1″ margin on all sides.
- Justify the left margin only.
- Type your name, address and phone number (fax and E-mail, if applicable) on the top left margin of the first page, single-spaced.
- Type the novel's genre, the word length and then the word "Synopsis" on the top right margin of the first page, single-spaced.
- Do not number the first page (but it is considered page one).

- Put the novel's title, centered and in all caps, about one-third of the way down the page (from the top margin).
- Drop four lines (double-space twice) below the title and begin the text of the synopsis.
- The text throughout the synopsis should be double-spaced (unless you intend to keep your synopsis to one or two pages, then single-space is OK).
- Use all caps the first time you introduce a character.
- After the first page, use a slug line (also called a header) in the top left of every page. The slug line should contain your last name, a slash, your novel's title in all capital letters, another slash and the word "Synopsis."
- Also after the first page, put the page number in the top right corner of every consecutive page, on the same line as the slug line.
- The first line of text on each page after the first page should be three lines (about ¾") below the slug line and page number.

Other Dos and Don'ts

- Do use present tense.
- Do write it in first person, even if your novel is written in third person.
- Do keep in mind that your synopsis is a sales pitch (make it a short, fast, exciting read).
- Do establish a hook at the beginning of the synopsis (introduce your lead character and set up a key conflict).
- Do try to introduce your most important character first.
- Do provide details about your central character (age, gender, marital status, profession, etc.), but don't do this for every character, only the primary ones.
- Do try to include the characters' motivations and emotions.
- Do highlight pivotal plot points.
- Do reveal the novel's ending.
- Don't go into detail about what happens; just tell what happens.
- Don't make your synopsis over twenty-five pages.
- Don't inject long sections of dialogue into your synopsis.

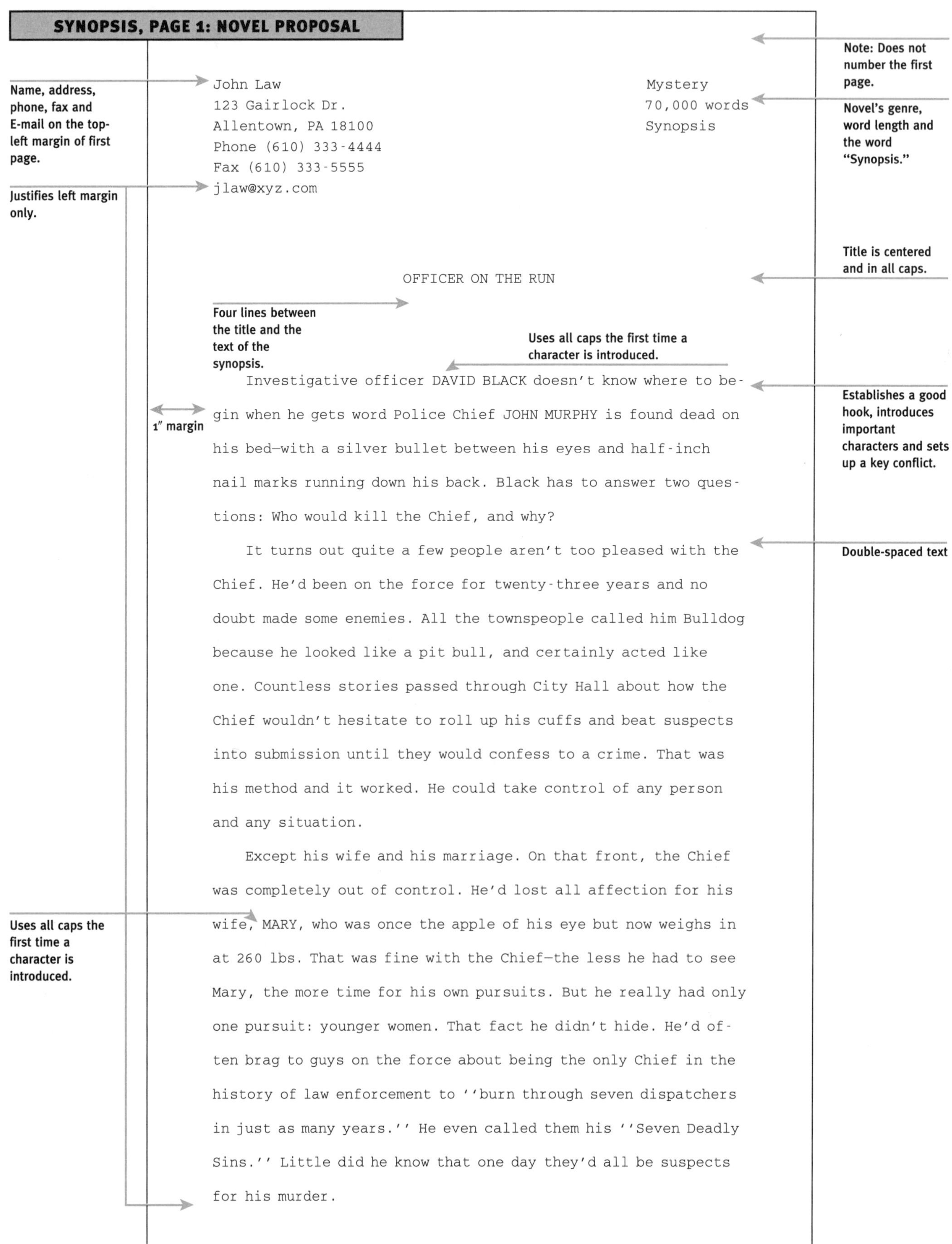
SYNOPSIS, PAGE 1: NOVEL PROPOSAL
Note: Does not number the first page.
Name, address, phone, fax and E-mail on the top-left margin of first page.
Novel's genre, word length and the word "Synopsis."
Justifies left margin only.
Title is centered and in all caps.
Four lines between the title and the text of the synopsis.
Uses all caps the first time a character is introduced.
Establishes a good hook, introduces important characters and sets up a key conflict.
1" margin
Double-spaced text
Uses all caps the first time a character is introduced.

John Law
123 Gairlock Dr.
Allentown, PA 18100
Phone (610) 333-4444
Fax (610) 333-5555
jlaw@xyz.com

Mystery
70,000 words
Synopsis

OFFICER ON THE RUN

Investigative officer DAVID BLACK doesn't know where to begin when he gets word Police Chief JOHN MURPHY is found dead on his bed—with a silver bullet between his eyes and half-inch nail marks running down his back. Black has to answer two questions: Who would kill the Chief, and why?

It turns out quite a few people aren't too pleased with the Chief. He'd been on the force for twenty-three years and no doubt made some enemies. All the townspeople called him Bulldog because he looked like a pit bull, and certainly acted like one. Countless stories passed through City Hall about how the Chief wouldn't hesitate to roll up his cuffs and beat suspects into submission until they would confess to a crime. That was his method and it worked. He could take control of any person and any situation.

Except his wife and his marriage. On that front, the Chief was completely out of control. He'd lost all affection for his wife, MARY, who was once the apple of his eye but now weighs in at 260 lbs. That was fine with the Chief—the less he had to see Mary, the more time for his own pursuits. But he really had only one pursuit: younger women. That fact he didn't hide. He'd often brag to guys on the force about being the only Chief in the history of law enforcement to ''burn through seven dispatchers in just as many years.'' He even called them his ''Seven Deadly Sins.'' Little did he know that one day they'd all be suspects for his murder.

SYNOPSIS, PAGE 2: NOVEL PROPOSAL

Slug line with last name, title (in all caps) and the word "Synopsis."

Law/OFFICER ON THE RUN/Synopsis 2

Page number goes on the same line as the slug line.

First line of text is three lines below the slug line and page number.

Paragraphs are short and fast reads, mentioning only the essentials of the story.

Black interviews all seven women and finds no leads until MARLENE PRESTON, the Chief's ''Seventh Deadly Sin,'' reveals how the Chief repeatedly would handcuff her arms and legs to four metal poles under the bleachers at the school football stadium. Marlene says she's never told anyone about any of it. Black then interrogates the six other ''sins,'' to see if they had also been physically mistreated. They all say the Chief never tried anything like that with them.

A new scene/twist begins with start of a new paragraph.

Black drinks himself into a stupor and pours out his problems to a young barmaid, SARAH, who just happens to be the best friend of the Police Lieutenant's daughter, KELLY LIEBERMAN. Sarah tells Black the Chief deserved to die and that he was a jerk, especially to Kelly when she'd baby-sit for the Chief and his wife. According to Sarah, the Chief used to talk dirty to Kelly and then threaten her not to tell her father because LIEUTENANT LIEBERMAN was in line for a promotion.

Black interviews Kelly. She denies the Chief did anything but make a few lewd comments on occasion. When Black approaches Kelly's father, Lieutenant Lieberman says Kelly never mentioned a word about the Chief. Black returns to talk with Kelly and asks why she's never mentioned anything to her father. She says she's afraid he'd get upset at her for bringing it up. Black presses further, asking Kelly if the Chief ever did anything other than verbally harass her. Kelly says no.

Black decides to walk back under the bleachers to the spot where Marlene says the Chief repeatedly handcuffed her. There, he notices two sneaker shoestrings on the ground by the four poles Marlene pointed out. The strings had been tied in knots and then cut Black shows the strings to Marlene and asks if the Chief ever tied her to the poles with them. ''Not once,'' she says. ''Handcuffs every time.''

Outline

Submission Tips

An outline is often used interchangeably with a synopsis. For most editors and agents, however, there is a distinction. While a synopsis is a brief, encapsulated version of the novel at large, an outline makes each chapter its own story, usually containing a few paragraphs per chapter. In short, you're breaking down the novel and synopsizing each chapter individually. Try to keep each chapter to about a page, and begin each new chapter on a different page (See Outline Novel Proposal on page 127).

Never submit an outline unless an agent or editor specifically asks for it. Keep in mind that fewer and fewer agents and editors want outlines these days. Most just request a cover letter, a few sample chapters and a short synopsis (or sometimes the entire manuscript). Outlines most often are requested by genre fiction editors, because genre books run for many pages and have numerous plot shifts.

Formatting Specs

- Use a 1″ margin on all sides.
- Justify the left margin only.
- Use a slug line in the top left of every page. The slug line should contain your last name, a slash, your novel's title in all capital letters, another slash and the word "Outline."
- Put the page number in the top right corner of every page.
- Drop four lines below the slug line, center and bold or underline the words "Chapter-by-Chapter Outline."
- Drop four more lines and type the chapter number (Chapter 3).
- Drop two lines and put the chapter's title on the left margin and the number of manuscript pages that chapter runs on the right margin.
- Drop two lines and begin the text of the outline.
- Double-space the text throughout the outline.
- Use all caps the first time you introduce a character.
- Use a separate page for each chapter.

Other Dos and Don'ts

- Do keep in mind that your outline is an extended, more detailed and structural version of your synopsis.
- Do explain the gist of the chapter.
- Do highlight pivotal plot points.
- Do write in the present tense.
- Do provide a hook for each chapter.
- Do reveal how the chapter begins and ends.
- Do make sure each succeeding chapter picks up where the previous chapter left off.
- Don't include extended dialogue.

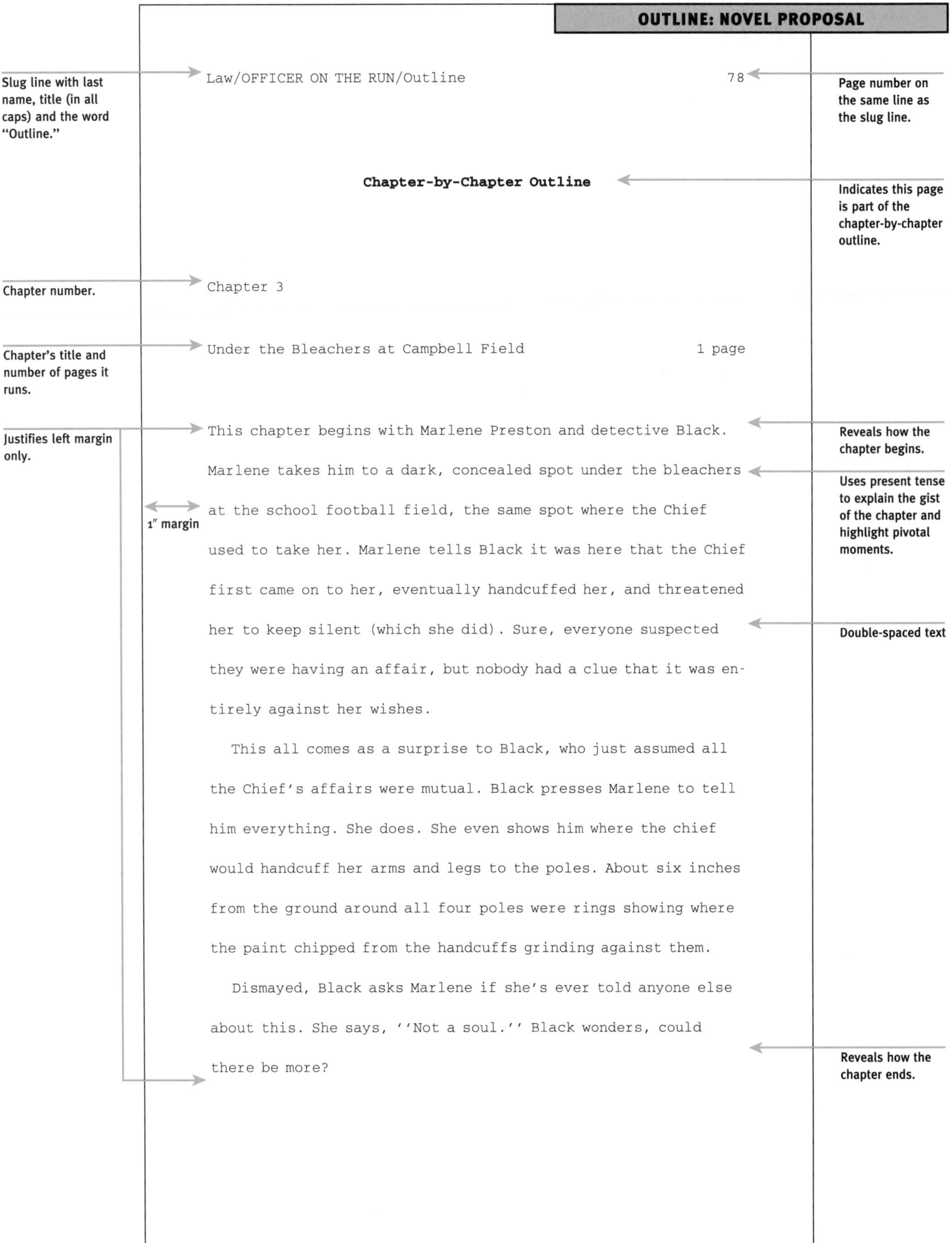

OUTLINE: NOVEL PROPOSAL

Law/OFFICER ON THE RUN/Outline 78

Chapter-by-Chapter Outline

Chapter 3

Under the Bleachers at Campbell Field 1 page

This chapter begins with Marlene Preston and detective Black. Marlene takes him to a dark, concealed spot under the bleachers at the school football field, the same spot where the Chief used to take her. Marlene tells Black it was here that the Chief first came on to her, eventually handcuffed her, and threatened her to keep silent (which she did). Sure, everyone suspected they were having an affair, but nobody had a clue that it was entirely against her wishes.

This all comes as a surprise to Black, who just assumed all the Chief's affairs were mutual. Black presses Marlene to tell him everything. She does. She even shows him where the chief would handcuff her arms and legs to the poles. About six inches from the ground around all four poles were rings showing where the paint chipped from the handcuffs grinding against them.

Dismayed, Black asks Marlene if she's ever told anyone else about this. She says, ''Not a soul.'' Black wonders, could there be more?

Slug line with last name, title (in all caps) and the word "Outline."
Page number on the same line as the slug line.
Indicates this page is part of the chapter-by-chapter outline.
Chapter number.
Chapter's title and number of pages it runs.
Justifies left margin only.
1" margin
Reveals how the chapter begins.
Uses present tense to explain the gist of the chapter and highlight pivotal moments.
Double-spaced text
Reveals how the chapter ends.

Author Biography

Submission Tips

Your author bio is about you, but only in the context of what makes you the perfect person to tell this story. Don't include any information that doesn't directly help the pitch. Including educational information is OK if you have an advanced degree. Unless there's something strikingly unusual about your family, don't mention them. It's OK to say where you live and to whom you're married. Mention your profession if it's pertinent to the novel. Definitely include any previous publishing credits. Remember, your bio should always be less than a page and should never include information not directly relevant to your novel's publication.

Formatting Specs

- Have a slug line in the top left corner with your last name, then backslash, then the novel's title in all caps, then backslash again, then "Author Biography."
- Put the page number in the top right corner on the same line as the slug line.
- Double-space the text.
- Write in third person.
- Use present tense.
- Keep it to one page. Standard length is 200–250 words.

Other Dos and Don'ts

- Don't mention your membership in any writer's organizations, unless it can help promote your novel (e.g., if you write a mystery, tell that you belong to the Mystery Writers of America, etc.).
- Do mention any publicity or promotion you've received, such as appearances on national TV or radio programs, or interviews in national magazines.
- Don't mention any "minor" publishing credits unrelated to your novel (e.g., that you had two poems published in your local paper).
- Don't spend too much time complimenting yourself.
- Do stick to the facts (don't exaggerate or lie).
- Don't include an author bio if you're a beginning writer with no publishing credits.
- Do have a separate bio if you're collaborating with another author, but make both bios fit on the same page.

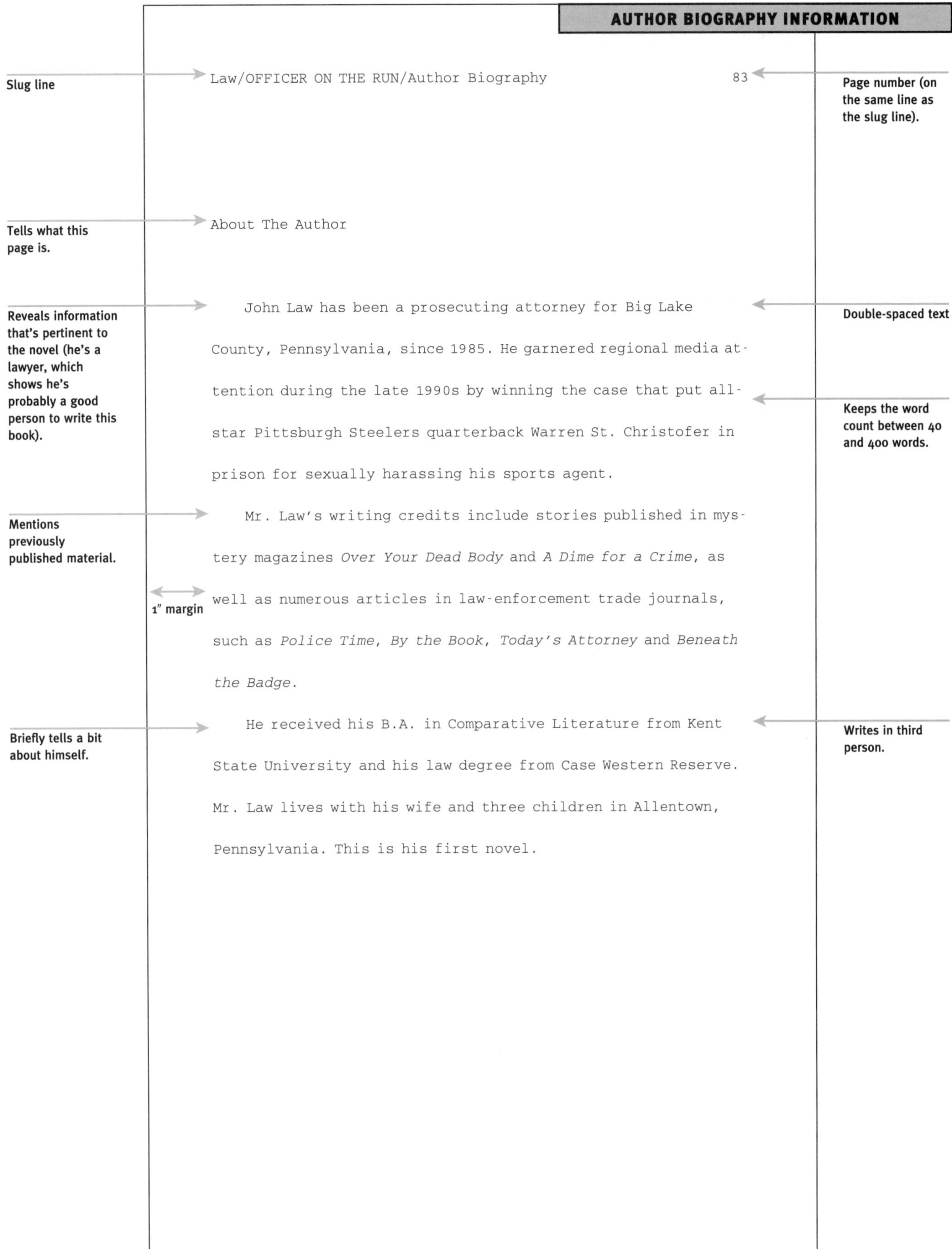
AUTHOR BIOGRAPHY INFORMATION
Slug line
Law/OFFICER ON THE RUN/Author Biography
83
Page number (on the same line as the slug line).
Tells what this page is.
About The Author
Reveals information that's pertinent to the novel (he's a lawyer, which shows he's probably a good person to write this book).
John Law has been a prosecuting attorney for Big Lake County, Pennsylvania, since 1985. He garnered regional media attention during the late 1990s by winning the case that put all-star Pittsburgh Steelers quarterback Warren St. Christofer in prison for sexually harassing his sports agent.
Double-spaced text
Keeps the word count between 40 and 400 words.
Mentions previously published material.
Mr. Law's writing credits include stories published in mystery magazines Over Your Dead Body and A Dime for a Crime, as well as numerous articles in law-enforcement trade journals, such as Police Time, By the Book, Today's Attorney and Beneath the Badge.
1" margin
Briefly tells a bit about himself.
He received his B.A. in Comparative Literature from Kent State University and his law degree from Case Western Reserve. Mr. Law lives with his wife and three children in Allentown, Pennsylvania. This is his first novel.
Writes in third person.

Endorsements Page

Submission Tips

An endorsements page is like a dishwasher—it's not essential, but it helps to have one. Putting the page together is simple because it's nothing more than a list of quotes. The trick, however, is that these quotes must come from noteworthy people, typically prominent industry insiders (well-known authors, agents, editors, experts on the topic) who've read your manuscript and have decided to comment favorably on it. Forget about including what your husband or neighbor or writing group said about your novel. While their words of praise matter to you, they don't matter to an agent or publisher—such opinions won't help sell your book.

Unless you have contacts, it is difficult to obtain a quote from someone noteworthy. Sure, you can send your manuscript to someone like Philip Roth and hope he'll take the time to read it and comment on it, but the chances of that happening are terribly slim. It's best not to include an endorsements page unless you have at least two good quotes from well-known, well-respected sources. Don't fret if you don't have an endorsements page—very few authors include one with fiction manuscripts. Most endorsements will come once the galleys go out to reviewers.

Formatting Specs

- Have a slug line (also called a header) in the top left corner with your last name, followed by a backslash, followed by the novel's title in all caps, followed by another backslash, then the word "Endorsements."
- The page number should be in the top right corner on the same line as the slug line.
- Single-space the text within each quote.
- Triple-space between quotes.
- Attribute the quotes (double-check for correct spelling of names and titles).
- Keep each endorsement short (fifty words or less).

Other Dos and Don'ts

- Don't worry too much about obtaining endorsements; fiction manuscripts stand on their own.
- Don't expect a response if you send your manuscript to some prominent person you don't know (certainly don't wait more than a few weeks for a response).
- Do get the source's permission to include the endorsement.
- Do send a thank-you note if someone provides a laudatory quote.

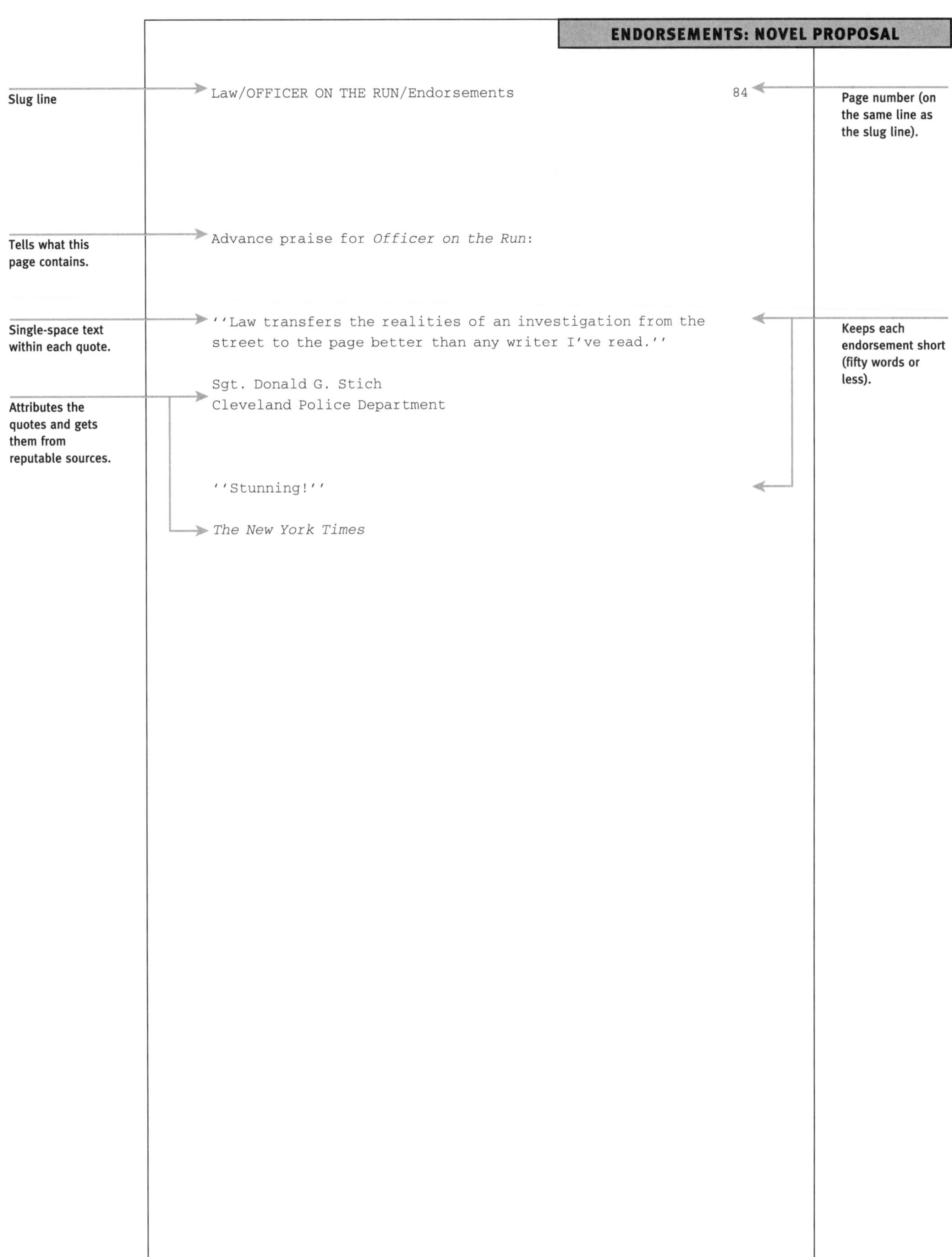
ENDORSEMENTS: NOVEL PROPOSAL
Slug line
Law/OFFICER ON THE RUN/Endorsements
84
Page number (on the same line as the slug line).
Tells what this page contains.
Advance praise for Officer on the Run:
Single-space text within each quote.
''Law transfers the realities of an investigation from the street to the page better than any writer I've read.''
Keeps each endorsement short (fifty words or less).
Sgt. Donald G. Stich
Cleveland Police Department
Attributes the quotes and gets them from reputable sources.
''Stunning!''
The New York Times

The Novel Manuscript

Your novel manuscript is easy to format and submit. What's most important is that you know when and what to submit. Never send an entire manuscript until you've been requested to do so. Unsolicited manuscripts are often ignored and returned (and sometimes even recycled or thrown away) when sent to an agent or publisher who does not accept them. Don't waste your time, energy, paper and postage; check the particular agent's or publisher's requirements to see if he accepts unsolicited manuscripts. Most don't.

Submission Tips

When a request for your manuscript does come, however, you'll need to know precisely what to send and how to organize it.

Proposal

If an agent or editor wants to consider representing or publishing your manuscript, here's what to send:

- Cover letter
- Title/Cover page
- Table of Contents
- Chapters
- SASE or postcard reply

Optional Front Matter:

- Author Biography (see page 129)
- Endorsements Page (see page 131)
- Epigraph (see page 147)

Accepted Proposal

If a publisher agrees to publish your novel, submit:

- Cover letter
- Title/Cover page
- Table of Contents
- Chapters
- SASE or postcard reply

Optional Front Matter:

- Acknowledgments (see page 143)
- Author Biography (see page 129)
- Dedication Page (see page 147)
- Endorsements Page (see page 131)
- Foreword (see page 149)
- Preface (see page 149)

Manuscript Pages

Formatting Specs

- Use a 1″ margin on all sides.
- Use a title page, set up the same as the title page in your proposal.
- Don't number the title page. Begin numbering with the first page of the text of the book, usually the introduction, prologue or chapter one.
- Use a slug line in the top left corner.
- Start each new chapter on its own page, one-third of the way down the page. The chapter number and chapter title should be in all caps, separated by two hyphens (CHAPTER 1--THE BODY).
- Begin the body of the chapter four to six lines below the chapter title.
- Indent five spaces for each new paragraph.
- Double-space the entire text.
- Underline anything that needs to be italicized.
- Use 10- or 12-point plain font: Times New Roman, Arial or Courier.
- Use 20-lb. bond paper.

Other Dos and Don'ts

- Do not staple anything.
- Do not punch holes in the pages or submit it in a three-ring binder.
- Do submit the manuscript loose-leaf in an envelope. That's why the slug line and page numbers are there.
- Don't number the page or use a slug line on the title/cover page.
- Don't justify or align the right margin.
- Don't put any copyright information on the manuscript. It's copyrighted when you write it, and the editor or agent knows this.

Cover Letter

Submission Tips

A cover letter accompanying a finished novel is brief. All you must do is let the editor know what's enclosed and how to contact you. Be cordial, of course, and feel free to thank the editor for working with you on the project, but don't go into great lengths about the novel or anything else. At this point in the game your editor is focused on one thing: grabbing your novel and reading it in its entirety. So get to the point in your cover letter and let the editor proceed at will.

Formatting Specs

- Use a standard font or typeface (no bold, script or italic).
- Place your name, address, phone (include E-mail and fax) in the top right corner.
- Use a 1″ margin on all sides.
- Keep it to one short page—a short paragraph will be fine.
- Use block or semi-block letter format.
- Single-space the body of the letter; double-space between paragraphs.
- Catalog every item you're sending in your enclosures (manuscript, reply postcard, etc.)

Other Dos and Don'ts

- Do thank the editor.
- Do tell the novel's exact word count.
- Do include a postcard for reply, and state in the letter that you have done so (but you'll probably already have a phone relationship with the editor at this point).
- Don't use "Dear Sir," "Dear Madame," etc. in your salutation.
- Don't tell how much time you've spent on the novel.
- Don't bring up payment (advances, royalties, etc.).
- Don't staple your cover letter to your novel.
- Don't put a page number on the cover letter.

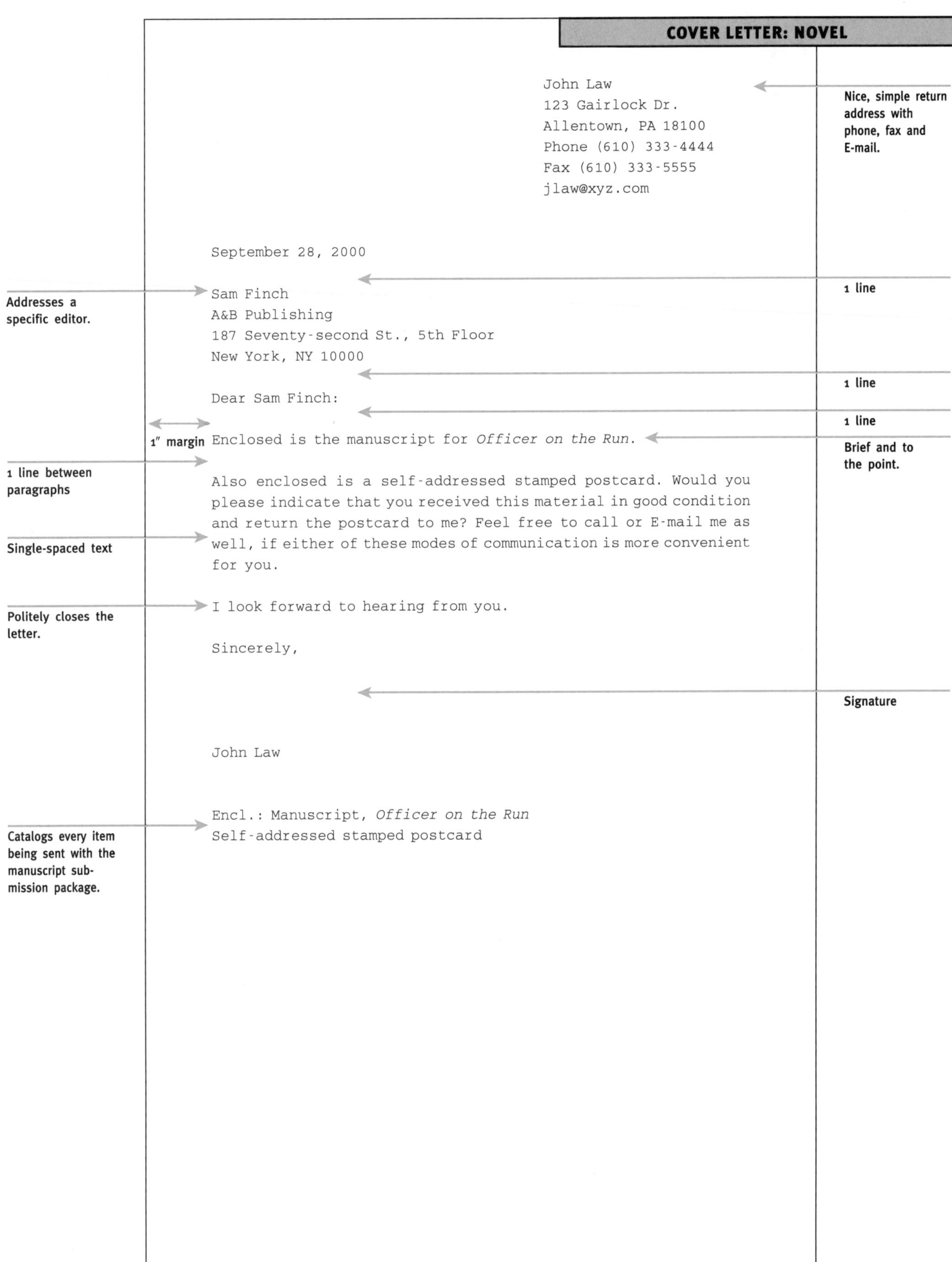

COVER LETTER: NOVEL

John Law
123 Gairlock Dr.
Allentown, PA 18100
Phone (610) 333-4444
Fax (610) 333-5555
jlaw@xyz.com

September 28, 2000

Sam Finch
A&B Publishing
187 Seventy-second St., 5th Floor
New York, NY 10000

Dear Sam Finch:

Enclosed is the manuscript for *Officer on the Run*.

Also enclosed is a self-addressed stamped postcard. Would you please indicate that you received this material in good condition and return the postcard to me? Feel free to call or E-mail me as well, if either of these modes of communication is more convenient for you.

I look forward to hearing from you.

Sincerely,

John Law

Encl.: Manuscript, *Officer on the Run*
Self-addressed stamped postcard

Nice, simple return address with phone, fax and E-mail.
1 line
Addresses a specific editor.
1 line
1 line
1" margin
Brief and to the point.
1 line between paragraphs
Single-spaced text
Politely closes the letter.
Signature
Catalogs every item being sent with the manuscript submission package.

Title Page

In the top right corner of the page, flush with the right margin, put the word count. Then, your novel's title should be centered, in bold and in all caps, about halfway down the page. Double-space again and type "A Novel" (do not type the quotation marks), and then double-space again and type "by" (do not type the quotation marks). Double-space again and type your name (if your novel is written with another person use an ampersand between your names). In the lower right-hand corner, put your name, address, and phone/fax/E-mail, single-spaced, in regular text (not all caps). If you have an agent, put the agent's name, address and phone number here and put your name, address and phone/fax/E-mail in the top left corner.

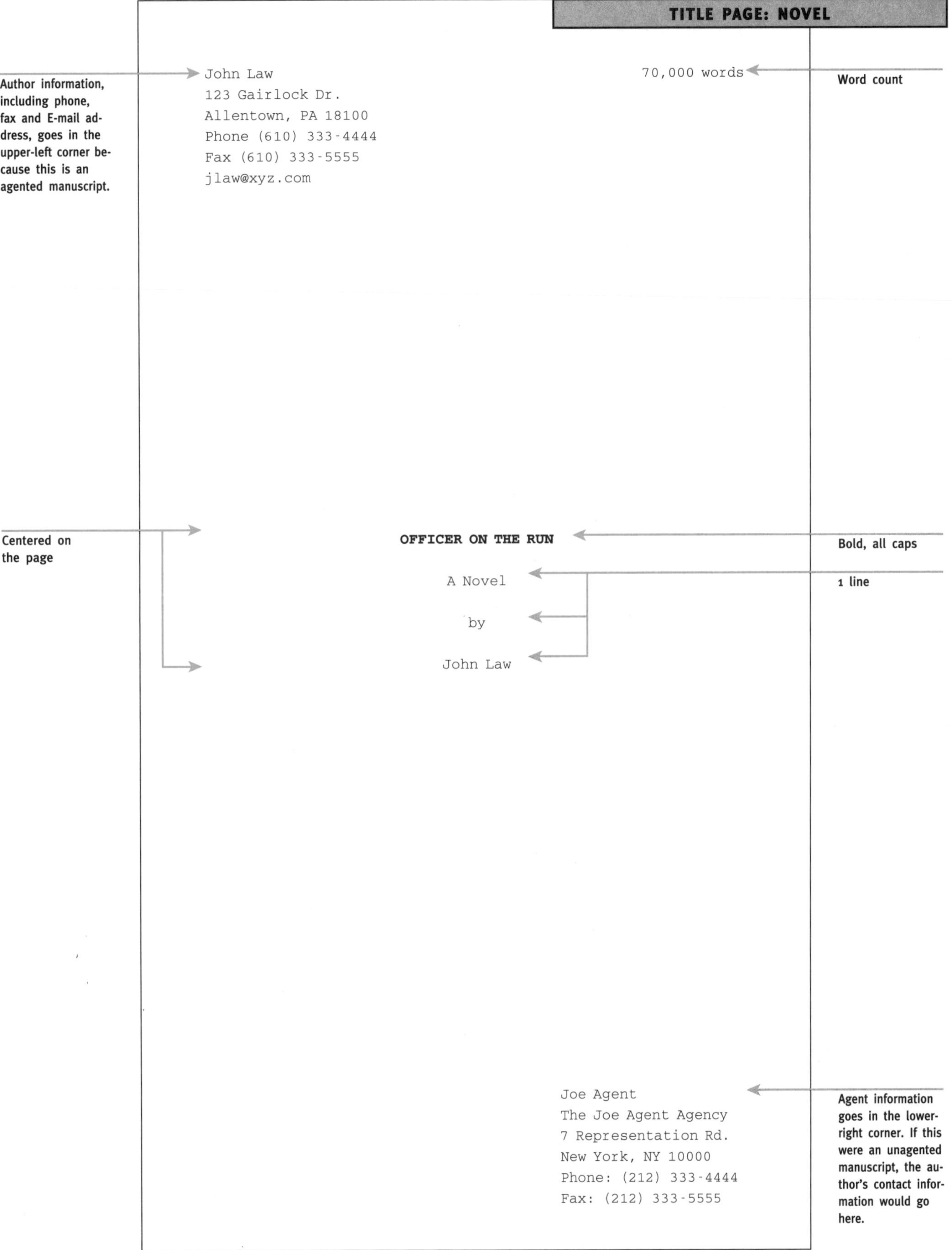
TITLE PAGE: NOVEL
Author information, including phone, fax and E-mail address, goes in the upper-left corner because this is an agented manuscript.
John Law
123 Gairlock Dr.
Allentown, PA 18100
Phone (610) 333-4444
Fax (610) 333-5555
jlaw@xyz.com
70,000 words
Word count
Centered on the page
OFFICER ON THE RUN
Bold, all caps
A Novel
1 line
by
John Law
Joe Agent
The Joe Agent Agency
7 Representation Rd.
New York, NY 10000
Phone: (212) 333-4444
Fax: (212) 333-5555
Agent information goes in the lower-right corner. If this were an unagented manuscript, the author's contact information would go here.

MANUSCRIPT, PAGE 1: NOVEL

Slug line with novel's title in all caps.

Law/OFFICER ON THE RUN 1

Page number (on the same line as the slug line).

Chapter number and chapter title in all caps, separated by two hyphens, one-third of the way down the page.

CHAPTER 1--THE BODY

Marlene Preston walked like a freak but sang like a bird. With aspirations to become a star, she sang in a band on weekends but was a nightshift dispatcher during the week. She was the Chief's latest affair, his Seventh Deadly Sin. He would joke about her with the other officers and refer to her as Lucky No. 7. To her face he only called her Lucky. She never figured out why. She just wanted him to call her Marlene.

Justifies left margin only.

Double-spaced text

Marlene grabbed the Chief's attention her second day on the job, when she arrived at work after a rare midweek gig. Because the band played until 11:30 and she had to start her shift at midnight, Marlene didn't have time to change into suitable work clothes. To everyone's surprise, she showed up at the station in skin-hugging black leather tights, six-inch silver pumps and a white halter top. Her long, dark, untamed hair wrapped around her shoulders, and her perfume smelled like a rose. Marlene Preston blazed a trail of lust.

1" margin

Indents five spaces for each new paragraph.

Every officer on the force was checking out Marlene. That was for her one of the perks of the job—being the only woman in the company of men. She loved the attention, especially from the Chief. He was, after all, The Man—the guy all the other officers aspired to be. Marlene was flattered by his flirtations. She knew she was looking good, and it pleased her that the Chief noticed. And notice he did.

MANUSCRIPT, PAGE 2: NOVEL

Slug line with novel's title in all caps.

Law/OFFICER ON THE RUN 2

Page number (on the same line as the slug line).

At 12:50, a call came in about a robbery. Two guys held up a 24-hour convenience store and shot a clerk in the shoulder. The Chief immediately directed all four officers on duty to hit the streets, two at the crime scene and two to find the getaway car. As soon as the station cleared, the Chief was alone with Marlene. And he let her know he liked that.

Starts each change of dialogue on a new line, with a five-space paragraph indent.

''So, Marlene, this is your first major dispatch, isn't it?''

''Well yeah.''

''You handled that call really well Marlene. Like a pro.''

''Thanks.''

''But then again you look like you could handle just about anything. You're so calm.''

''Thanks.''

''You gotta admit it's kind of exciting, isn't it?''

''Yeah. But it's really sad somebody would go and shoot a poor clerk just for some cash register change.''

''People do crazy things for personal gain, Marlene. Stay on this job and it won't take you long to figure that out.''

''I guess not. I mean it's only my second day and already a robbery. What's next?''

''Oh, who knows. Maybe it could be something really exhilarating . . . like a murder. Like maybe an angry wife murdered her husband because he was having an affair with a colleague. Now that sounds fun.''

The Chief then walked out the door and left Marlene to ponder such a scenario. She was nervous. What did he mean by that? Marlene thought about that for a while but decided she was probably just reading too much into it. Everyone knew the Chief was a happily married man, a father of two lovely children and well respected in the community. Surely she must have misunderstood.

Reply Postcard

If you're a bit paranoid about whether your novel actually makes it to the publisher, you may send a reply postcard along with your novel. Having it signed by the editor (or someone on the staff) and sent back to you will alleviate any worries that the package didn't make it to its destination. Two caveats: 1) Not all editors are gracious enough to send your reply postcards back—but most are. 2) Just because you receive a postcard reply from an editor, you cannot assume your novel has been read or will be read in the next few days or even weeks. Your reply postcard's only function is to let you know your package has been received.

Your best bet to ensure an editor will return your reply postcard is to make it neat and simple to use. That means typing your postcard and not asking the editor to do anything other than note your submission has been received. Although it's OK to leave a small space for "Comments," keep the space very small and never expect it to be filled in—most editors don't have the time or a reason to write anything in it. You'll turn off an editor if you ask him to do too much.

Creating a suitable and functional reply postcard is easy. If you create a reply postcard similar to the one on the following page you'll be just fine. Above all, remember to keep things short and sweet—and, of course, always be sure the postcard has a stamp in the top right corner on the side with your address.

REPLY POSTCARD: NOVEL

John Law
123 Gairlock Dr.
Allentown, PA 18100

John Law, 123 Gairlock Dr., Allentown PA 18100, (610) 333-4444

Date: ______________________________

Your novel *Officer on the Run* was received in my office on

______________________.

Other comments:

Signature ______________________________

Company ______________________________

Acknowledgments Page

Optional. Your acknowledgments page is the place where you spend time thanking everybody who helped you throughout the process of writing the book. Most people thanked in an acknowledgments page are friends who gave you ideas and offered criticisms, family and friends who supported you, any institution that awarded you a grant or sabbatical, and, of course, your agents and editors. Don't forget anyone who helped in preparation of the book when you write acknowledgments, unless they don't want to be mentioned. It can pay to keep a running file of names and ways that people helped so you don't have to scramble for this information at the end. Sometimes, what would normally go in an acknowledgments page ends up in a preface, if you have one—unless there are more people and/or institutions than can be acknowledged in the preface.

Put the acknowledgments page on its own page, do not number the page, use a slug line, and double-space the text. Be sure to drop about a third of the way down the page and use a centered heading that says, "Acknowledgments" underlined. At the end of your acknowledgments, you may sign your initials and indicate the place and date.

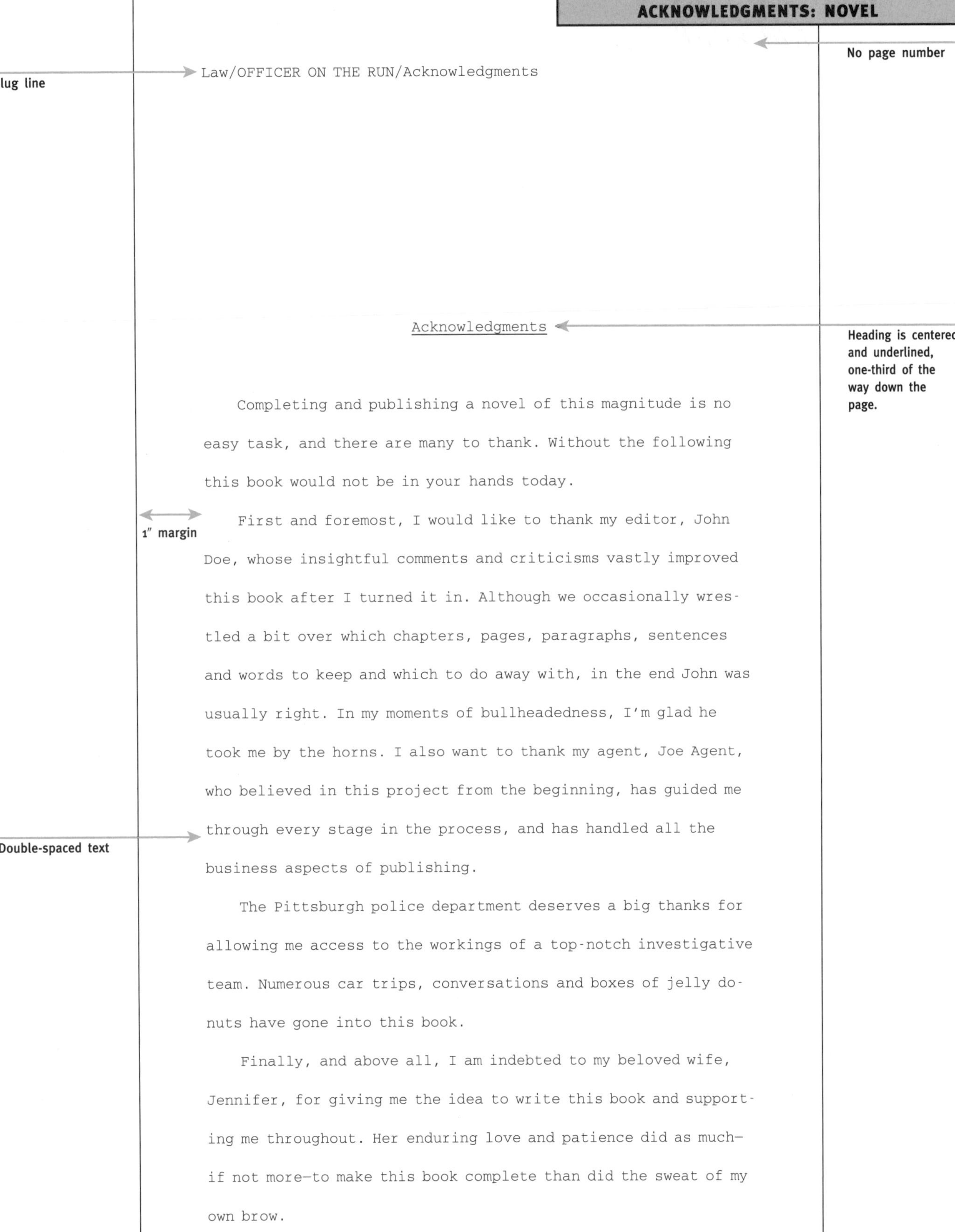

Law/OFFICER ON THE RUN/Acknowledgments

Acknowledgments

Completing and publishing a novel of this magnitude is no easy task, and there are many to thank. Without the following this book would not be in your hands today.

First and foremost, I would like to thank my editor, John Doe, whose insightful comments and criticisms vastly improved this book after I turned it in. Although we occasionally wrestled a bit over which chapters, pages, paragraphs, sentences and words to keep and which to do away with, in the end John was usually right. In my moments of bullheadedness, I'm glad he took me by the horns. I also want to thank my agent, Joe Agent, who believed in this project from the beginning, has guided me through every stage in the process, and has handled all the business aspects of publishing.

The Pittsburgh police department deserves a big thanks for allowing me access to the workings of a top-notch investigative team. Numerous car trips, conversations and boxes of jelly donuts have gone into this book.

Finally, and above all, I am indebted to my beloved wife, Jennifer, for giving me the idea to write this book and supporting me throughout. Her enduring love and patience did as much—if not more—to make this book complete than did the sweat of my own brow.

Table of Contents

Submission Tips

The table of contents for fiction manuscripts is often pretty spare—merely listing the chapter title and page numbers.

Formatting Specs

- Center the heading "Table of Contents" or "Contents" at least a third of the way down the page.
- Provide an extra-wide margin, at least 1½".
- Don't number pages as part of the manuscript.
- Use a slug in the same place in the header as the rest of the manuscript.
- At the very least, include the chapter titles.
- Include such front-matter elements as prefaces, forewords and prologues.
- Don't include acknowledgments, dedications and other short bits of front matter.

TABLE OF CONTENTS: NOVEL

Slug

Law/OFFICER ON THE RUN/Contents

No page number

Table of Contents

Centered, one-third of the way down the page.

Wide margins (2″)

Page numbers correspond to manuscript pages.

Double-spaced text

Dedication Page

Optional. The dedication is a brief inscription in which you express affection or respect for a person (or persons) who may or may not be directly related to the subject matter of your book. This is the place for you to write things like, "For Jennifer—the light of my life." Be sure to keep your dedication short (only a few lines). The dedication gets its own page (do not number) and must have a slug line that should look like this: Law/OFFICER ON THE RUN/Dedication. The dedication should be centered about a third of the way down the page. Do not put a heading that labels this page a "Dedication."

Epigraph

Optional. The epigraph is a short quotation used at the beginning of the novel and/or at the beginning of each chapter. Its content should have relevance to the contents of the book. The source should be cited. When used at the beginning of the novel, type on separate page (do not number). Be sure if the epigraph is on its own page to use a slug lien that should look like this: Law/OFFICER ON THE RUN/Epigraph. The epigraph should be centered about a third of the way down the page. Do not put a heading that labels this page an "Epigraph." When used at the beginning of a chapter, type on the same page as the chapter begins (do not number).

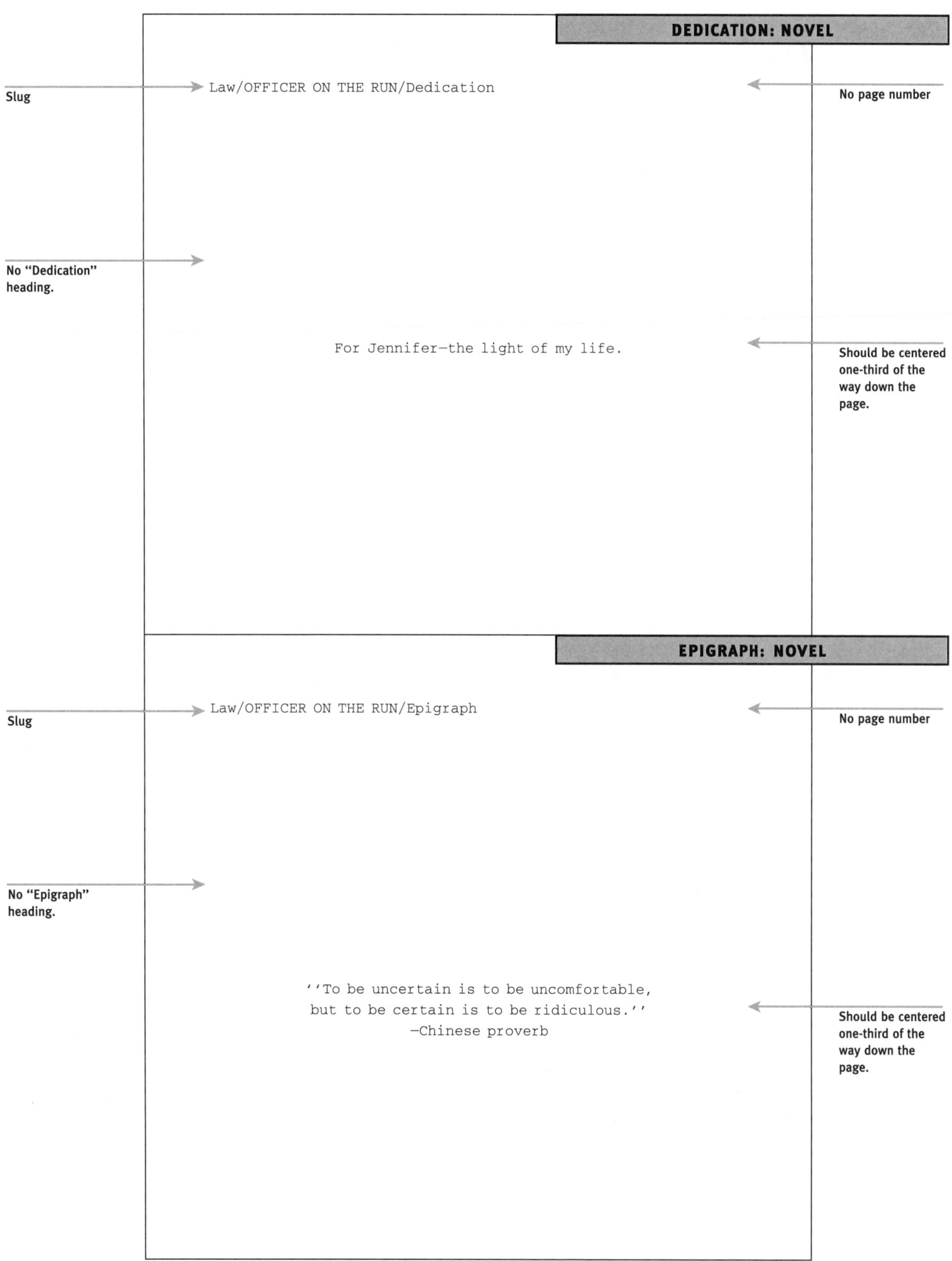
DEDICATION: NOVEL
Slug
Law/OFFICER ON THE RUN/Dedication
No page number
No "Dedication" heading.
For Jennifer—the light of my life.
Should be centered one-third of the way down the page.
EPIGRAPH: NOVEL
Slug
Law/OFFICER ON THE RUN/Epigraph
No page number
No "Epigraph" heading.
''To be uncertain is to be uncomfortable,
but to be certain is to be ridiculous.''
—Chinese proverb
Should be centered one-third of the way down the page.

Foreword

Optional. A brief commentary, included in a book's front matter, in which the author or another person remarks on the book's contents. A foreword is sometimes written by a well-known author or authority to add credibility and sales appeal to the work. Although the publisher often makes arrangements for the foreword to be written, the author's suggestions about experts in the book's particular subject field are usually welcome. Like the rest of the front matter, the Foreword has a slug but no page numbers. Be sure to use a heading that explicity states "Foreword" about one-third of the way down the page. The name of the foreword's author goes flush right at the end of the text, followed by title and affiliation. The foreword's author may want to indicate the city, year, and place the foreword was written.

Preface

Optional. You might want to write a preface if you feel you need to explain why you wrote the book. It's rarely done with fiction, so talk with your agent or editor about it. The preface can also be used as an acknowledgments page—to thank the people and/or the institutions that helped bring the book to fruition. You, the author, write the preface. Make sure you sign your initials, tell the place where you're writing from and include the date. Type the preface on a separate page, double-space the text, do not number the page, and be sure to use a slug line. Finally, use a heading, starting about a third of the way down the page, that clearly indicates this is the preface.

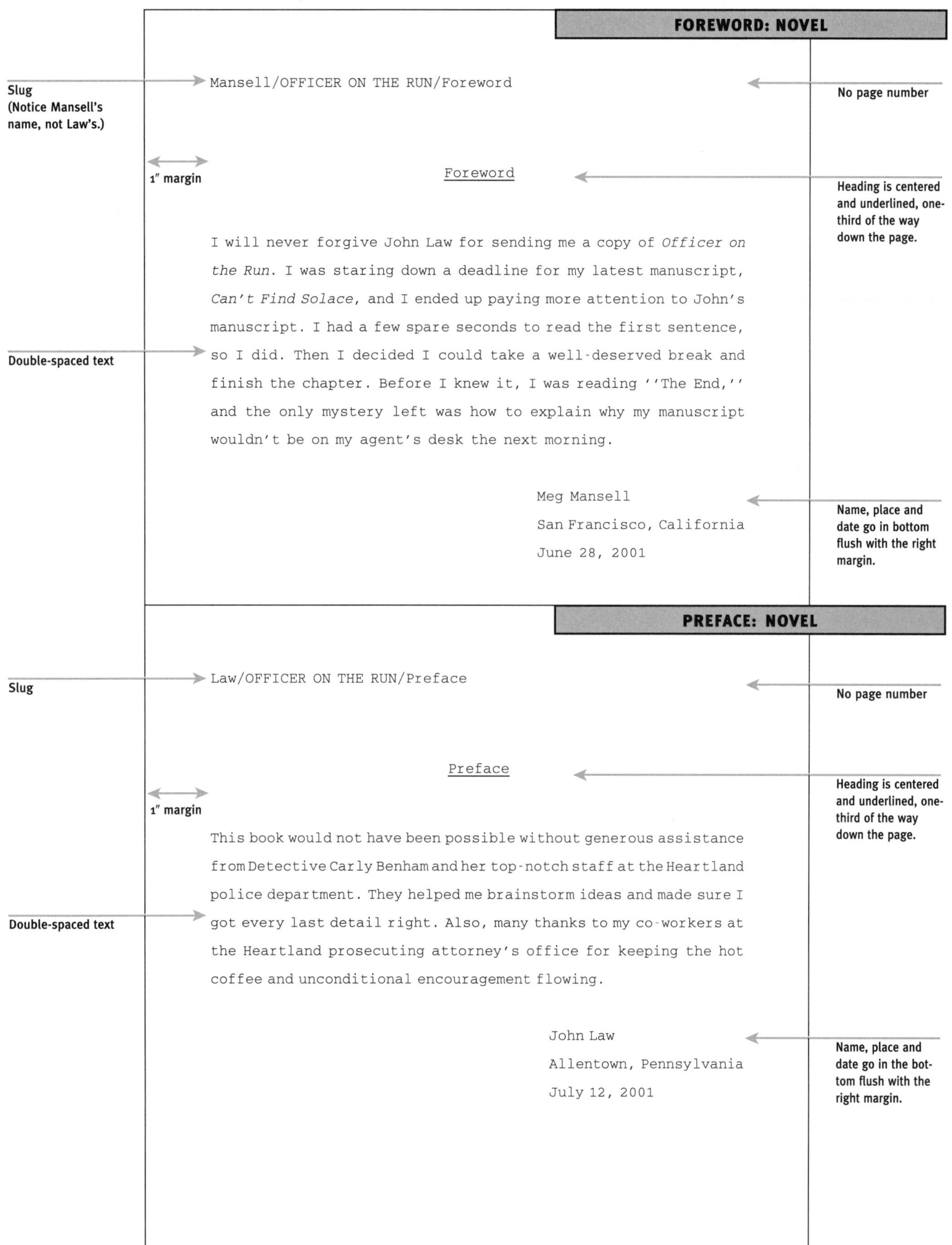
FOREWORD: NOVEL
Slug
(Notice Mansell's name, not Law's.)
Mansell/OFFICER ON THE RUN/Foreword
No page number
1" margin
Foreword
Heading is centered and underlined, one-third of the way down the page.
I will never forgive John Law for sending me a copy of *Officer on the Run*. I was staring down a deadline for my latest manuscript, *Can't Find Solace*, and I ended up paying more attention to John's manuscript. I had a few spare seconds to read the first sentence, so I did. Then I decided I could take a well-deserved break and finish the chapter. Before I knew it, I was reading ''The End,'' and the only mystery left was how to explain why my manuscript wouldn't be on my agent's desk the next morning.
Double-spaced text
Meg Mansell
San Francisco, California
June 28, 2001
Name, place and date go in bottom flush with the right margin.
PREFACE: NOVEL
Slug
Law/OFFICER ON THE RUN/Preface
No page number
Preface
1" margin
Heading is centered and underlined, one-third of the way down the page.
This book would not have been possible without generous assistance from Detective Carly Benham and her top-notch staff at the Heartland police department. They helped me brainstorm ideas and made sure I got every last detail right. Also, many thanks to my co-workers at the Heartland prosecuting attorney's office for keeping the hot coffee and unconditional encouragement flowing.
Double-spaced text
John Law
Allentown, Pennsylvania
July 12, 2001
Name, place and date go in the bottom flush with the right margin.

CHAPTER SIX

SPECIALIZED FICTION

To submit and format your short stories and novels for genre fiction please consult the appropriate pages (short stories appear on page 97; novel proposals on page 109). Here, however, is information on the four major genres of fiction, with specifics pertaining to the peculiarities of each, as well as contact information for each genre's primary writing organization. Also included in this chapter is information on two additional specialized markets: children's books and comics.

Horror

Howard Phillips (H.P.) Lovecraft, generally acknowledged to be the master of the horror tale in the twentieth century and the most important American writer of this genre since Edgar Allan Poe, maintained that "the oldest and strongest emotion of mankind is fear, and the oldest and strongest kind of fear is fear of the unknown. These facts few psychologists will dispute, and their admitted truth must establish for all time the genuineness and dignity of the weirdly horrible tales as a literary form."

Lovecraft distinguishes horror literature from fiction based entirely on physical fear and the merely gruesome. "The true weird tale has something more than secret murder, bloody bones or a sheeted form clanking chains according to rule. A certain atmosphere of breathless and unexplainable dread of outer, unknown forces must be present; there must be a hint, expressed with a seriousness and portentousness becoming its subject, of that most terrible concept of the human brain—a malign and particular suspension or defeat of the fixed laws of Nature which are our only safeguards against the assaults of chaos and the daemons of unplumbed space." It is that atmosphere—the creation of a particular sensation or emotional level—that, according to Lovecraft, is the most important element in the creation of horror literature.

The earliest predecessor of the modern horror genre was the gothic romance novel of the eighteenth century. The nineteenth century produced classic works of horror fiction such as Robert Louis Stevenson's *The Strange Case of Dr. Jekyll and Mr. Hyde* and Guy de Maupassant's *The Horla.* The nineteenth century also marked the emergence of Edgar Allan Poe, whose work set a new standard of realism in the history of literary horror and had a profound impact on the mainstream of macabre writing.

Early twentieth-century writers of note include Lovecraft, Arthur Machen (*The Great God Pan*), and Algernon Blackwood (*The Willows*). Contemporary writers enjoying considerable success in the horror fiction genre include Stephen King (*Rose Madder, Four*

Past Midnight, Needful Things), Robert Bloch (*Psycho, Night of the Ripper*), Peter Straub (*Houses Without Doors, Julia, The Throat*), Charles L. Grant (*The Black Carousel, In a Dark Dream, In the Fog*) and Dean Koontz (*The Bad Place, The Door to December, Dragon Tears*).

Writers can research current trends in the genre by studying anthologies such as Charles L. Grant's *Shadows*, Kirby McCaulley's *Dark Forces*, and *The Year's Best Horror Stories*, edited by Karl Edward Wagner.

Horror Writers Association (Formerly Horror Writers of America.)

An organization with more than seven hundred members in two classes: active members (professional writers who have sold work), and affiliate members (professionals in the genre other than writers and those interested in horror).

HWA awards the Bram Stoker Award for Superior Achievement annually. It publishes a bimonthly newsletter and a membership directory. For information, visit the HWA Web site (www.horror.org) or write to the HWA at P.O. Box 418, Annapolis Junction, MD 20701.

Mystery

The mystery is a form of fiction in which one or more elements remain unknown or unexplained until the end of the story. The modern mystery story contains elements of the serious novel: a convincing account of a character's struggle with various physical and psychological obstacles in an effort to achieve his goal, good characterization and sound motivation. Publishers of mystery stories often look for one or more of these eleven categories:

- **Amateur sleuth**. In an amateur sleuth, the main character does the detection, but isn't a professional private investigator or police detective. Two detectives work together in a bickering team or cohort mystery series. The crime is the main focus, but the relationship—be it marriage or friendship—is also developed in the series.
- **Caper**. A caper is a crime story usually told from the viewpoint of the perpetrator. The tone may be lighthearted and the crime is often theft rather than murder.
- **Cozy**. A murder mystery set in a small English or New England town that features an amateur sleuth is called a cozy or English cozy. The "detective" is usually a genteel old lady or gentleman.
- **Gothic**. A gothic mystery is one with a dark and brooding tone. Usually set at an old estate, a gothic contains elements of romantic suspense.
- **Hard-boiled**. A story that features a streetwise and hardened detective is a hard-boiled detective story. Often a male, this character type was popularized in the 1940s and 1950s.
- **Heist**. More serious than a caper, a heist focuses on solving the theft, as well as on the planning and execution of the theft.
- **Malice domestic**. A mystery involving a family member's murder is a malice domestic.
- **Police procedural**. A police procedural is a mystery featuring a police detective or officer who uses standard professional police practices to solve the crime.

• **Romantic suspense**. In a romantic suspense, strong elements of romance appear, usually between the detective and the victim or the detective and the suspect.

• **True crime**. Nonfiction about real murders and serial killings is true crime. Truman Capote is credited with beginning this genre with *In Cold Blood.*

• **Whodunit**. The focus is on discovering the identity of the murderer in a whodunit.

Mystery Writers of America, Inc

This organization of 2,500 members is "dedicated to the proposition that the detective story is the noblest sport of man." The membership includes published writers, novice writers and people in writing-related fields, such as publishers, editors and agents. Annual activities include a convention, presentation of the Edgar Allan Poe and Raven Awards, and publication of an anthology of members' work. A newsletter, *The Third Degree*, is issued ten times a year. The headquarters of this organization is at 17 E. Forty-seventh St., Sixth Floor, New York, NY 10017 (212) 888-8171; Fax: (212) 888-8107. You can send E-mail to mwa_org@earthlink.net, or visit the Web site: www.mysterynet.com/mwa/.

Romance

The romance novel is a type of category fiction in which the love relationship between a man and a woman pervades the plot. The story is told from the viewpoint of the heroine, who meets a man (the hero), falls in love with him, encounters a conflict that hinders their relationship, then resolves the conflict. As opposed to many gothic romances, settings in these stories are contemporary; the characters are modern. Though marriage is not necessarily the outcome of the story, the ending is always happy.

Romance is the overriding element in this kind of story: The couple's relationship determines the plot and tone of the book. The theme of the novel is the woman's sexual awakening. Although she may not be a virgin, she has never before been so emotionally aroused. Despite all this emotion, however, characters and plot both must be well-developed and realistic: Contrived situations and flat characters are unacceptable. Throughout a romance novel, the reader senses the sexual and emotional attraction between the heroine and hero. Lovemaking scenes, though sometimes detailed, are generally not too graphic; more emphasis is placed on the sensual element than on physical action.

Romance novels fall into three distinct formats.

• **Sensual**. The sensual romance, which is currently the best-selling type, is illustrated by the Silhouette Desire line. The emphasis in these plots is on the sensual tension between the hero and heroine, as well as the sizzling sexual scenes.

• **Spicy**. The spicy romance, which includes Harlequin SuperRomances and Harlequin Presents, is exemplified in stories in which married characters resolve (to a happy end) their problems. Books in these lines consist of less sex and more story, compared to some other lines of romances.

• **Sweet**. The sweet romance, which is on the wane at the moment, is published in Harlequin Romances, Silhouette Romances and Bantam's Loveswept. Many of the heroines in sweet romances are virgins, and the stories contain little if any sex.

The appeal of the romance reaches the teenaged market, as well, with romances highlighting relationships of sixteen-year-old contemporary heroines and their seventeen- to eighteen-year-old boyfriends. The stories concern the problems of growing up and the difficulties of romantic encounters in youth. Explicit sex and highly controversial issues such as abortion and unmarried pregnancy are not considered by editors of teenage romance novels.

Today's adult romance novel differs from its counterpart of the past in that it reflects society's increasing respect for women. "Bodice-rippers" and "rape sagas," though still being published in the historical romance field, are becoming less popular than category romances, as authors and readers increasingly subscribe to the values fostered by the women's movement. Some publishers now recommend in their guidelines that the heroine have a career; others are loosening the restrictions on the status of women deemed acceptable heroines.

Each publisher of romances has detailed, specific guidelines regarding her line. The publisher will stipulate, for example, whether the setting may be a foreign country or within the U.S., whether the heroine may engage in sex outside of marriage, whether marriage will occur at novel's end, and whether the heroine is in her twenties, thirties or another age group. In addition, publishers specify lengths for romances, which usually are from 50,000 to 60,000 words; books in some lines, however, are longer, such as Harlequin's Worldwide SuperRomances, which run about 85,000 words.

Romance Writers of America (RWA)

This organization was established in 1979. Writers need not be published to join RWA, whose more than 7,700 members include individuals in foreign countries and more than 150 local chapters. RWA strives to make romantic fiction a recognized genre, to increase interest in it, to support and encourage writers in their careers and to provide market information. The Golden Heart Award, presented annually, recognizes an RWA member who is an unpublished writer of romantic fiction. Rita Awards, presented annually, recognize the best in published romantic fiction. RWA has 7,700 members and publishes a monthly newspaper, *Romance Writers Report.* It holds an annual conference and regional conferences.

You can visit the RWA's Web site at www.rwanational.com, or write to 3767 F.M. 1960, Suite 555, Houston, TX 77068; (281) 440-6885; fax (281) 440-7510.

Science Fiction

Science fiction can be defined as literature involving elements of science and technology as a basis for conflict, or as the setting for a story. The science and technology are generally extrapolations of existing scientific fact, and most (though not all) science fiction stories take place in the future. There are other definitions of science fiction, and much disagreement in academic circles as to just what constitutes science fiction and what constitutes fantasy. This is because in some cases the line between science fiction and fantasy is virtually nonexistent. Despite the controversy, it is generally accepted that, to be science fiction, a story must have elements of science. Fantasy, on the other hand, rarely utilizes science, relying instead on magic, mythological and neo-mythological beings and devices, and outright invention for conflict and setting.

Some of the basic elements of science fiction have been in existence for thousands of years. There have always been fortune-tellers, prophets, clairvoyants and other extraordinary people who sought to foretell the future. The grand adventure in an exotic setting—a recurring story structure in science fiction—has been a literary theme almost as long as the desire to know the future. Tales of mythological gods and their involvement with humans are echoed by modern-day science fiction stories of encounters with alien beings. The heroic quest, occurring so often in all mythologies, is paralleled by stories of pioneering space explorers.

There is some disagreement about when the first true science fiction story was written, but most scholars feel that "True History," written by a Greek, Lucian of Somosata, about 175 A.D., was the first real science fiction story. This tale dealt with a trip to the moon in a ship borne aloft by a great whirlwind.

The direct ancestor of modern science fiction is generally considered to be Mary Shelley's *Frankenstein: or, The Modern Prometheus* (1818). Over the next few decades, authors such as Poe, Stevenson and Verne expanded the field, developing what was known as the "scientific romance." H.G. Wells capped the development of the scientific romance and, in 1926, science fiction emerged as a distinct genre (under the name "scientifiction") with the publication of the first all-science fiction magazine, *Amazing Stories.*

The pulp magazine era was just beginning, and the explosion of markets for short stories in magazines helped science fiction gain a firm foothold in the American literary scene. The market for original paperback novels opened up in the 1950s. Major talents such as Robert A. Heinlein, Isaac Asimov and Arthur C. Clarke emerged during this period and brought the field to maturity. Under the influence of scores of writers and editors—as well as TV and films—science fiction has reached its current state of development.

Contemporary science fiction, while maintaining its focus on science and technology, is more concerned with the effects of science and technology on people. Since science is such an important factor in writing science fiction, accuracy with reference to scientific fact is important. Most of the science in science fiction is hypothesized from known facts, so in addition to being firmly based in fact, the extrapolations must be consistent. Science fiction writers make their own rules for future settings, but the field requires consistency. For example, if a future is established in which mass transit is the only form of personal transportation, a character cannot be shown driving a personal vehicle just because it is convenient to the plot. In the same manner, in a setting derived from our own world, it would be inconsistent to introduce a human being who has reached the stage of evolution in which it reproduces asexually.

Whatever the background, science fiction, as other forms of fiction, is dependent upon the "standard" elements of storytelling—plot, characterization, theme, motivation, etc.—for success. Many would-be science fiction writers miss this fact, and attempt to dazzle readers with gimmicks and gadgets, to no effect. Beyond inconsistency and an overabundance of gadgetry in place of a good story, there are few taboos in science fiction. Anyone wishing to write science fiction should spend time reading both current and past work to gain insight into its distinct characteristics.

There are several subcategories of science fiction, including dark fantasy, sociological SF, humorous SF, space opera, military SF, alternate history and cyberpunk, each having its own peculiarities. Extensive reading in the field can aid the neophyte in identifying these subcategories, and is recommended for anyone wishing to write science fiction.

Locus Magazine is considered the genre's bible. (Beginners should also note that editors and writers prefer the abbreviation SF to SciFi for their specialty genre.)

Science-fiction and Fantasy Writers of America (SFFWA)

Formerly the Science Fiction Writers of America, this organization was founded in 1965 by Damon Knight. More than twelve hundred SF/Fantasy writers, artists, editors and allied professionals are members. The SFFWA has four categories of membership: Active, for published authors and their estates; Associate, for beginning writers with one professional publication; Affiliate, for allied professionals such as agents, editors, artists and publishers; and Institutional, for organizations such as schools and universities. All members receive the quarterly bulletin, the annual membership directory, the *SFFWA Handbook* and copies of the model paperback and hardcover contracts. Active and Associate members also receive the *SFFWA Forum*, an in-house journal, six times a year. SFFWA supports a Grievance Committee, legal counsel, a Speaker's Bureau and a Circulating Book Plan, which offers members access to new hardcover books. Various committees monitor contracts and royalty statements, maintain contact with other writers' organizations, set standards for author/agent relationships, and help members deal with the strange world of science fiction conventions. SFFWA presents the Nebula Awards for the best SF or Fantasy short story, novelette, novella and novel of the year.

Visit the SFFWA's Web site at www.sfwa.org, or write to Sharon Lee, executive director, SFFWA, Inc., P.O. Box 171, Unity, ME 04988-0171.

Children's Picture Books

Written for children to read or have read to them, a picture book usually contains 150-1,500 words and thirty-two pages. The text of a picture book is well-organized and carefully constructed, since its audience has little experience with literature. Because picture books are often read aloud and children have an instinctual fondness for rhythm, poetic techniques (e.g., alliteration, consonance, assonance and onomatopoeia) can enhance a picture book's story. Other techniques that appeal to children are the repeated anecdote, used in *The Three Little Pigs*, and the refrain, used in *The Gingerbread Man.* Vocabulary in this category of writing is simple and sentence construction is likewise uncomplicated; it often uses the active voice and mimics speech patterns.

Submitting

The primary difference between submitting a picture book and an adult book is that you must send the entire manuscript of your picture book, not just a proposal or a few sample chapters. For longer work (young adult, lengthy nonfiction picture books), however, some children's publishers prefer to see a query letter instead. Check each publisher's specific submission guidelines in *Children's Writer's & Illustrator's Market* before you send anything. (Note: even though the text for a picture book is short, publishers do not want you to submit more than one manuscript at a time.)

Cover Letter

The cover letter accompanying your manuscript should be brief and professional, yet friendly. Jean E. Karl, in *How to Write and Sell Children's Picture Books*, says the cover letter should "interest the reader who receives it, and not put that person off by overcleverness or cuteness . . . ." Karl recommends mentioning the title of the work being sent, a sentence or two about the material, and a brief summary of previous writing experience. If you don't have any previous experience, you shouldn't mention it; simply thank the editor for her consideration. Olga Litowinsky, in *Writing and Publishing Books for Children in the 1990s*, suggests finding out something about the editor or the publisher's list and complimenting her: "Perhaps your friendly tone will result in a friendly answer."

Don't include a sentence like this in your cover letter: "I read my work to my kids/grandkids/second grade class and they just loved it." This definitely does not sway an editor's opinion; it even seems amateurish. Think about it: If you wrote a novel for adults, would you say, "I read this to my wife and my next-door neighbor and they just loved it"? Of course not. For more information on query and cover letters, consult pages 110-117.

Formatting

As far as manuscript formats for picture books, chapter books or young adult novels, follow the same format as you would for any fiction manuscript (see formats for a novel on pages 138-139). One note: When submitting a picture book manuscript, you shouldn't indicate page breaks—the editor will decide. You should, however, keep in mind that most picture books are almost always thirty-two pages (including the copyright page and front and back matter) and be aware of how your text flows and where illustrations might be placed as you're writing your manuscript.

Illustrations

A common misconception among many new writers of picture books is that they must find illustrators for their work before they submit. This is absolutely not the case; in fact, most editors frown upon a writer and illustrator teaming up on a submission. Once a publisher accepts your material, the publisher will select an appropriate illustrator for your project. So even if your sister-in-law or co-worker is an illustrator, it's best not to send their illustration samples with your manuscript. Most likely a publisher will not be interested in the whole package, and including those illustrations will only hurt your chances of getting published. Also, if you enclose unprofessional art samples with your manuscript, you're destined for rejection.

Remember that the biggest taboo in picture book publishing is submitting finished artwork with the proposal: This is the unmistakable mark of an amateur—worse, an amateur who has not researched the field. The size, color and method of printing the art can only be determined after a book is budgeted and designed. Your best bet is to write a thirty-two-page story, forget about the illustrations, make your cover letter professional and submit your manuscript.

Other Types of Writing for Young Readers

Fantasy in Children's Literature

If fantasy is introduced in a children's story, it must be on a separate plane from reality, according to Claudia Lewis, educator and author of *Writing for Young Children*. She points out that the two worlds may be juxtaposed, as when a character awakens from a dream, but that one world may not be evidenced in the other—e.g., a character bringing back a material possession from a dream or a fantasy world is unacceptable to most editors. In some stories, such as A.A. Milne's *Winnie the Pooh*, reality and fantasy coexist but only seem to be in conflict with each other. In Milne's story, while Christopher Robin appears to be a real boy, the fact that he lives alone in a treehouse helps the reader realize that Christopher is partially fantastic—and so he is believable when conversing with animals.

In some juvenile stories, you can shift to a fantasy setting credibly if you transport the characters near the start of the piece, before readers are accustomed to the realistic scene. Lewis contends that fantasy is ineffective when you violate the reader's sense of logic: She gives the example of a personified train whose lights fail because of its emotional state, but then are repaired mechanically by an engineer. Before submitting fantasy to an editor, you should research her preferences and prejudices by reading specific requirements in the latest edition of *Children's Writer's & Illustrator's Market.*

Novels for Young People (Young Adult)

Books written for children (excluding picture books) are divided into two groups according to the readers' ages: novels written for children younger than twelve, and those written for children older than twelve. The main character in a children's novel should be no younger than the age group of the book's intended audience; however, the character can be a year or two older than the novel's oldest reader.

Novels for teenagers revolve around characters aged fourteen to seventeen who are involved in more complex plots and show more depth than those characters in novels for the under-twelve group. Also, novels for the older group employ a more sophisticated writing style, vocabulary, subject matter and general treatment.

In writing a novel for children older than twelve, you should remember that this work will be read predominantly by young teenagers, since older teenagers are likely to read fiction written for an adult audience. Therefore, the plot and the situations of the characters should be identifiable to the child of junior high school age. Reading children's novels and talking to public or school librarians are important steps toward understanding your audience.

Society of Children's Book Writers and Illustrators (SCBWI)

Formerly the Society of Children's Book Writers, this organization has about 10,000 members who are published or unpublished authors and illustrators of children's books. The SCBWI acts as a professional guild and offers workshops, conferences, meetings and critique groups throughout the country. Members receive the bimonthly SCBWI Bulletin, which contains current information about the children's book publishing industry. The organization also presents grants for writers and illustrators, the Golden Kite Award for published children's books, and the Magazine Merit Award. SCBWI is located at 22736 Vanowen St., Suite 106, West Hills, CA 91307.

Comics

Before you submit to any comics publisher, read their submission guidelines (you can usually obtain a free copy by sending a self-addressed, stamped envelope to the publisher with your request or by downloading it from the publisher's Web site). You should also become familiar with comic-book techniques and terminology. You might want to consult *Comics and Sequential Art*, by Will Eisner, which is considered the "bible" for comics writing.

Where to Find More on Comics

The following Web sites are thorough and provide good links to other comics-related sites:

http://members.tripod.com/~comics_faq or rec.arts.comics.info
http://www.anotheruniverse.com/newsarama/
http://www.icomics.com
http://www.comicbookresources.com
http://aaa.wraithspace.com
http://www.hoboes.com
http://www.yahoo.com/Entertainment/Comics

Submission Tips

Editors don't have time to read complete scripts, which is why you should only submit a brief story idea, not an entire story. This story idea is called a springboard—a one-page, double-spaced typed story concept/synopsis.

When writing your springboard, think of it as the sales copy on a novel's back jacket—if it's well-written and interesting, the person reading it will want to look inside. Make sure your springboard story has a beginning, a middle and an ending, so your story idea seems complete. Don't forget to introduce your main characters, develop conflicts, and have some resolution. The first sentence of your springboard should have a hook to grab the editor's attention and make her want to keep reading. What works best is condensing the gist of your story in one fast, catchy, interesting sentence.

Be aware that most publications will not allow a new writer to make any major changes in the series. You must be very familiar with a character's history before trying to write about him or her, so make sure you've read enough to understand what's been going on in the series over the past few months. Also, try not to rely on new powers, new worlds, death of an existing character or personality changes to make your story different—it won't work. If you are writing for a new character you've created, you should have a brief paragraph about the character and how he or she will fit into the larger story.

Other Dos and Don'ts

- Do include your name, address and phone number on each page of your submission.
- Do handle all submissions-related correspondence through the mail.
- Do submit copies of your work (never send originals).

- Do include an SASE (self-addressed, stamped envelope) for reply, with enough return postage.
- Do type your material and use only one side of the paper.
- Do make your submission professional (neat, typed, spell-checked, brief).
- Do include a short cover letter that briefly states your background in comics or any related assignments.
- Don't send portfolios or other expensive packages.
- Don't call.
- Don't send a resume.
- Don't staple pages.
- Don't drop by the office.
- Don't send proposals for your own series or characters.

Formatting Specs

Full-length comic stories for most magazines tend to run from twenty-two to twenty-five typed pages, depending, of course, on the publication and the required format. There are several formats that have been used by comic writers and illustrators over the years, including the Two-Column Method, the Marvel Methods (Marvel Method I, Modified Marvel Method I, Modified Marvel Method II), the Funny-Animal Methods (Funny Animal Method and the Modified Funny Animal Method), and the Screenplay Method. Of all these, the most accepted one is the Screenplay Method. It's very similar to formatting a movie or television script—but a little easier. All you have to do is describe each panel with the narrative, scene and dialogue underneath and to the right of each panel (see sample). Also be sure to use Courier 12-point font.

Tab and Margin Settings

(These are approximations—just try to make your pages look neat with consistent tab markings, as in the sample on page 161.)

- 17 left margin
- 22 NARRATIVE and SCENE headings
- 27 speaking character's NAME
- 38 dialogue
- 72 right margin

All Caps

- PANEL
- NARRATIVE
- SCENE
- speaking character's NAME
- Loud sounds (GONG!)

Underline

- PANEL
- NARRATIVE
- SCENE

Single Space

- within dialogue
- within scene descriptions
- within narrative

Double Space

- between the narrative and scene descriptions
- between the scene descriptions and dialogue
- between the speeches of the different characters

Triple Space

- between panels

Other Dos and Don'ts

- Do leave 1″ to 1½″ at the top and bottom of each page.
- Do keep dialogue short.
- Do number your pages (number goes at top of page, centered, about four lines down).
- Do number your panels.
- Don't number the first page.
- Don't use too many special visual directions (let the artist handle the visuals).
- Don't number your scenes.

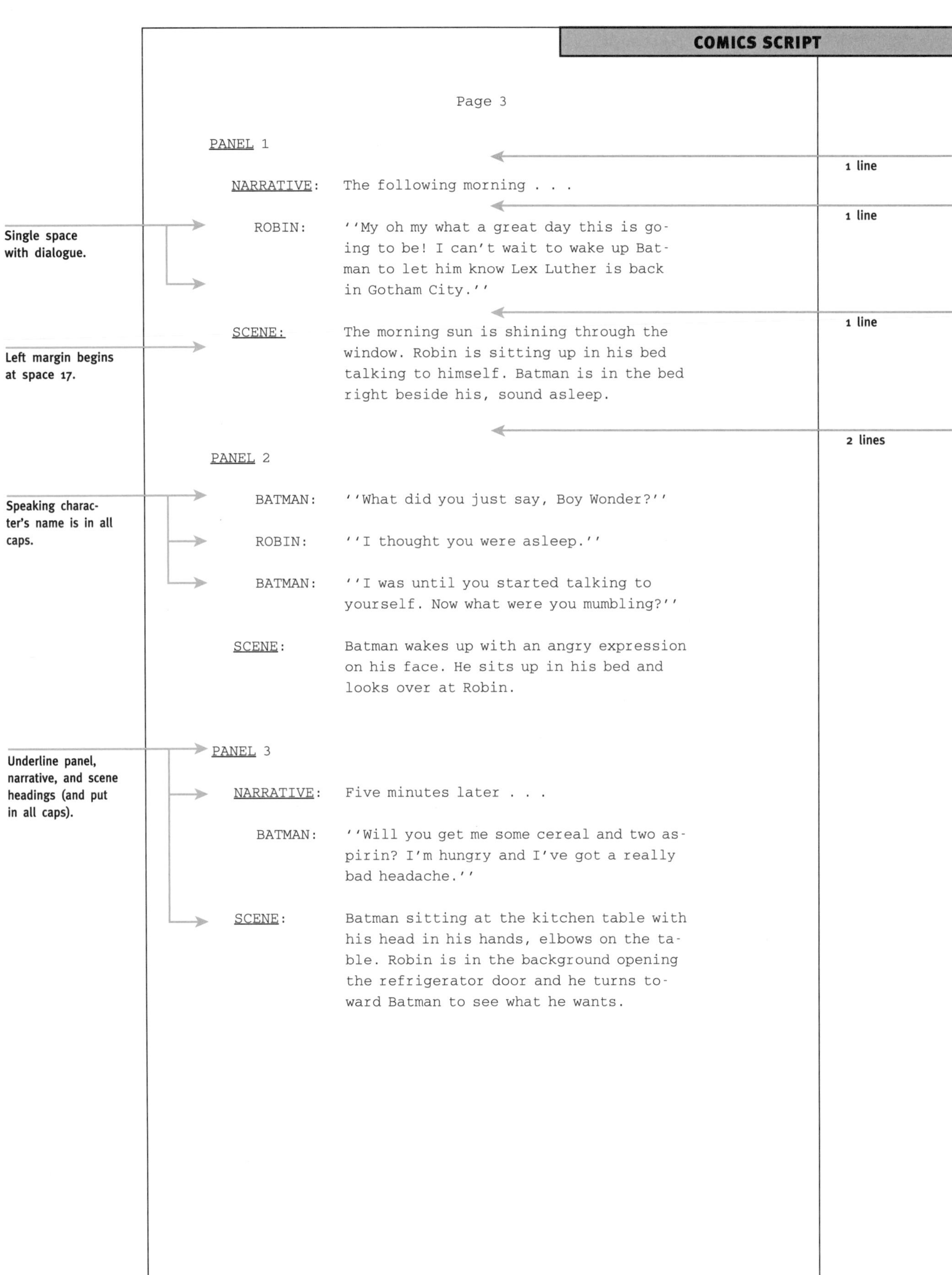
COMICS SCRIPT
Page 3
PANEL 1
NARRATIVE: The following morning . . .
ROBIN: ''My oh my what a great day this is going to be! I can't wait to wake up Batman to let him know Lex Luther is back in Gotham City.''
SCENE: The morning sun is shining through the window. Robin is sitting up in his bed talking to himself. Batman is in the bed right beside his, sound asleep.
PANEL 2
BATMAN: ''What did you just say, Boy Wonder?''
ROBIN: ''I thought you were asleep.''
BATMAN: ''I was until you started talking to yourself. Now what were you mumbling?''
SCENE: Batman wakes up with an angry expression on his face. He sits up in his bed and looks over at Robin.
PANEL 3
NARRATIVE: Five minutes later . . .
BATMAN: ''Will you get me some cereal and two aspirin? I'm hungry and I've got a really bad headache.''
SCENE: Batman sitting at the kitchen table with his head in his hands, elbows on the table. Robin is in the background opening the refrigerator door and he turns toward Batman to see what he wants.
1 line
1 line
1 line
2 lines
Single space with dialogue.
Left margin begins at space 17.
Speaking character's name is in all caps.
Underline panel, narrative, and scene headings (and put in all caps).

Part Three
SCRIPTS

CHAPTER SEVEN

THE SCREENPLAY

Although a screenplay can be difficult to sell, formatting one is pretty simple. Most motion picture scripts run from 90 to 120 pages (comedy scripts usually run about 90 to 105 pages, dramatic scripts 105 to 120 pages). Figure on one minute of screen time for each manuscript page (hence a 120-page script will run two hours), in a Courier 12-point type. Scripts should include dialogue and action descriptions but few to no camera directions and no soundtrack suggestions. Do not number your scenes, and always leave 1″-1½″ at the top and bottom of each page.

(Note: Screenplay writers today use one of the many software programs available to format their screenplay. For more information about these programs, see page 227–229).

Your screenplay can be broken down into six basic parts. Here they are in the order they are likely to appear in your script:

- Transitions
- Slug Line (Scene Heading)
- Action
- Character Cue
- Dialogue
- Parenthetical Comment

Now let's take a closer look at each of these.

Transitions

Transitions simply indicate that a shot or scene is either beginning, ending or shifting to another shot or scene. These include such directions as FADE IN:, FADE TO:, CUT TO:, and DISSOLVE TO:. Transitions appear in all caps and are flush with the right margin, except FADE IN:, which is flush with the left margin. Every screenplay begins with FADE IN: at the top left margin.

Slug Line (Scene Heading)

The slug line sets the scene and specifies the shot. It begins on the left margin (17 spaces from the left edge of the page) and is written in all caps, with a double-spaced line before and after it. Most slug lines begin with either EXT. (exterior shot) or INT. (interior shot). After you determine whether the shot is outside or inside, identify the specifics of the shot, such as a particular building or house, and then if necessary, precisely where the shot takes place. With the slug line, organize the details by going from the more general to the more specific. End each slug line by indicating whether it's day or night. For example:

```
INT. WOODROW WILSON ELEMENTARY SCHOOL—PRINCIPAL'S
OFFICE—DAY.
```

Action

The action descriptions are sentences or very short paragraphs that describe what happens during the scene. They should always be written in present tense. The text within the action descriptions begins on the left margin (17 spaces from the left edge of the page) and is single-spaced, with regular capitalization. Do not justify the right margin. There should be one double-spaced line before and after the action text. If you have lots of description, break up the text to leave some white space—try not to allow a block of text to run more than five or six lines without a double-spaced break for the eyes (the more white space in a script, the better).

Character Cue

The speaking character's name should be typed in all caps, and should appear 43 spaces from the left edge of the page. A double-spaced line should appear before the character's name, but there should be no double-space between the name and the dialogue, or between the name and the parenthetical comment (see below).

Dialogue

Dialogue should be in regular text (not all caps) and begin on the line below the speaking character's name. The left margin for dialogue is at space 28, and the right margin is at space 60 (do not justify the right margin). Try to avoid large blocks of dialogue that run seven or more lines. If your character needs to say more than can be fit in seven lines, add a blank line space between the text so it's more visually pleasing (e.g., a fourteen-line section of dialogue should be broken into two blocks of seven lines each).

Parenthetical Comment

Parenthetical comments, also known as parentheticals, help the speaker of the dialogue know what emotion you intend for the delivery. Parenthetical comments are typically short (often a word or two), typed in regular text (not all caps), appear one line below the character's name (and thus one line above dialogue) and are set in parentheses. A parenthetical should look like this:

```
             ANN
        (panicking)
What's wrong with Mrs. Browning?
```

Many screenwriters are shying away from using parentheticals. They prefer to detail the emotion in a descriptive action line instead. So the previous parenthetical would look like this:

```
ANN paces back and forth in a panic.
```

```
      ANN
   What's wrong with Mrs. Browning?
```

In addition to the aforementioned regular elements of your screenplay, you will probably find yourself in situations where you need some special formatting and cues. Here are some of the more common script tricks you can inject in your screenplay.

Narrative Voice-Over

Many films have a first-person narrator who relates parts of the story to the viewer. If your script calls for voice narration, indicate it as such by typing "(V.O.)" next to the name of the character who's narrating. A scene with a voice narration should look like this:

```
INT. ROGER'S CHILDHOOD HOME—LIVING ROOM—DAY

Many young kids are running around the room yelling and
screaming at each other. The mother has no control over the
situation.

      ROGER (V.O.)
   Mine wasn't what you'd call a typical childhood. With
   ten brothers and sisters running around, I never got
   the sense that I was unique. I was always just one of
   the boys. My poor mom spent all her time trying to keep
   us from killing each other, so making each of us feel
   loved and special just wasn't possible. But she did
   the best she could.
```

Carrying Dialogue From One Page to the Next

Do your best not to make a character (actor) flip a page in the middle of dialogue. If, however, you can't avoid carrying a character's dialogue on to the next page, use the indicator "(MORE)" on the bottom of the first page and "(cont'd)" next to the speaker's name at the top of the next page:

```
      ROGER
   I'm sorry, Marcia. I've tried and tried to please you
   but you never appreciate a damn thing I do.
                        (MORE)

____________________NEW PAGE____________________

      ROGER (cont'd)
   I just can't go on being your slave. You never clean
   up after yourself. You never do the laundry. Hell,
   you've never given me even a penny for the rent.
```

Having a Character Speak Off-Camera

In movies, characters often speak off-camera, and you'll probably write at least one scene in which this happens. When you have a character speaking off-camera, use "(O.C.)" next to the character's name. Let's say Roger is on camera in the bedroom while talking to Marcia who's off-camera in the bathroom.

```
     ROGER
Marcia, did you just say something? I thought I heard
you say something.

     MARCIA (O.C.)
I asked if you would bring me towel. I'm soaking wet
for God's sake. Are you deaf?

     ROGER
What did you say?
```

Employing Continuing Shots

Although as a screenwriter you should refrain from giving camera directions (that's the director's job), you might want to tell part of your story with a series of camera shots without dialogue or narration. These kinds of "moving pictures" usually tell their own little story. They are often accompanied by a musical score and are used to quickly advance the plot. Try doing it like this:

```
SERIES OF SHOTS: ROGER AND MARCIA EXPLORE NEW YORK

(A) On a ferry to the Statue of Liberty.
(B) Eating hot dogs from a vendor on Times Square.
(C) Walking arm in arm through Central Park.
(D) Kissing outside the Guggenheim.
(E) Driving across the Washington Bridge.

BACK TO SCENE
```

Another way to use continuing shots is with a montage. A montage is pretty much the same as a series of shots except it's used for a briefer sequence of shots and doesn't really have to tell its own story. A montage is formatted a little differently, too, with a double hyphen instead of letters in parentheses:

```
MONTAGE--ROGER AND MARCIA AT DISNEY WORLD

--They get their pictures taken with Mickey and Minnie.

--They ride Magic Mountain.

--Roger offers Marcia some cotton candy. She makes a mus-
tache out of it and Roger eats it. They laugh.

END MONTAGE
```

With both a series of shots and montages, be sure to end with either "BACK TO SCENE" or "END MONTAGE."

Other Dos and Don'ts

- Do spell out numbers (one through ninety-nine), but use numbers for 100 and over.
- Do spell out personal titles (Father Niehaus, Pastor Karl) except for Mr., Mrs. and Ms.
- Do spell out time indicators: eleven-thirty, not 11:30.
- Do spell out "okay," not OK or o.k.
- Do number your pages and put a period after the number (the page number goes at the top of the page, flush right, about four lines down).
- Do keep dialogue short.
- Don't use special effects directions, such as FX (visual).
- Don't use sound effects directions, such as SFX (sound).
- Don't use camera directions and camera angles.
- Don't number the first page.
- Don't number your scenes.
- Do leave 1″-1½″ at the top and bottom of each page.

What follows are formatting specifications for your screenplay as well as a sample screenplay title page and a sample first page of a screenplay.

Tab and Margin Settings

- 17 left margin
- 28 dialogue left margin
- 35 parenthetical comments
- 43 character cue
- 60 dialogue right margin
- 66 transitions
- 72 page number followed by a period (in top right-hand corner, four lines from top of page)
- 75 right margin

All Caps

- Type of shot (INT. and EXT.)
- Setting or scene location (ITALIAN RIVIERA)
- Time of day (DAY or NIGHT)
- The first time you introduce a character (JOHN walks in)
- The speaking character's name (PHIL), followed by dialogue
- Camera directions (PAN, CLOSE-UP, etc.)
- Important sound cues (Ted hears a GUNSHOT in the hallway.)
- Scene transitions (CUT TO:, DISSOLVE TO:, etc.)
- (MORE)

Single Space

- within dialogue
- within action/scene descriptions (also called narrative)
- within camera directions, sound cues
- within stage directions
- between the character's name and dialogue

Double Space

- between the scene location and action/scene descriptions
- between the action/scene descriptions and the speaking character's name
- between the speeches of the different characters
- between the paragraphs of lengthy dialogue or action descriptions
- between dialogue and a new speaking character's name
- between dialogue and stage or camera directions

Triple Space

- before each new scene

Title Page

The screenplay title should be in all caps, centered, about one-third of the way down the page. Double-space twice, and type either "Written by," "Screenplay by" or just "by" (do not type the quotation marks). Double-space again and type your name (if your script is written with another person, use an ampersand between your names). Also, if your script is based on a novel, drop six lines and type "Based on the novel *Novel's Title*," drop two more lines and type "by" and "Author's Name" (see the following sample). In the lower right-hand corner, put your name, address and phone number, single-spaced, in regular text (not all caps). If you have an agent, put "Representation:," skip a line and put the agent's name, address and phone number instead of yours. Note: Some writers will type the draft number and the date in the bottom left corner. Do not do this for a spec script—including the draft number is irrelevant and including the date of a script can show that it has been circulating for a long time.

Cover Page Paper

Preferred is a white, gray, cream, rust or pale blue cover of card stock, 40 to 60 lbs., with no picture or artwork on it—only the title and the author's name. The pages should be bound in brass brads, short enough so they don't cut through an envelope when mailed. Never use spiral or other machine-type bindings. Although your script should have three holes punched in it, only the top and bottom holes need to have brads in them. Be sure to use a backing with the same stock as the cover page.

Note: Your script should be registered with the Writer's Guild of America (WGA), but you do not need to put the WGA registration number on the title or cover page.

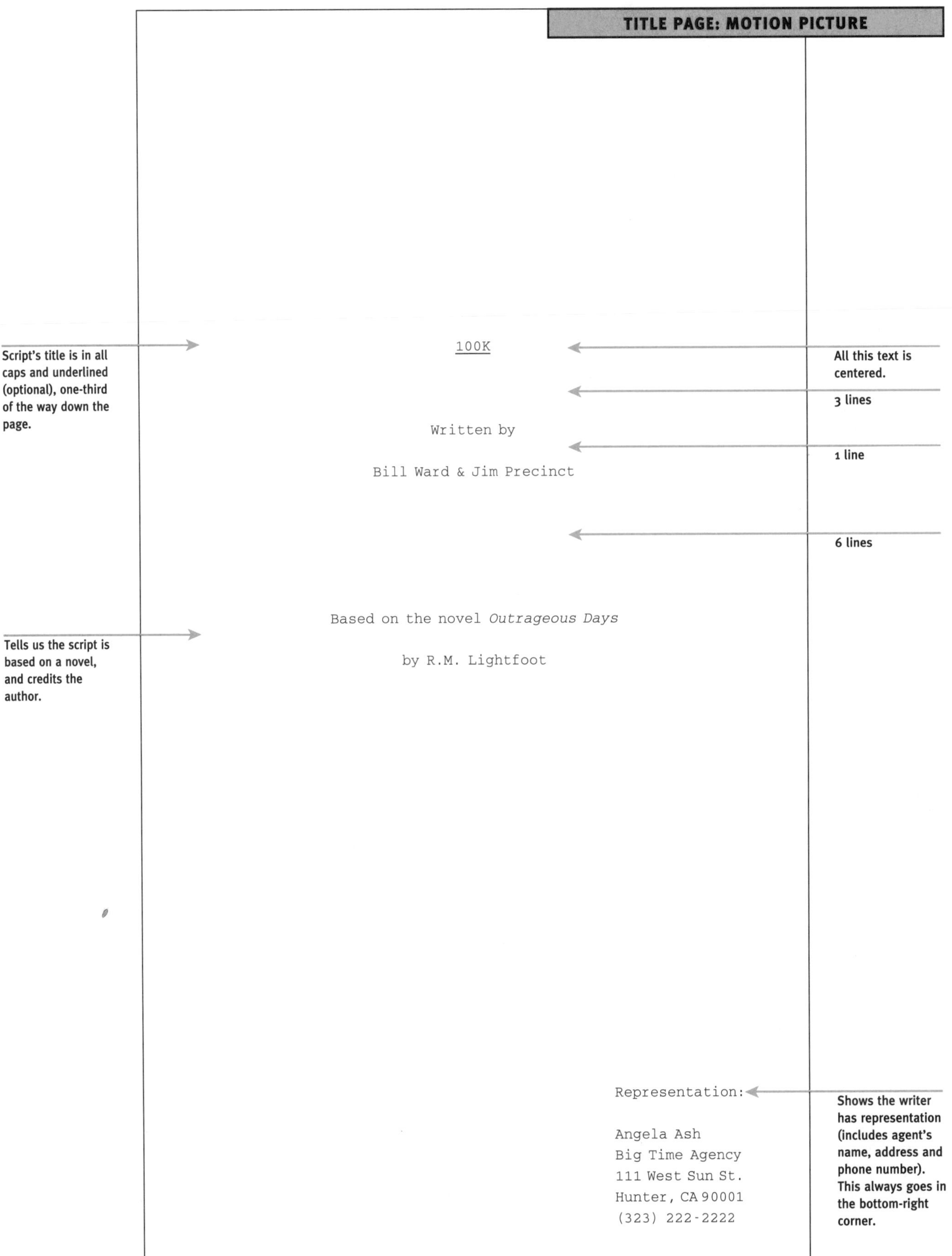
TITLE PAGE: MOTION PICTURE
100K
Written by
Bill Ward & Jim Precinct
Based on the novel *Outrageous Days*
by R.M. Lightfoot
Representation:
Angela Ash
Big Time Agency
111 West Sun St.
Hunter, CA 90001
(323) 222-2222
Script's title is in all caps and underlined (optional), one-third of the way down the page.
Tells us the script is based on a novel, and credits the author.
All this text is centered.
3 lines
1 line
6 lines
Shows the writer has representation (includes agent's name, address and phone number). This always goes in the bottom-right corner.

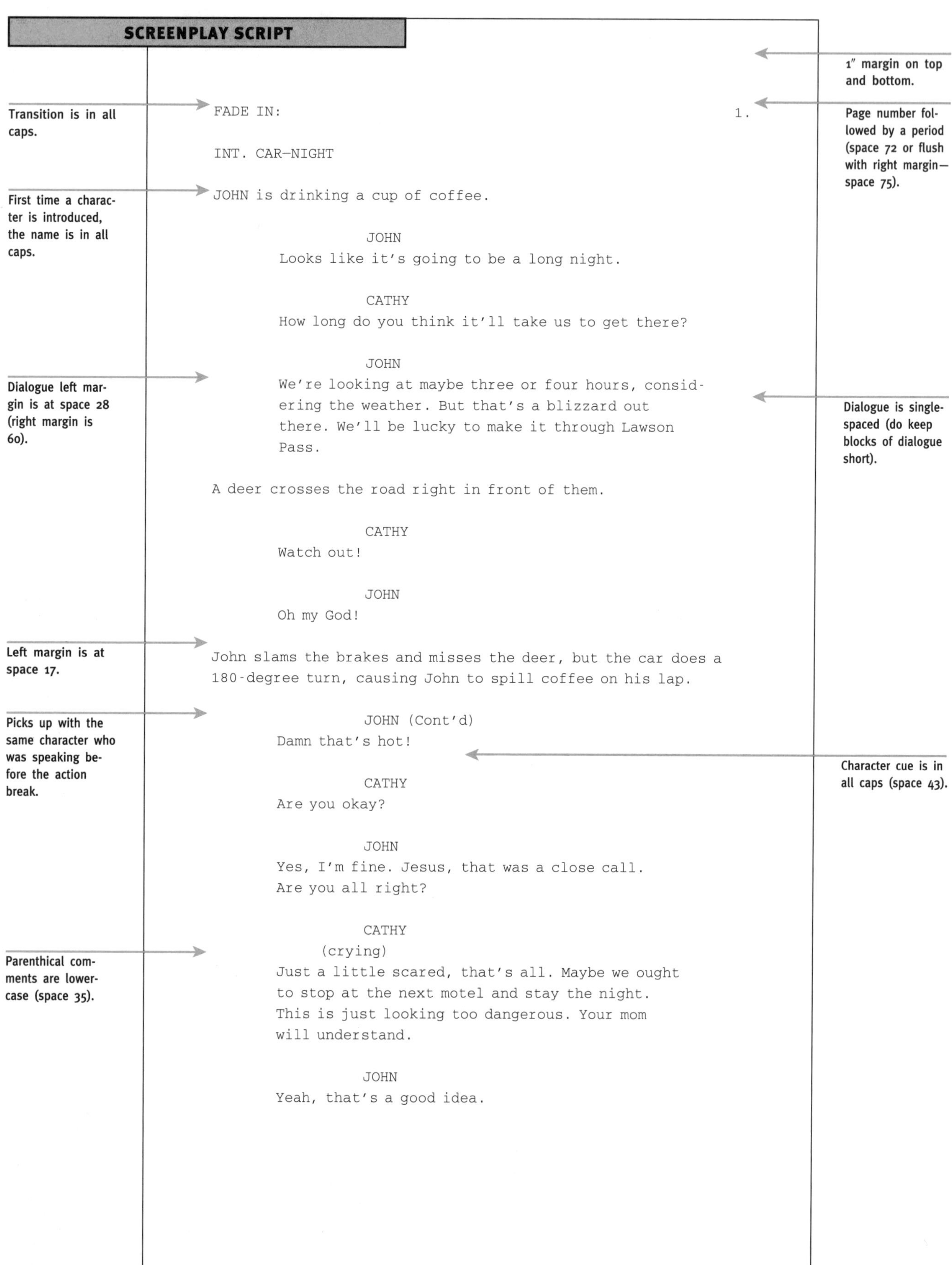
SCREENPLAY SCRIPT
1" margin on top and bottom.
Transition is in all caps.
FADE IN:
1.
Page number followed by a period (space 72 or flush with right margin—space 75).
INT. CAR—NIGHT
First time a character is introduced, the name is in all caps.
JOHN is drinking a cup of coffee.
JOHN
Looks like it's going to be a long night.
CATHY
How long do you think it'll take us to get there?
Dialogue left margin is at space 28 (right margin is 60).
JOHN
We're looking at maybe three or four hours, considering the weather. But that's a blizzard out there. We'll be lucky to make it through Lawson Pass.
Dialogue is single-spaced (do keep blocks of dialogue short).
A deer crosses the road right in front of them.
CATHY
Watch out!
JOHN
Oh my God!
Left margin is at space 17.
John slams the brakes and misses the deer, but the car does a 180-degree turn, causing John to spill coffee on his lap.
Picks up with the same character who was speaking before the action break.
JOHN (Cont'd)
Damn that's hot!
Character cue is in all caps (space 43).
CATHY
Are you okay?
JOHN
Yes, I'm fine. Jesus, that was a close call. Are you all right?
Parenthetical comments are lowercase (space 35).
CATHY
(crying)
Just a little scared, that's all. Maybe we ought to stop at the next motel and stay the night. This is just looking too dangerous. Your mom will understand.
JOHN
Yeah, that's a good idea.

SCREENPLAY SCRIPT, PAGE 2

Slug line is in all caps.

```
EXT. MOTEL PARKING LOT—NIGHT                                 2.

Snow is falling heavily and we see the car pull into a very crow-
ded lot. John gets out, goes inside, and immediately returns to
the car.

                    CATHY
        Boy that was fast. Are they booked?

                    JOHN
        Of course they're booked.

                    CATHY
        I wonder if we should go back home?

                    JOHN
        We're not going back home now. I'll just keep driv-
        ing until we get there. I'll drive all night if I
        have to.

Car speeds out of parking lot.

                                                       FADE OUT
```

Action description is single-spaced and flush with left margin.

Transition is at space 66 (or flush with right margin).

Submitting Your Screenplay to an Agent or Production Company

After you finish your screenplay you'll want to submit it to an agent or a production company. Ideally, you'll find an agent to represent you, someone who knows the ins and outs of Hollywood. Having a good agent who believes in your work and is willing to go to great lengths to get it sold is invaluable. Almost every screenwriter in Hollywood has an agent, and so should you.

The Value of an Agent

So, what is a good agent? Aside from being someone who believes in your work, a good agent knows who is working where, who has deals with whom and who wants what. A good agent will direct your script to the most suitable producer and will negotiate payments on your behalf. Many beginning writers try to become a client at a major agency but that's not always such a good idea. Newcomers often don't get much attention at major agencies. Your best bet is to find an agent who will appreciate your writing and do his or her best to champion it—no matter how large or small the agency. Just be sure the agent is a signatory of the WGA—signatory agents have signed and agreed to abide by industry rules and standards. All reputable agencies belong to the WGA; those who do not should be avoided.

Finding the Right Agent for You

A good way to acquire an agent who will appreciate your writing is to find one who already represents material similar to yours. Seek out movies already made that are similar to yours. See or rent them, and pay close attention to the credits. Write down the names of the writers or the story editors.

Once you get these names, call the Writer's Guild, West (323) 951-4000, request to speak to the agency department, then ask which agency represents those writers or story editors. The agency department will grant your request if you have three names or less (no more). After you get the agency's name, consult the WGA's list of signatory agents to make sure that agent is a signatory. The WGA offers the list free on its Web site (http://www.wga.org), or you can write or call: 7000 W. Third St., Los Angeles, CA 90048-4329, (323) 951-4000.

Also check the following directories if you wish to do research on agents:

ANNUAL AGENCY GUIDE, published by The Writers Network, Inc., lists over 1,500 literary agents, managers and entertainment lawyers. The directory indicates if the agency represents motion picture and/or television writers, and if there is a fee involved.

GUIDE TO LITERARY AGENTS, published by Writer's Digest Books, contains the most detailed listings of five hundred literary and script agents. The guide divides its listings according to nonfee-charging and fee-charging agents. It also includes a variety of insider information (profiles, interviews, articles, query samples) on marketing your work and getting your script in the right agent's hands (1507 Dana Ave., Cincinnati, OH 45207, [800] 289-0963).

HOLLYWOOD AGENTS & MANAGERS DIRECTORY, published by the Hollywood Creative Directory, offers probably the most complete list of agents and managers. It boasts

4,100 names (3000 W. Olympic Blvd., Suite 2525, Santa Monica, CA 90404, [800] 815-0503).

Selling the Script Yourself

You may wish to shop your script to a studio or production company without first finding an agent. This will likely be difficult but it is still an option, and many first-time writers go this route. Fortunately, a few resources do exist for finding information about producers, studio executives and other industry insiders. In fact, some of the following publications provide extensive lists of studios and production companies that might take an interest in your script:

Hollywood Creative Directory (3000 W. Olympic Blvd., Suite 2525, Santa Monica, CA 90404, [800] 815-0503) is a great place to locate the person you're looking for. This is the film and television industry bible, with the most complete, up-to-date information about who's who in film and TV development and production. It lists production companies, studios and networks; their addresses, phone and fax numbers; and provides cross-referencing.

Hollywood Literary Sales Directory, edited by Howard Meibach (In Good Company Products, 2118 Wilshire Blvd., #934, Santa Monica, CA 90403, [310] 828-4946), catalogs sales and deals of all sorts. This can be quite helpful because it tells what material production companies and studios are buying. The sales information is divided into three sections: screenplay sales, book sales and pitch/treatment sales. The directory is cross-referenced.

Hollywood Reporter Bluebook (5055 Wilshire Blvd., Los Angeles, CA 90036) also provides information about numerous production companies and their needs.

Pacific Coast Studio Directory (P.O. Box V, Frazier Park, CA 93222, [213] 467-2920) could be your best bet. Published quarterly, it contains comprehensive listings of television and film production companies, and also provides a list of agents, artist representatives, publicity organizations, television stations and unions.

Spec Screenplay Sales Directory, Deluxe Edition (edited by Howard Meibach) lets you in on what screenplays have been selling, who's buying them and how much your potential script could be worth. It lists 750 screenplays, including log line, genre, writer, producer, agent, buyer, attorney and sales. This is also cross-referenced.

If you want to stay tuned to the day-to-day operations in Hollywood, check out *Daily Variety* (5700 Wilshire Blvd., Los Angeles, CA 90036) and *The Hollywood Reporter* (5055 Wilshire Blvd., Los Angeles, CA 90036), both of which will keep you up on industry news. *Boxoffice* is a monthly trade magazine geared more toward movie distributors than scriptwriters, but it still offers a lot of information about what kinds of films studios are producing.

After you figure out which studio or production company you're interested in, call and ask for the story department then ask for the name of the story editor. That's it. Don't ask to speak with the story editor—just get his or her name, then get ready to write your letter of inquiry.

The Query Letter

Once you know who to contact (agent, producer or story editor), send that person a query letter. *Do not submit an outline, a treatment, or a script to anyone in the industry unless you've been asked to do so*—they'll return it because they can't look at anything without a signed release form. In your query letter, say that you've written a script and would like the person you're soliciting to consider it. Keep your query letter to a few short paragraphs (less than a page). J. Michael Straczynski, in *The Complete Book of Scriptwriting*, suggests mentioning the following:

- That you know the films they produce (or the agency represents, if you're soliciting an agent).
- That you've written an original screenplay that fits in quite well with what they've been producing (or with an agency, representing) over the past few years.
- That you own the rights to the story.
- That you would like to submit your screenplay on a spec basis. (Do not go into detail about the contents of your spec script—you'll ruin your chances of selling it.)
- That when you send your script you will enclose a standard release form or use the production company's or agency's preferred release form.
- That you have writing credits or a professional background that qualifies you to write this screenplay. (If you've spent ten years as an attorney and your screenplay is a legal thriller, mention your background.)

Basically, that's all you need to include in your query. Again, never send an unsolicited script, treatment or synopsis to an agent, producer or story editor—it will be returned, the package unopened. Producers and agents will not look at unsolicited scripts because they are afraid of getting sued for plagiarism. That's why you need to send the release form. Of course, mention your script idea in your query letter, but do so only in general terms.

Follow these formatting specifications when composing your query letter:

Formatting Specs

- Use a standard font or typeface (no bold, script or italic).
- Place your name, address and phone number (include E-mail and fax, if applicable) in the top right corner.
- Use a 1″ margin on all sides.
- Address it to a specific agent, producer or story editor.
- Keep it to one page.
- Use block or semiblock letter format.
- Single-space the body of the letter; double-space between paragraphs.
- Catalog every item you're sending in your enclosures.

Other Dos and Don'ts

- Do make the letter pointed and persuasive.
- Do include an SASE or postcard for reply, and state in the letter that you have done so.

- Do offer to sign a release form.
- Do offer to send the script.
- Don't use "Dear Sir," "Dear Madame," etc. in your salutation.
- Don't use Mr., Ms., Mrs. or Miss unless you're certain of the person's gender and marital status.
- Don't mention that you're a first-time writer or that you've never sold any piece of writing.
- Don't spend much time trying to sell yourself.
- Don't tell how much time you've spent on the script.
- Don't ask for advice or criticism.
- Don't mention anything about yourself not pertinent to the script.
- Don't bring up payment.
- Don't include your social security number.

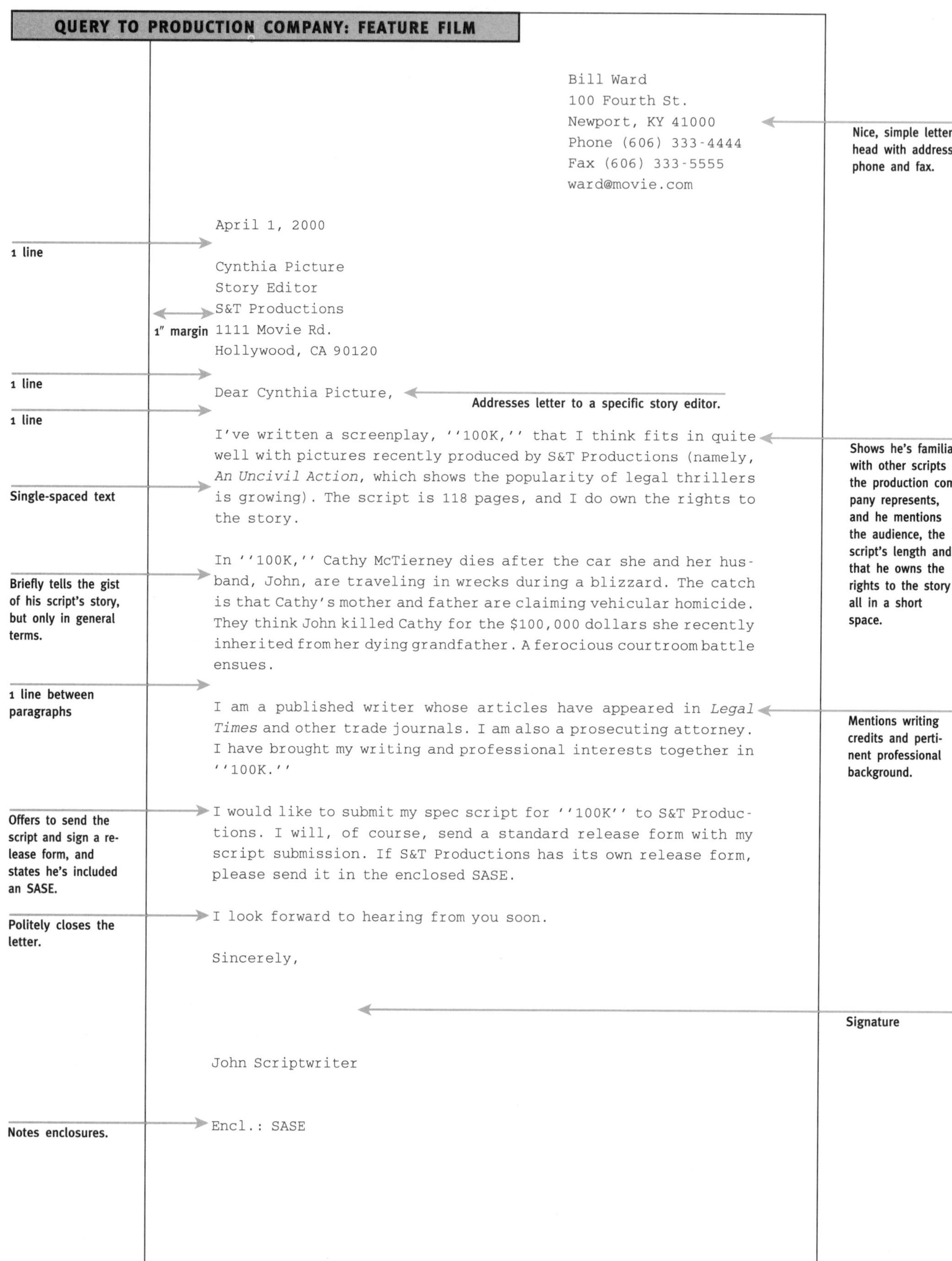

QUERY TO PRODUCTION COMPANY: FEATURE FILM

Bill Ward
100 Fourth St.
Newport, KY 41000
Phone (606) 333-4444
Fax (606) 333-5555
ward@movie.com

April 1, 2000

Cynthia Picture
Story Editor
S&T Productions
1111 Movie Rd.
Hollywood, CA 90120

Dear Cynthia Picture,

I've written a screenplay, ''100K,'' that I think fits in quite well with pictures recently produced by S&T Productions (namely, *An Uncivil Action*, which shows the popularity of legal thrillers is growing). The script is 118 pages, and I do own the rights to the story.

In ''100K,'' Cathy McTierney dies after the car she and her husband, John, are traveling in wrecks during a blizzard. The catch is that Cathy's mother and father are claiming vehicular homicide. They think John killed Cathy for the $100,000 dollars she recently inherited from her dying grandfather. A ferocious courtroom battle ensues.

I am a published writer whose articles have appeared in *Legal Times* and other trade journals. I am also a prosecuting attorney. I have brought my writing and professional interests together in ''100K.''

I would like to submit my spec script for ''100K'' to S&T Productions. I will, of course, send a standard release form with my script submission. If S&T Productions has its own release form, please send it in the enclosed SASE.

I look forward to hearing from you soon.

Sincerely,

John Scriptwriter

Encl.: SASE

Nice, simple letterhead with address, phone and fax.
1 line
1" margin
1 line
Addresses letter to a specific story editor.
1 line
Shows he's familiar with other scripts the production company represents, and he mentions the audience, the script's length and that he owns the rights to the story all in a short space.
Single-spaced text
Briefly tells the gist of his script's story, but only in general terms.
1 line between paragraphs
Mentions writing credits and pertinent professional background.
Offers to send the script and sign a release form, and states he's included an SASE.
Politely closes the letter.
Signature
Notes enclosures.

Submitting Your Script

If your query letter does what you want it to, you'll receive a request for your script. Before you do anything else, register your script with the WGA (you don't need to be a WGA member to do so). To register, contact the WGA and ask them to send you an application (7000 W. Third St., Los Angeles, CA 90048-4329, [323] 951-4000).

Then you need to get your script ready for submission. Print your script on standard three-hole, 20-lb. paper. Use heavy (40- to 60-lb. bond), colored stock paper (use either cream, gray, rust or pale blue paper) for your cover/title page and your back cover. Bind your script with two brass paper fasteners (sometimes called brads), one in the top hole and one in the bottom. Enclose a simple letter that says the requested script and release form are enclosed. Also include an SASE. Do not forget to sign and include the release form, and on the outside of the package's envelope be sure to write "REQUESTED RELEASE FORM ENCLOSED." Then send your script and wait four to six weeks for a reply.

Outlines and Treatments

Outlines and treatments are stepping stones on the way to selling your full-length script. Both are summaries of your script, and both share the same format. The outline is a short precursor followed by a longer, more detailed (and more important) treatment. Although your script is composed almost entirely of dialogue, your outline or treatment covers the overarching story behind (and without) the dialogue and scene descriptions.

Outlines

An outline briefly synopsizes your script. You likely will not have to show anyone your outline, but you could be asked for one—if so, focus only on the major points of your story, keep the outline informal and write it in paragraph form. With an outline, less is more, especially when you use it as a pitch to sell your idea. You don't want to bore anyone, and the rule of thumb in Hollywood is that "high-concept" story ideas can be described quickly (ideally, one sentence!) and are the most saleable. The outline is an informal but crucial starting point from which you can successfully pitch your story idea, which leads to writing a compelling treatment, which ultimately leads to selling a script.

Most outlines run anywhere from a few pages for a half-hour sitcom to as many as seven or more pages for a feature film. Rarely should your outline go over 5,000 words. Outlines always have the title centered in all caps about one-fourth of the way down the page, followed by a blank line and then the words "An Outline by" (centered), then one more blank line followed by "Your Name" (centered). Drop four lines and begin the text, which should be double-spaced, written in present tense and void of sample dialogue, directions or narration.

Treatments

Unlike outlines, which tend to be a bit informal and more skeletal, treatments are carefully constructed, extremely well-written summaries of your script (in fact, treatments are similar to a novel synopsis). You get to expand on the outline and go into more detail about your characters, settings and plot twists. You can even weave some samples of dialogue into the narrative. Try to keep the number of dialogue lines minimal, however, and be sure to inject them only at points where they can tell something significant about the character uttering them.

Treatments can run anywhere from four to twenty or more pages, depending on the type of script at hand. If you're writing a treatment for a half-hour sitcom, it will probably run from four to six pages, whereas a treatment for an hour episodic drama might run six to nine pages, and one for a motion picture feature or movie of the week (MOW) might be ten to fifteen pages. No specific stipulations apply to the length of your treatment, but remember that shorter is usually better (especially with spec treatments—try to keep them under ten pages). The two imperatives are that you double-space the text and write in present tense. The script title for your treatment should be in all caps, centered, followed by a blank line and the words "A Treatment by" (centered), then one more blank line followed by "Your Name" (centered). Then drop four lines and begin the text of the treatment.

Ideally, your treatment should clearly delineate the major scenes in your script, with a new paragraph devoted to each scene or plot shift in the script. Writers typically break up their treatments according to the conventions of the type of script they're writing. You can break up your treatment by using subheads to denote when a new act begins. Doing so shows you've thought out the structure and timing of the script.

- Most sitcoms are divided into two acts; a few are broken down into three acts. Some series use a teaser at the show's beginning and/or a tag at the show's conclusion.
- One-hour dramas typically have four acts; some shows also use a teaser at the show's beginning and/or a tag at the ending.
- MOWs (movies of the week) contain seven acts. The act breaks coincide with the seven commercial breaks that typically occur during a two-hour time slot for movies on television.
- Motion picture feature films consist of three acts.

Why You'll Need an Outline and Treatment

Whether you're writing for television or the silver screen, to get your foot in the door you will need a sample spec script that showcases your talent as a writer. (That's why you must send a complete script after you've queried—a mere outline or treatment won't do at this stage in the game because you still need to prove yourself as a writer.) If that spec script impresses the right person (hopefully, the producer), you might be invited to pitch ideas for other scripts. This, by the way, is where knowing how to write an outline comes in handy—you use an outline to ensure you cover all the major points in your pitch. If your pitch is successful, you might get an assignment to write a treatment, and if that goes well, you will be asked to write the script.

To make sure you understand the process, let's walk through a dream-come-true hypothetical scenario. You've written a spec motion picture script called "The Summer of Love," and you've been fortunate enough to get a producer at (since we're dreaming) DreamWorks to read your script. He loves it but he refuses to buy it. Why? Because DreamWorks just bought a similar script called "1967." However, he was so impressed with your writing that he wants you to come up with a few other movie ideas that he might consider optioning. You agree, come up with three ideas, write pitch outlines for each and make an appointment to pitch your story ideas to him. Your first two ideas don't go over so well, but your third one does. He tells you he'll talk to other producers and get back to you. A few weeks go by, and lo and behold, you get a call from the producer telling you that everybody at DreamWorks loves your idea, and DreamWorks would like to offer you a development deal, or a step deal. Are you interested? Of course.

You then sign a contract for the development or step deal, which means that you get a step-by-step commitment—and payment—from the producer as the deal goes through development. It works like this: The producer can stop the development of your script at any step in the process, but he must pay you for what you've already written. And because he's paid you for what you've done, he owns and can do what he wants with it.

So what are the steps in a development deal? The first step is a treatment, next comes the first draft of a script, then a second draft, and finally the perfected script. Once the producer asks you to write the initial treatment for your story idea, he must pay you the negotiated fee for that step (step one) of the process. If, unfortunately, you turn in your treatment and DreamWorks doesn't like it, they have the option to drop you from the project and pass it on to other writers (you still, of course, get paid for the treatment). If they do like it, however, you're asked to write (and get paid for) a complete draft of the script. Even if your final draft goes over well and you get paid lots of money for it, keep in mind that DreamWorks has the right to pass your script on to other writers to make improvements to it—sorry, that's just the way the business works. You'll still get the credit for the screenplay, of course, but your story could get changed quite a bit. Just be prepared.

Formatting Specs

- Use a 1″ margin on all sides.
- Justify the left margin only.
- Type your name, address and phone number on the top left margin of the first page, single-spaced.
- Put the script's title, centered and in all caps, about one-fourth of the way down the page (from the top margin).
- Drop one line below the title and type "A Treatment by" or "An Outline by" (centered).
- Drop one line and type your name (centered).
- Drop four lines and begin the text of the treatment.
- Do not number the first page (but it is considered page one).
- After the first page, use a slug line (also called a header) at the top left of every page. The slug line should contain your last name, a backslash, your script's title in all capital letters, another backslash and the word "Treatment."
- After the first page, put the page number in the top right corner of every consecutive page, on the same line as the slug line.
- The text throughout the treatment should be double-spaced.
- Use all caps the first time you introduce a character.
- The first line of text on each page after the first page should begin three lines (about ¾″) below the slug line and page number.

Other Dos and Don'ts

- Do use present tense.
- Do write in first person.
- Do keep in mind that you're writing a sales pitch (make it a short, fast, exciting read).
- Do establish a hook at the beginning of the treatment (introduce your lead character and set up a key conflict).
- Do try to introduce your most important character first.
- Do provide details about your central character (age, gender, marital status, profession, etc.), but don't do this for every character—only the primary ones.
- Do try to include characters' motivations and emotions.
- Do highlight pivotal plot points.
- Do reveal the story's ending.
- Don't go into too much detail about what happens; just tell what happens (plot twists, etc.).
- Don't insert long sections of dialogue into your treatment.

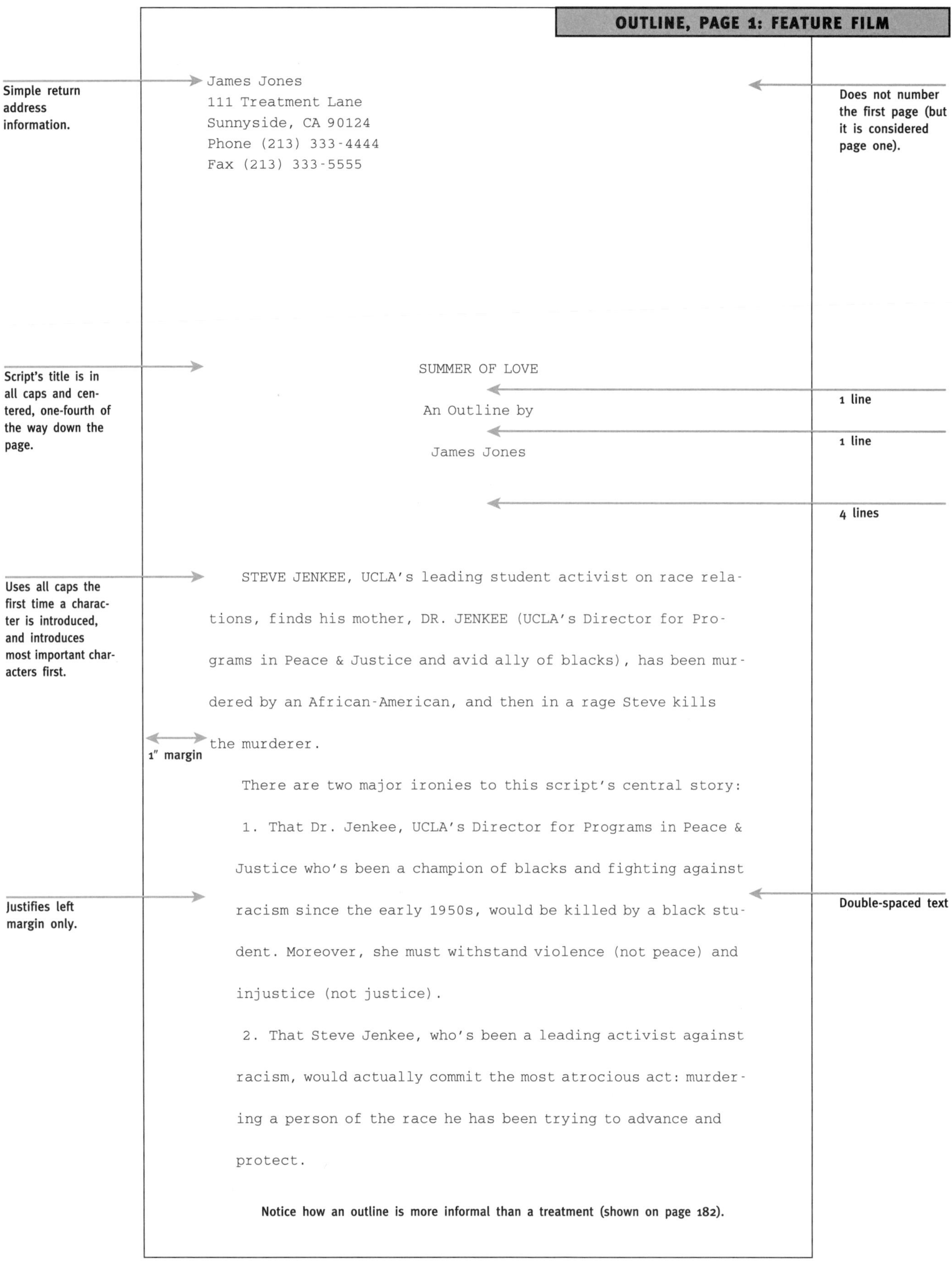
OUTLINE, PAGE 1: FEATURE FILM
Simple return address information.
James Jones
111 Treatment Lane
Sunnyside, CA 90124
Phone (213) 333-4444
Fax (213) 333-5555
Does not number the first page (but it is considered page one).
Script's title is in all caps and centered, one-fourth of the way down the page.
SUMMER OF LOVE
1 line
An Outline by
1 line
James Jones
4 lines
Uses all caps the first time a character is introduced, and introduces most important characters first.
STEVE JENKEE, UCLA's leading student activist on race relations, finds his mother, DR. JENKEE (UCLA's Director for Programs in Peace & Justice and avid ally of blacks), has been murdered by an African-American, and then in a rage Steve kills the murderer.
1" margin
There are two major ironies to this script's central story:
1. That Dr. Jenkee, UCLA's Director for Programs in Peace & Justice who's been a champion of blacks and fighting against racism since the early 1950s, would be killed by a black student. Moreover, she must withstand violence (not peace) and injustice (not justice).
Justifies left margin only.
Double-spaced text
2. That Steve Jenkee, who's been a leading activist against racism, would actually commit the most atrocious act: murdering a person of the race he has been trying to advance and protect.
Notice how an outline is more informal than a treatment (shown on page 182).

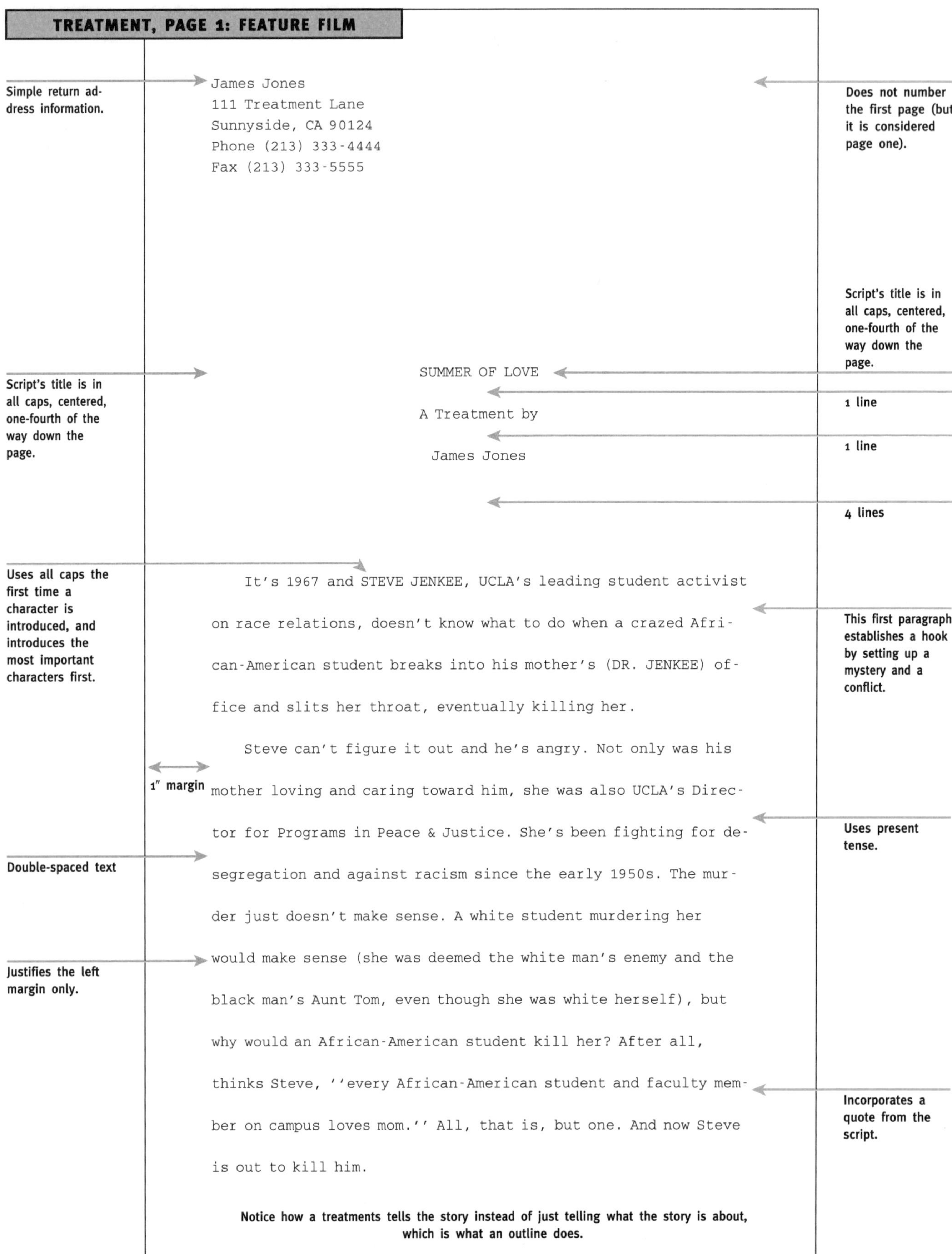
TREATMENT, PAGE 1: FEATURE FILM
Simple return address information.
James Jones
111 Treatment Lane
Sunnyside, CA 90124
Phone (213) 333-4444
Fax (213) 333-5555
Does not number the first page (but it is considered page one).
Script's title is in all caps, centered, one-fourth of the way down the page.
SUMMER OF LOVE
1 line
A Treatment by
1 line
James Jones
4 lines
Uses all caps the first time a character is introduced, and introduces the most important characters first.
It's 1967 and STEVE JENKEE, UCLA's leading student activist on race relations, doesn't know what to do when a crazed African-American student breaks into his mother's (DR. JENKEE) office and slits her throat, eventually killing her.
This first paragraph establishes a hook by setting up a mystery and a conflict.
Steve can't figure it out and he's angry. Not only was his mother loving and caring toward him, she was also UCLA's Director for Programs in Peace & Justice. She's been fighting for desegregation and against racism since the early 1950s. The murder just doesn't make sense. A white student murdering her would make sense (she was deemed the white man's enemy and the black man's Aunt Tom, even though she was white herself), but why would an African-American student kill her? After all, thinks Steve, ''every African-American student and faculty member on campus loves mom.'' All, that is, but one. And now Steve is out to kill him.
1" margin
Uses present tense.
Double-spaced text
Justifies the left margin only.
Incorporates a quote from the script.
Notice how a treatments tells the story instead of just telling what the story is about, which is what an outline does.

CHAPTER EIGHT

TV SCRIPTS

Submitting Television Scripts

To get your television script (sitcom, episodic drama, soap opera, movie of the week) through the Hollywood maze, you need to put your script in the right hands. There are a few ways to go about this. The ideal way is to acquire an agent to represent you, but a few writers sneak through the cracks by contacting the production company first.

Before soliciting anyone, however, you should know a couple peculiarities about submitting scripts for television.

First, you might want to have more than one spec script ready to showcase. Some writers actually have a portfolio of scripts for each *type* of show they want to work on (if they want to write sitcoms, for instance, they'll have one script each for shows like *Friends, Frasier, Dharma & Greg,* and *The Drew Carey Show*).

Second, in choosing the shows you write spec scripts for, know that you probably will not be able to submit a script for the exact show you want to work on. It sounds crazy, but that's the way television works. So if you want to write for *The Practice,* for example, you'll need to send a *Law and Order* script and vice versa. You must do this because it reduces the chances of plagiarism lawsuits (plus the show's writers and producers might not be objective enough to fairly evaluate your writing). By submitting a similar type of script, you avert these problems while still demonstrating your writing skills in that medium.

Whether you plan to solicit a production company or an agent, you must first target the show you plan to write for, watch it and pay close attention to the opening and closing credits.

Contacting the Production Company

To contact the production company directly, look at the show's credits for the name of the production company and the producer or story editor. (Tape the show if you have to, so you get the correct names and spellings.) Then find the phone number and address of the production company and send the producer or story editor a query letter (see the following sources for information on contacting production companies).

The best way to find the production company's address is to call directory assistance or consult one of the following publications:

Hollywood Creative Directory (3000 W. Olympic Blvd., Suite 2525, Santa Monica, CA 90404, [800] 815-0503) is great place to locate the person you're looking for. This is the film and television industry bible, with the most complete, up-to-date information about who's who in film and TV development and production. It lists production companies, studios and networks; addresses, phone and fax numbers; and provides cross-referencing.

HOLLYWOOD LITERARY SALES DIRECTORY, edited by Howard Meibach (In Good Company Products, 2118 Wilshire Blvd., #934, Santa Monica, CA 90403, [310] 828-4946), catalogs sales and deals of all sorts. This can be quite helpful because it tells what material production companies and studios are buying. The sales information is divided into three sections: screenplay sales, book sales and pitch/treatment sales. The directory is cross-referenced.

HOLLYWOOD REPORTER BLUEBOOK (5055 Wilshire Blvd., Los Angeles, CA 90036) also provides information about numerous production companies and their needs.

PACIFIC COAST STUDIO DIRECTORY (P.O. Box V, Frazier Park, CA 93222, [213] 467-2920) could be your best bet. Published quarterly, it contains comprehensive listings of television and film production companies, but it does not list the names of individual shows (and who produces them). That's why you need to check out the show's credits to find the name of the production company.

Contacting Agents

If you don't want to go directly to the production company, contact an agent who represents the show's writers. To do this, pay close attention to the show's credits to find the names of the writers or story editors. Once you get these names, call the Writer's Guild, West (323) 951-4000, request to speak to the agency department, then ask which agency represents those writers or story editors. The agency department will grant your request if you have three names or less, so don't call with a long list of names.

After you get the agency's name, consult the WGA's list of signatory agents to make sure that agent is a signatory (the WGA offers the list free on its Web site: http://www.wga.org), or write or call for the list: 7000 W. Third St., Los Angeles, CA 90048-4329, (323) 951-4000. Signatory agents have signed a membership contract agreeing to abide by industry rules and standards. All reputable agents belong to the WGA; those who do not should be avoided.

Also check the following directories if you wish to find out more about agents:

ANNUAL AGENCY GUIDE, published by The Writers Network, Inc., lists over 1,500 literary agents, managers and entertainment lawyers. The directory indicates if the agency represents motion picture and/or television writers, and if there is a fee involved.

GUIDE TO LITERARY AGENTS, published annually by Writer's Digest Books (1507 Dana Ave., Cincinnati, OH 45207, [800] 289-0963), contains the most detailed listings of five hundred literary and script agents. The guide divides its listings according to nonfee-charging and fee-charging agents. It also includes a variety of insider information (profiles, interviews, articles, query samples) on marketing your work and getting your script in the right agent's hands.

HOLLYWOOD AGENTS & MANAGERS DIRECTORY, published by the Hollywood Creative Directory (3000 W. Olympic Blvd., Suite 2525, Santa Monica, CA 90404, [800] 815-0503), offers probably the most complete list of agents and managers—it boasts 4,100 names.

Other Television Resources

Other excellent publications for breaking into television include: *Written By: The Journal of the Writers Guild of America, West* (7000 W. Third St., Los Angeles, CA 90048-4329,

[888] 974-8629, writtenby@wga.org) provides a TV Market List with information about every television show in production, including the person responsible for freelance writers and the phone number of the production company. Non-WGA members may subscribe. Also, *The Hollywood Scriptwriter* (P.O. Box 10277, Burbank, CA 91510, [818] 845-5525, http://www.hollywoodscriptwriter.com) offers interviews with successful writers as well as agent and market information. If you want to stay tuned to the day-to-day operations in Hollywood, check out *Daily Variety* (5700 Wilshire Blvd., Los Angeles, CA 90036) and *The Hollywood Reporter* (5055 Wilshire Blvd., Los Angeles, CA 90036), both of which publish charts with television production information and will keep you up on industry news.

The Query Letter

After you've done your research and know how to contact the right agency, producer or story editor, send a query letter. That's all you should send at this point; do not submit your spec script. In your query letter, say you'd like to write for the show and ask if the production company or agency is interested in new writers. J. Michael Straczynski, in *The Complete Book of Scriptwriting* (Writer's Digest Books), suggests mentioning the following:

- That you're enthusiastic about the show and have studied it.
- That you've written a spec script and would like to submit it. (Do not go into detail about the contents of your spec script—you'll definitely ruin your chances of writing for the show.)
- That when you send your spec script you will enclose a standard release form or will use the production company's or agency's release form.
- That you have writing credits or a profession that qualifies you to write for this show. (If you've spent ten years working in an emergency room, mentioning that could really help if you want to write for a show like *ER*.)

That's basically all you need to include in your query. Again, never send a spec script to an agent, producer or story editor unless you are requested to do so. Do not mention any specifics about your story idea in your query letter or it will be returned immediately. Producers and agents refuse to look at unsolicited spec scripts and story ideas because they are afraid of getting sued for plagiarism. Just keep your query letter to a few short paragraphs and ask for permission to send your spec script. Follow these guidelines:

Formatting Specs

- Use a standard font or typeface (no bold, script or italic).
- Place your name, address and phone number (include E-mail and fax, if applicable) in the top right corner.
- Use a 1″ margin on all sides.
- Address it to a specific agent, producer or story editor.
- Keep it to one page.
- Use block or semiblock letter format.
- Single-space the body of the letter; double-space between paragraphs.
- Catalog every item you're sending in your enclosures.

Other Dos and Don'ts

- Do include an SASE or postcard for reply, and state in the letter that you have done so.
- Do offer to sign a release form.
- Do offer to send the spec script.
- Don't use "Dear Sir," "Dear Madame, etc." in your salutation.
- Don't use Mr., Ms. Mrs. or Miss unless you're certain of the person's gender and marital status.
- Don't mention that you're a first-time writer or that you've never sold any piece of writing.
- Don't spend much time trying to sell yourself.
- Don't tell how much time you've spent writing the script.
- Don't ask for advice or criticism.
- Don't mention anything about yourself not pertinent to the script.
- Don't bring up payment.
- Don't mention copyright information.

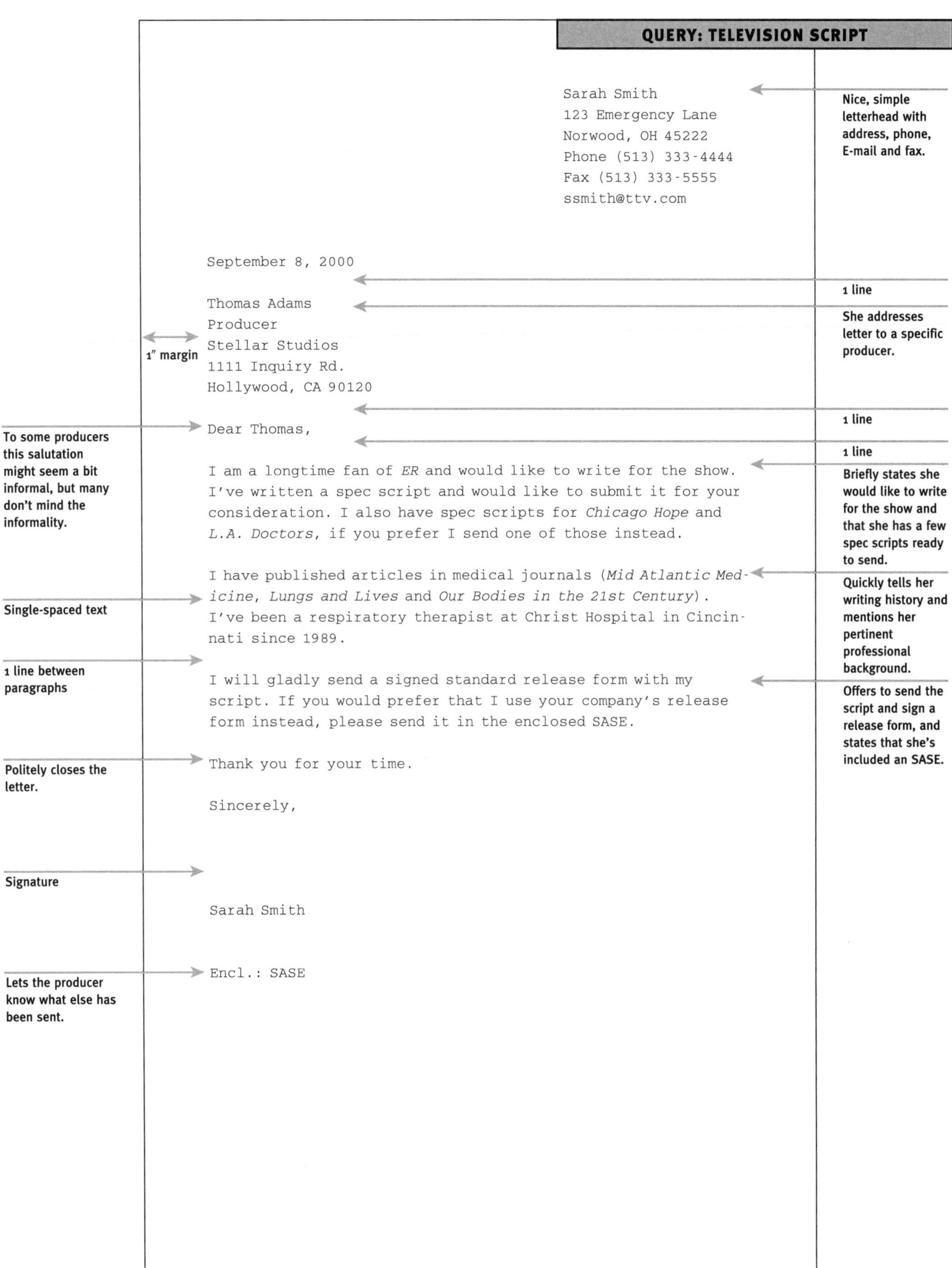

QUERY: TELEVISION SCRIPT

Sarah Smith
123 Emergency Lane
Norwood, OH 45222
Phone (513) 333-4444
Fax (513) 333-5555
ssmith@ttv.com

September 8, 2000

Thomas Adams
Producer
Stellar Studios
1111 Inquiry Rd.
Hollywood, CA 90120

Dear Thomas,

I am a longtime fan of *ER* and would like to write for the show. I've written a spec script and would like to submit it for your consideration. I also have spec scripts for *Chicago Hope* and *L.A. Doctors*, if you prefer I send one of those instead.

I have published articles in medical journals (*Mid Atlantic Medicine*, *Lungs and Lives* and *Our Bodies in the 21st Century*). I've been a respiratory therapist at Christ Hospital in Cincinnati since 1989.

I will gladly send a signed standard release form with my script. If you would prefer that I use your company's release form instead, please send it in the enclosed SASE.

Thank you for your time.

Sincerely,

Sarah Smith

Encl.: SASE

Nice, simple letterhead with address, phone, E-mail and fax.
1 line
She addresses letter to a specific producer.
1" margin
1 line
1 line
To some producers this salutation might seem a bit informal, but many don't mind the informality.
Briefly states she would like to write for the show and that she has a few spec scripts ready to send.
Quickly tells her writing history and mentions her pertinent professional background.
Single-spaced text
1 line between paragraphs
Offers to send the script and sign a release form, and states that she's included an SASE.
Politely closes the letter.
Signature
Lets the producer know what else has been sent.

Sitcoms

Unlike movie features and one-hour dramas that are shot on film, half-hour sitcoms are shot entirely on videotape and have a unique script format tailored for them. (Actually, each sitcom has its individual formatting quirks, so try to obtain a copy of the show's "bible" and a sample script.) What sets a sitcom script apart from other scripts is that almost everything is in all caps and double-spaced. There are good reasons for these differences, most notably that sitcom scripts often get revised up until the taping sessions (there are usually two sessions in front of live audiences, held on the same day), and sitcoms have directions for three cameras written alongside the script. A script written in a single-spaced format wouldn't allow enough room for the handwritten changes and camera directions. Basically, a sitcom script has a lot of much-needed white space.

Structure

Most sitcoms have only two acts, with three scenes per act (some shows use a teaser or a tag, which we'll discuss later). Because of all the double-spacing, plan on about thirty seconds per script page. Consider that the viewing time of the average sitcom is about twenty-two to twenty-four minutes, so your script should be forty to fifty pages (with each act running about twenty to twenty-five pages; six to eight pages per scene). Acts are in all caps. At the end of the act, type "END OF ACT ONE" (or two), centered and underlined two or three spaces below the last line of the act.

Teasers and Tags

Many sitcoms today begin with a teaser or end with a tag; some use both. A teaser is a short scene that airs at the beginning of the show, and a tag is a short scene that appears after the final act has been resolved. The tag almost always follows a commercial break and has the show's credits rolling alongside it. Both tags and teasers should run about two pages. Sometimes tags and teasers have little or nothing to do with that episode's story.

First-Page Particulars

The series title should be ten lines from the top of the page and centered. Two lines under the series title should be the episode title, with the act number centered eight lines below that (the act number should be completely spelled out). The series title and act number should be in all caps and underlined, whereas the episode title should be in regular text (not all caps), underlined and enclosed in quotation marks. Drop both the series title and the episode title from the first page of act two, but remember to include the act number (spelled out)—it should be fifteen lines from the top of the page and centered.

Page Numbers

Page numbers should appear in the top right corner of the page, flush with the right margin (about 75 spaces from the left edge of the page), about four lines from the top of the page, and followed by a period (e.g., 17.).

Act and Scene Number Notations

In the top right corner two lines below the page number should appear an act and scene number notation (although many sitcoms use letters for their scenes—A, B, C—instead of numbering them; check the formatting rules for each show). This notation should be in all caps on the first page of the act:

```
First page in act: ACT 2, SCENE 2
```

After the first page of the act, the heading should be underlined on the rest of the pages, and only the act should be capitalized:

```
All other pages in the act: ACT 2, scene 2
```

Cast Member Lists

Also in the top right corner of the page is the cast member list. It appears only on the first page of each new scene, in parentheses, two lines under the act and scene notation. The cast member list includes just the names of the actors in that scene, with the names in regular text (not all caps) separated by commas:

```
15.

ACT 2, scene 2

(Tom, Jerry, Stan)
```

Some scripts, however, have the character list two lines under the slug line (scene heading) on the left margin (see Slug Lines below). Again, check the show's specifications.

Transitions

Transitions indicate that a shot or scene is either beginning, ending or shifting to another shot or scene. These include such directions as FADE IN:, FADE OUT, DISSOLVE TO: and CUT TO:. Transitions appear in all caps and are justified with the right margin (about 75 spaces from the left edge of the page), except FADE IN:, which is flush with the left margin (15 spaces from the left edge of the page). FADE OUT is used only at the end of an act and CUT TO: at the end of a scene (to indicate a new scene should begin). Some shows underline transitions.

Slug Lines

The slug line, also called a scene heading, specifies the scene. It begins on the left margin (15 spaces from the left edge of the page) and is written in all caps and underlined, with a double-spaced line before and after it. Your first slug line should appear two lines below FADE IN:. In sitcoms, the slug line will usually be INT. (interior shot), but occasionally you'll need to use EXT. (exterior shot). With the slug line, organize the details by going from the more general to the more specific. End each slug line by indicating whether the action takes place during the day or at night. For almost every sitcom, the slug line typically contains three parts: INT. or EXT., the scene location and DAY or NIGHT. Your slug line will look like this:

INT. FRASIER'S LIVING ROOM—NIGHT

Some shows have the character list for that particular scene in parentheses one line below the slug line:

INT. FRASIER'S LIVING ROOM—NIGHT
(Frasier, Niles, Daphne)

Action Directions

The action directions are sentences that describe specifics about what happens, when, where, how and anything else that's important to the scene. The text within the action sentences begins on the left margin (15 spaces from the left edge of the page), is single-spaced, in all caps and should always be written in present tense (in some scripts, the action is in parentheses). Do not justify the right margin (which is at 75 spaces). Many shows underline entrances and exits (either the entire sentence or just the verb):

JONATHAN ENTERS THE DINING ROOM.

Or:

JONATHAN ENTERS THE DINING ROOM.

There should be one double-spaced line before and after the action description. If you have lots of description, break up the text to leave some white space—try not to allow a block of text to run more than four or five lines without a double-spaced break for the eyes (the more white space in a sitcom script, the better).

Character Names

The speaking character's name (also called the character cue) should be in all caps and should appear 35 spaces from the left edge of the page. A double-spaced line should appear before and after the character's name. Note: The first time you introduce a character into the script, put that character's name in all caps and/or underline it.

JACK
I think I just saw SUSAN walk up the steps. Maybe she's coming up here.

Parentheticals

Parenthetical comments, also known as parentheticals, help the speaker of the dialogue know what emotion or expression you intend with the delivery. A parenthetical is typically short (often a word or two), typed in all caps and appears either on the same line as the first line of dialogue or on a line by itself (in which case it appears flush with the left margin):

VERONICA
(EMBARRASSED) He really said I was cute?

Or:

```
          VERONICA
(EMBARRASSED)
        He really said I was cute?
```

Dialogue

Dialogue is double-spaced, typed in regular text (not all caps) and begins two lines below the speaking character's name (and parenthetical). The left margin for dialogue is at space 25 and the right margin is at space 60 (do not justify the right margin).

Continuations

If you must continue dialogue from one page to the next, use what are called continuations, which are just the words (MORE) and (CONT'D). Use them like this: Put (MORE) under the last line of dialogue on the first page and (CONT'D) to the right of the character's name on the following page:

```
     PAUL
Ira, if you don't knock before you come in here
                    (MORE)

______________________NEW PAGE______________________

     PAUL (CONT'D)
I'm going to sick Murray on you.
```

Using a Narrative Voice-Over

You will rarely need to use a narrative voice-over with sitcoms, but if you do, make sure you indicate it as such by typing "(V.O.)" to the right of the character's name:

```
     DHARMA (V.O.)
Wait a minute, now how did that happen?
```

Having a Character Speak Off-Camera

When you have a character speaking off-camera, type "(O.C.)" to the right of the character's name. Let's say Joey is on camera in the hallway talking to Chandler who's off-camera inside the apartment.

```
     JOEY
Come on, Chandler. You gotta let me in.
     CHANDLER (O.C.)
Joey, that's you, right?
```

Other Dos and Don'ts

- Do keep dialogue short (break it up every four or five lines).
- Do spell out one- and two-digit numbers (one, ten, fifty), but use numbers for 100 and over.

- Do spell out personal titles except for Mr., Mrs. and Ms.
- Do spell out time indicators: eleven-thirty, not 11:30.
- Do spell out "okay," not OK or o.k.
- Don't use any font other than Courier 12-point.
- Don't justify right margins.
- Don't date your script.
- Don't include a cast of characters or set list page.
- Don't use camera directions and camera angles.
- Don't use special effects directions, such as FX (visual).
- Don't use sound effects directions, such as SFX (sound).

What follows are formatting specifications for your sitcom script, a sample first page of a mock script for *Frasier*, and a sample sitcom script title page.

Tab and Margin Settings

- left 15; right 55 camera and stage directions
- left 15; right 70 action/scene descriptions
- left 15; right 70 slug line
- left 25; right 60 dialogue
- 35 character name
- 15 FADE IN
- 60 transitions

All Caps

- Act and scene headings
- Act breaks
- All action/scene/stage directions
- Speech delivery (e.g., SLURRY)
- Transitions (FADE IN:, FADE OUT)
- Tags
- Teasers
- Slug lines (EXT. or INT., DAY or NIGHT)
- All descriptions
- Character names (except when part of dialogue or character list)
- Continuations (MORE or CONT'D)
- Act and show endings (END OF SHOW)

Underline

- Act headings
- Scene headings
- Locale designations
- Important sounds
- Slug lines
- When a character is first introduced

Single Space

- within action directions

- within scene descriptions

Double Space

- between scene heading and first lines of directions or scene descriptions
- between character's name and dialogue
- within dialogue lines
- between dialogue lines and directions or scene descriptions
- before and after transitions

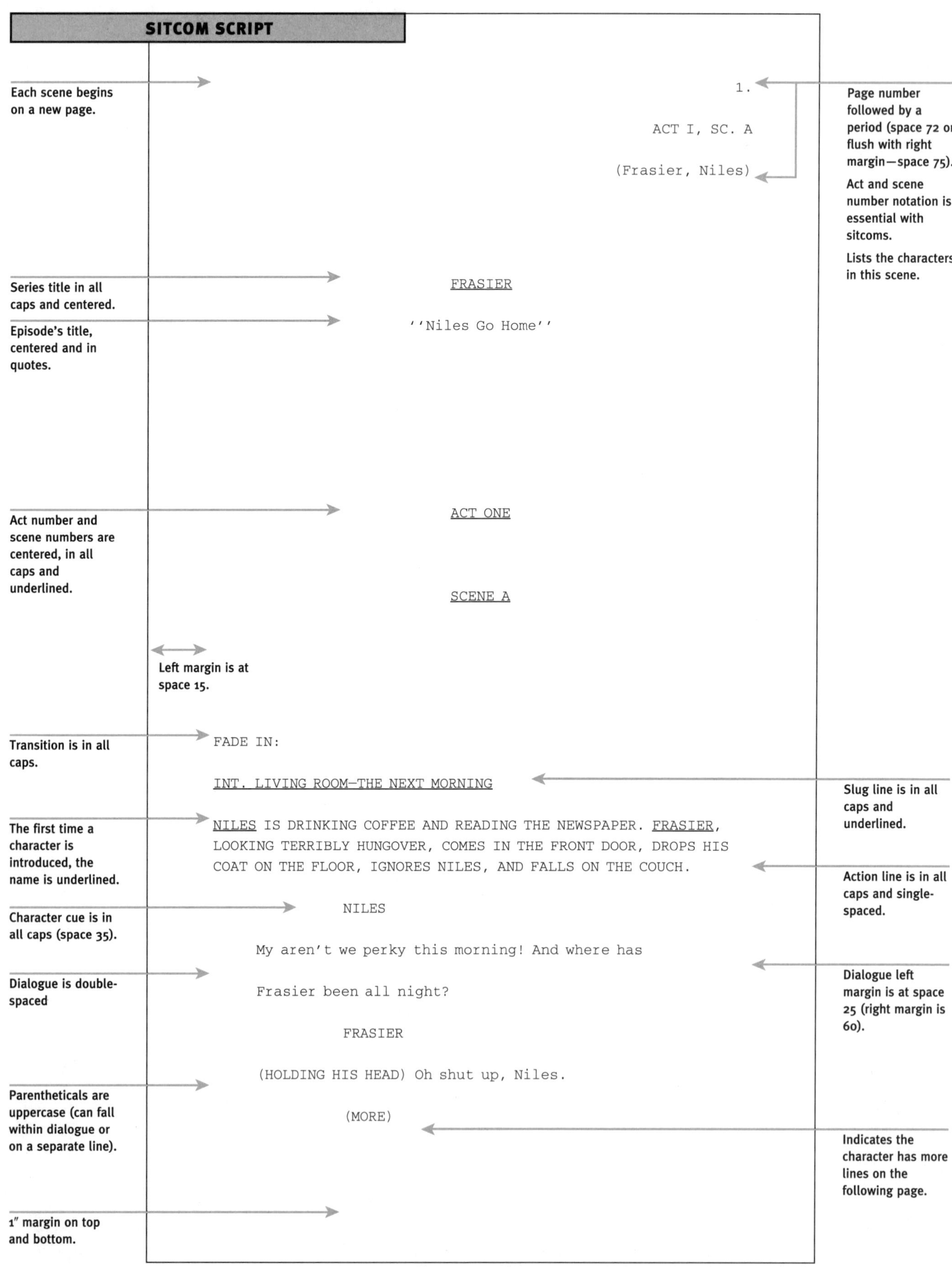
SITCOM SCRIPT
Each scene begins on a new page.
1.
ACT I, SC. A
(Frasier, Niles)
Page number followed by a period (space 72 or flush with right margin—space 75).
Act and scene number notation is essential with sitcoms.
Lists the characters in this scene.
Series title in all caps and centered.
FRASIER
Episode's title, centered and in quotes.
''Niles Go Home''
Act number and scene numbers are centered, in all caps and underlined.
ACT ONE
SCENE A
Left margin is at space 15.
Transition is in all caps.
FADE IN:
INT. LIVING ROOM—THE NEXT MORNING
Slug line is in all caps and underlined.
The first time a character is introduced, the name is underlined.
NILES IS DRINKING COFFEE AND READING THE NEWSPAPER. FRASIER, LOOKING TERRIBLY HUNGOVER, COMES IN THE FRONT DOOR, DROPS HIS COAT ON THE FLOOR, IGNORES NILES, AND FALLS ON THE COUCH.
Action line is in all caps and single-spaced.
Character cue is in all caps (space 35).
NILES
My aren't we perky this morning! And where has
Frasier been all night?
Dialogue is double-spaced
Dialogue left margin is at space 25 (right margin is 60).
FRASIER
(HOLDING HIS HEAD) Oh shut up, Niles.
Parentheticals are uppercase (can fall within dialogue or on a separate line).
(MORE)
Indicates the character has more lines on the following page.
1" margin on top and bottom.

SITCOM SCRIPT, PAGE 2

2.

Second page numbered

Picks up with same character who was speaking before the page break.

FRASIER (CONT'D)

You're no ray of sunshine.

NILES

I'm no hungover drunk either.

FRASIER

Well at least I have a home.

NILES

Oh you cruel man. You know my marriage is on the rocks. You know that MARIS wouldn't let me back in the house if I sawed my left leg off for her. She's such a cold woman.

Dialogue is double-spaced (do keep blocks of dialogue short).

FRASIER

Yeah, but she's your woman. Now go back home.

NILES

Are you saying you don't want me here? Are you saying you won't help your brother out in a time of need?

FRASIER

That's exactly what I'm saying.

NILES

Dad!

HE GETS UP AND RUNS INTO THE KITCHEN, POUTING.

FADE OUT

Transition goes at space 66 (or flush with right margin).

END OF ACT ONE

Title Page

The sitcom series title should be in all caps, centered, about one-third of the way down the page. Drop one line and put the episode title in quotes. Drop four lines and type either "Written by" or just "by." Drop one line and type your name. In the lower right-hand corner, put your name, address and phone number, single-spaced, in regular text (not all caps). If you have an agent, type "Representation:," double-space, then put the agent's name, address and phone number instead of yours.

Cover Page Paper

Preferred is a white, gray, cream, rust or pale blue cover of card stock, between 40 and 60 lbs., with no picture or artwork on it. The pages should be bound in brass brads, short enough so they don't cut through an envelope when mailed. Never use spiral or other machine-type bindings. Although your script should have three holes punched in it, only the first and third holes should have brads in them. Be sure the back cover is the same stock as the front cover.

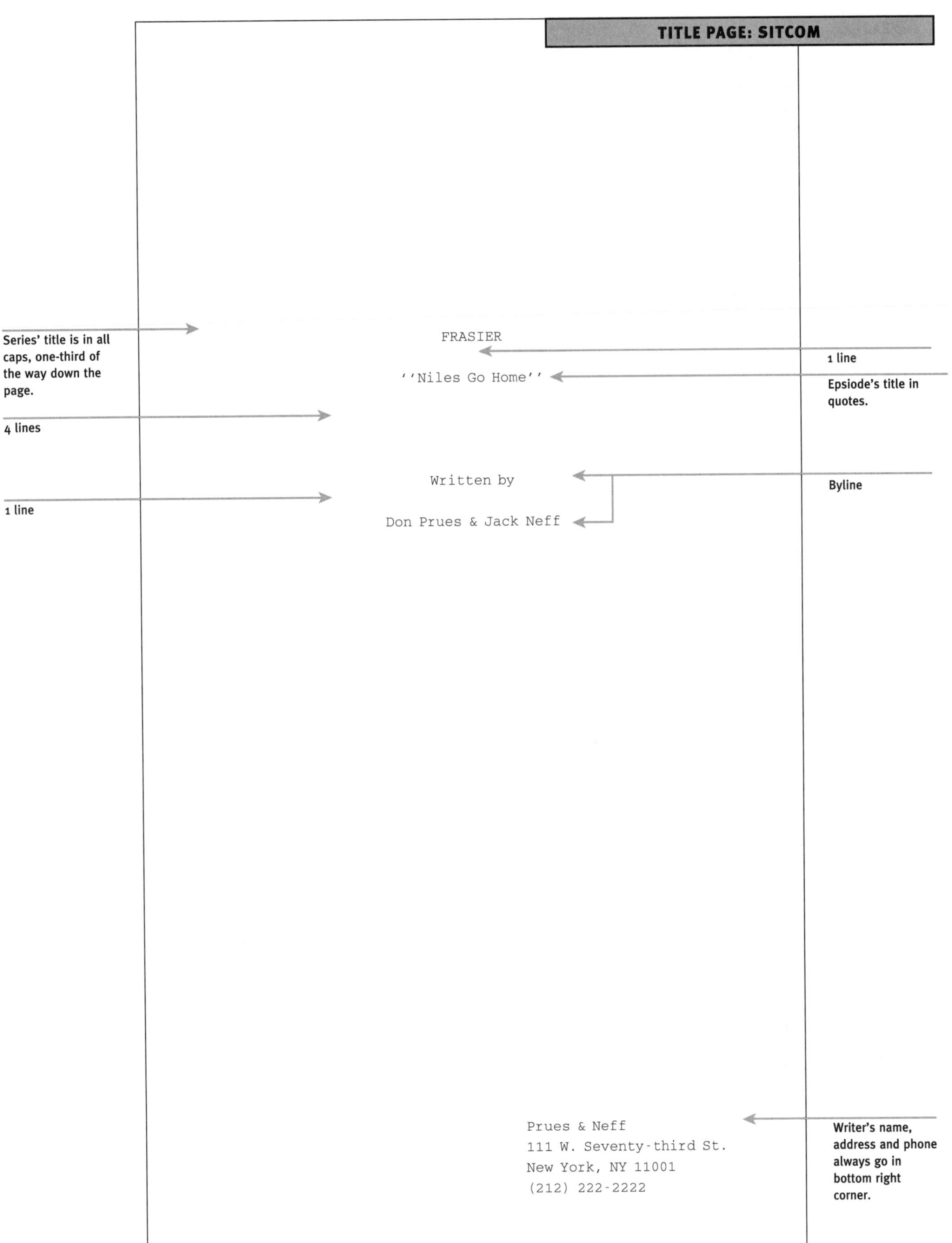
TITLE PAGE: SITCOM
Series' title is in all caps, one-third of the way down the page.
FRASIER
1 line
''Niles Go Home''
Epsiode's title in quotes.
4 lines
Written by
Byline
1 line
Don Prues & Jack Neff
Prues & Neff
111 W. Seventy-third St.
New York, NY 11001
(212) 222-2222
Writer's name, address and phone always go in bottom right corner.

The One-Hour Episodic Drama

Structure

Your hour-long script will be roughly fifty pages. Most one-hour dramas run forty-eight minutes, and as with the motion picture format, you can average about one minute of viewing time per manuscript page. Nearly all hour-long dramas contain four acts that occur at roughly twelve- to fifteen-minute intervals (so your script should change acts every twelve to fifteen pages). The act breaks will correspond with the network's commercials, which occur about every thirteen minutes. Because networks want viewers to hang around through the commercial breaks, your story needs to have a cliffhanger or an emotional moment at the end of each act (except the last one).

Transitions

Transitions simply indicate that a shot or scene is beginning, ending or shifting to another shot or scene. These include such directions as FADE IN:, FADE TO:, CUT TO: and DISSOLVE TO:. Transitions appear in all caps and are justified with the right margin (about space 75), except FADE IN:, which is flush with the left margin and should appear two lines below the act number. FADE OUT is used only at the end of an act (and is on the right margin).

Slug Line (Scene Heading)

The slug line sets the scene and specifies the shot. It begins on the left margin (17 spaces from the left edge of the page) and is written in all caps, with a double-spaced line before and after it. Your first slug line should appear two lines below FADE IN:. Most slug lines begin with either EXT. (exterior shot) or INT. (interior shot). After you determine whether the shot is outside or inside, identify the specifics of the shot, such as a particular building or house, and then, if necessary, precisely where the shot takes place. With the slug line, organize the details by going from the more general to the more specific. End each slug line by indicating whether it's day or night. For example, your slug line will look like this:

```
INT. YMCA—MEN'S LOCKER ROOM—NIGHT
```

Action

The action descriptions are sentences or very short paragraphs that describe specifics about what happens, location, the time of year and anything else important to the scene. The text within the action sentences begins on the left margin (17 spaces from the left edge of the page), is single-spaced (with regular capitalization) and should always be written in present tense. Do not justify the right margin (75). There should be one double-spaced line before and after the action text. If you have lots of description, break up the text to leave some white space—try not to allow a block of text to run more than five or six lines without a double-spaced break for the eyes (the more white space in a script, the better).

Character's Name

The speaking character's name (also called the character cue) should be in all caps and appear 43 spaces from the left edge of the page (about 30 spaces from the left margin).

A double-spaced line should appear before the character's name, but there should be no double-space between the name and the dialogue, or between the name and the parenthetical (see below). Note: The first time you introduce a character into the script you must put that character's name in all caps (this occurs either in dialogue when one character refers to another or in the narrative description line, "JOE enters the room"). After the character has been introduced, use regular capitalization.

Parenthetical Comment

Parenthetical comments, also known as parentheticals, help the speaker of the dialogue know what emotion you intend for the delivery. Parenthetical comments are typically short (often a word or two), typed in regular text (not all caps), appear one line below the character's name (and thus one line above dialogue) at space 35 and are set in parentheses. A parenthetical should look like this:

```
                SCULLY
          (antagonistic)
What in the hell's going on around here, Mulder?
```

Dialogue

Dialogue is typed in regular text (not all caps) and begins on the line below the speaking character's name (or one line below the parenthetical). The left margin for dialogue is at space 28 and the right margin is at space 60 (do not justify the right margin). Try to avoid large blocks of dialogue that run seven or more lines. If your character needs to say more than can fit in seven lines, add a blank line space between the text so it's more visually pleasing (e.g., a fourteen-line section of dialogue should be broken into two blocks of seven lines each).

In addition to the aforementioned regular elements of your one-hour episodic script, you will probably find yourself in situations where you might need some special formatting and cues. Here are some of the more common script elements you might need to inject in your one-hour episodic script.

Carrying Dialogue From One Page to the Next

Do your best not to make a character flip to the next page in the middle of speaking. Sometimes, however, this cannot be avoided, and you must use what's called a continuation. To carry a character's dialogue onto the next page, use the indicator (MORE) on the bottom of the first page and (CONT'D) next to the speaker's name at the top of the next page:

```
          JOE
I swear if I ever see you in this town again I'm going
                         (MORE)
_________________________NEW PAGE_________________________

          JOE (CONT'D)
to kill you.
```

Using a Narrative Voice-Over

If your script calls for a narrative voice-over, make sure you indicate it as such by typing "(V.O.)" next to the name of the character who's narrating. A scene with a voice narration should look like this:

```
    CAPTAIN SMITH (V.O.)
Now how did she get into the apartment when the keys
are inside?
```

Having a Character Speak Off-Camera

When you have a character speaking off-camera, type "(O.C.)" next to the character's name. Let's say Steve is on camera in the kitchen while talking to Maggie who's off-camera on the back porch.

```
    STEVE
Can you bring that old broom in here?

    MAGGIE (O.C.)
What? You want me to put that filthy thing in our
kitchen? You're crazy.

    STEVE
I need it to sweep up all this flour I just spilled on
the floor.

    MAGGIE (O.C.)
Oh, you're pathetic.
```

Other Dos and Don'ts

- Do number your pages and put a period after the number.
- Do keep dialogue short (keep to seven lines per block, then insert a double-space).
- Do spell out one- and two-digit numbers (one, ten, fifty), but use numbers for 100 and over.
- Do spell out personal titles except for Mr., Mrs. and Ms.
- Do spell out time indicators: eleven-thirty, not 11:30.
- Do spell out "okay," not OK or o.k.
- Don't use special effects directions, such as FX (visual).
- Don't use sound effects directions, such as SFX (sound).
- Don't use camera directions and camera angles.
- Don't number the first page.
- Don't number scenes (this is done in the final stages of story editing, before the script moves into preproduction).

What follows are formatting specifications for your one-hour episodic script as well as a sample one-hour episodic script title page and a sample first page of a one-hour episodic script.

Tab and Margin Settings

- 17 left margin
- 28 dialogue left margin
- 35 parenthetical directions
- 43 character's name (above the dialogue)
- 60 dialogue right margin
- 66 transitions
- 72 page number followed by a period (in top right-hand corner, four lines from top of page)
- 75 right margin

All Caps

- Type of shot (INT. and EXT.)
- Setting or scene location (JOE'S ROOM)
- Time of day (DAY or NIGHT)
- The first time you introduce a character (JOHN walks in)
- The speaking character's name (PHIL), followed by dialogue
- Camera directions (PAN, CLOSE-UP, etc.)
- Important sound cues (Ted hears a GUNSHOT in the hallway.)
- Scene transitions (CUT TO:, DISSOLVE TO:, etc.)
- (MORE)

Single Space

- within dialogue
- within action/scene descriptions (also called narrative)
- within camera directions, sound cues
- within stage directions
- between the character's name and dialogue
- between character's name and parenthetical
- between parenthetical and dialogue

Double Space

- between the scene location and action/scene descriptions
- between the action/scene descriptions and the speaking character's name
- between the speeches of the different characters
- between the paragraphs of lengthy dialogue or action descriptions
- between dialogue and a new speaking character's name
- between dialogue and stage or camera directions

Triple Space

- before each new scene

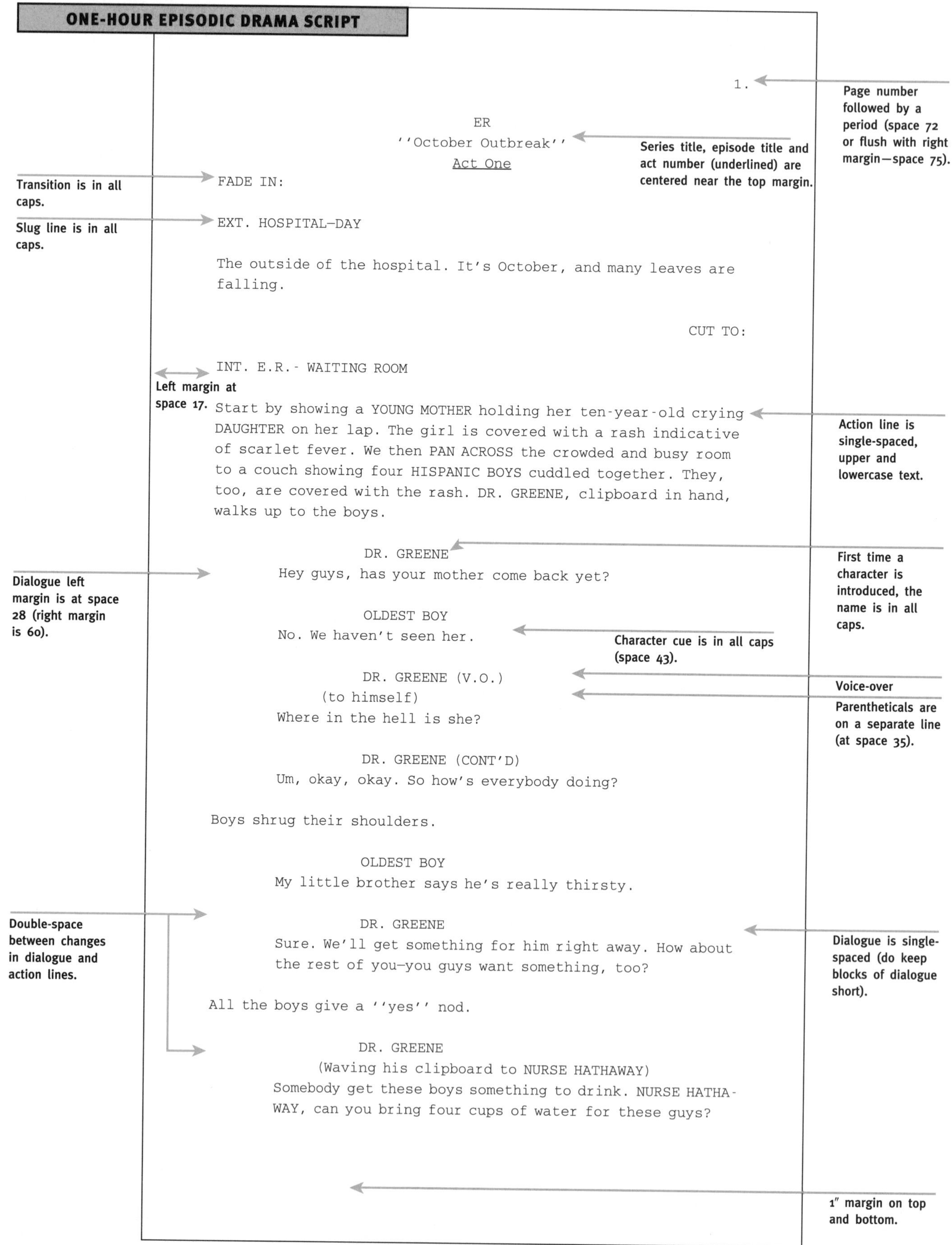
ONE-HOUR EPISODIC DRAMA SCRIPT
1.
ER
''October Outbreak''
Act One
FADE IN:
EXT. HOSPITAL-DAY
The outside of the hospital. It's October, and many leaves are falling.
CUT TO:
INT. E.R.- WAITING ROOM
Start by showing a YOUNG MOTHER holding her ten-year-old crying DAUGHTER on her lap. The girl is covered with a rash indicative of scarlet fever. We then PAN ACROSS the crowded and busy room to a couch showing four HISPANIC BOYS cuddled together. They, too, are covered with the rash. DR. GREENE, clipboard in hand, walks up to the boys.
DR. GREENE
Hey guys, has your mother come back yet?
OLDEST BOY
No. We haven't seen her.
DR. GREENE (V.O.)
(to himself)
Where in the hell is she?
DR. GREENE (CONT'D)
Um, okay, okay. So how's everybody doing?
Boys shrug their shoulders.
OLDEST BOY
My little brother says he's really thirsty.
DR. GREENE
Sure. We'll get something for him right away. How about the rest of you—you guys want something, too?
All the boys give a ''yes'' nod.
DR. GREENE
(Waving his clipboard to NURSE HATHAWAY)
Somebody get these boys something to drink. NURSE HATHA-WAY, can you bring four cups of water for these guys?
Page number followed by a period (space 72 or flush with right margin—space 75).
Series title, episode title and act number (underlined) are centered near the top margin.
Transition is in all caps.
Slug line is in all caps.
Left margin at space 17.
Action line is single-spaced, upper and lowercase text.
First time a character is introduced, the name is in all caps.
Dialogue left margin is at space 28 (right margin is 60).
Character cue is in all caps (space 43).
Voice-over
Parentheticals are on a separate line (at space 35).
Double-space between changes in dialogue and action lines.
Dialogue is single-spaced (do keep blocks of dialogue short).
1" margin on top and bottom.

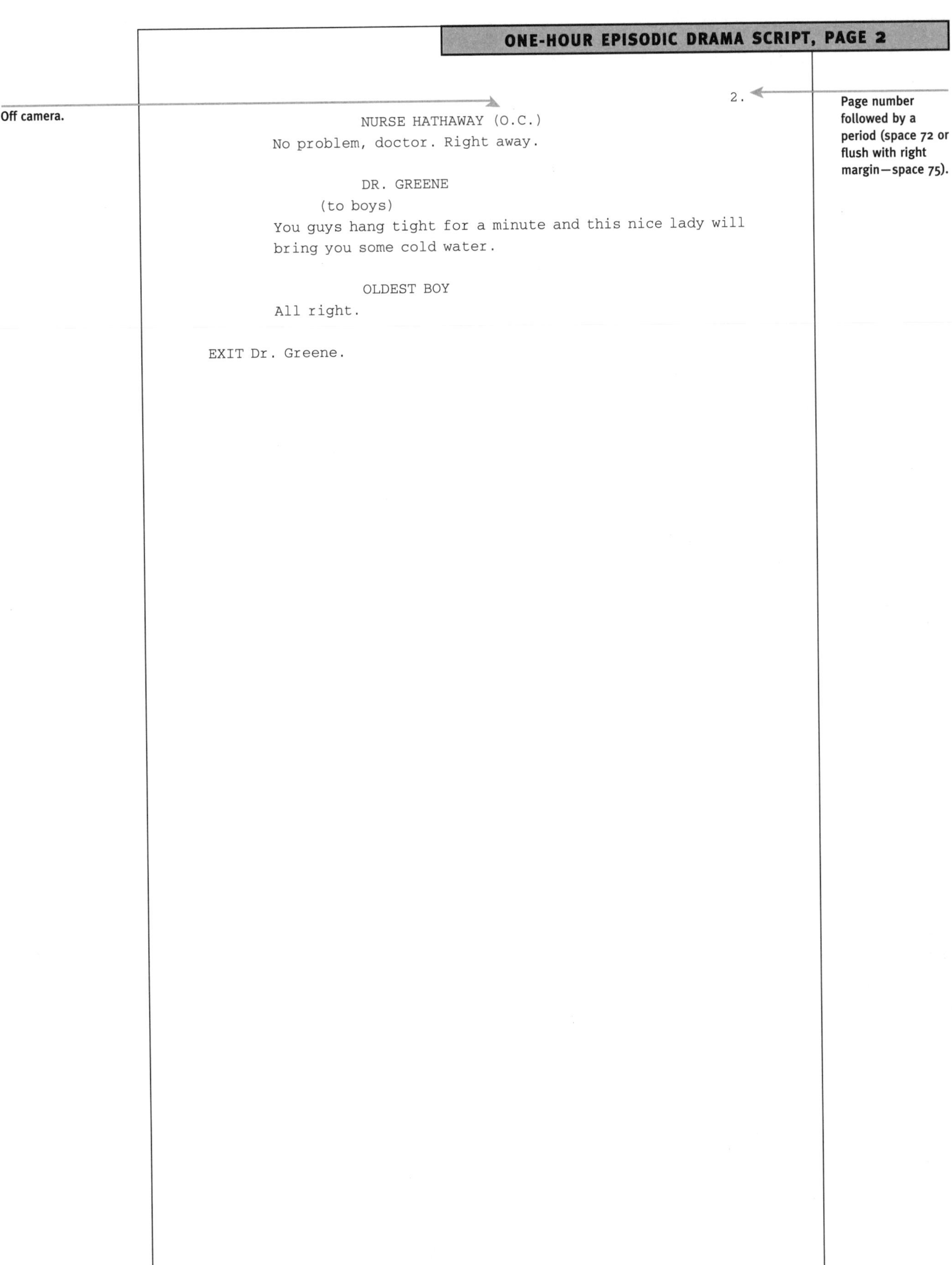
ONE-HOUR EPISODIC DRAMA SCRIPT, PAGE 2

2.

NURSE HATHAWAY (O.C.)
No problem, doctor. Right away.

DR. GREENE
(to boys)
You guys hang tight for a minute and this nice lady will bring you some cold water.

OLDEST BOY
All right.

EXIT Dr. Greene.

Off camera.

Page number followed by a period (space 72 or flush with right margin—space 75).

Title Page

The one-hour episodic script title should be in all caps, centered, about one-third of the way down the page. Drop ten lines and put the episode title in quotations: "October Outbreak." Then drop four lines and type "Story and Script." Drop one line and type "by". Double-space again and type your name. In the lower right-hand corner, put your name, address and phone number (single-spaced) in regular text (not all caps). If you have an agent, put "Representation:," double-space, then put the agent's name, address and phone number instead of yours.

Cover Page Paper

Preferred is a white, gray, cream, rust or pale blue cover of card stock, between 40 to 60 lbs., with no picture or artwork on it. The pages should be bound in brass brads, short enough so they don't cut through an envelope when mailed. Never use spiral or other machine-type bindings. Although your script should have three holes punched in it, only the first and third holes should have brads in them. Be sure to use a back cover of the same stock as the front cover.

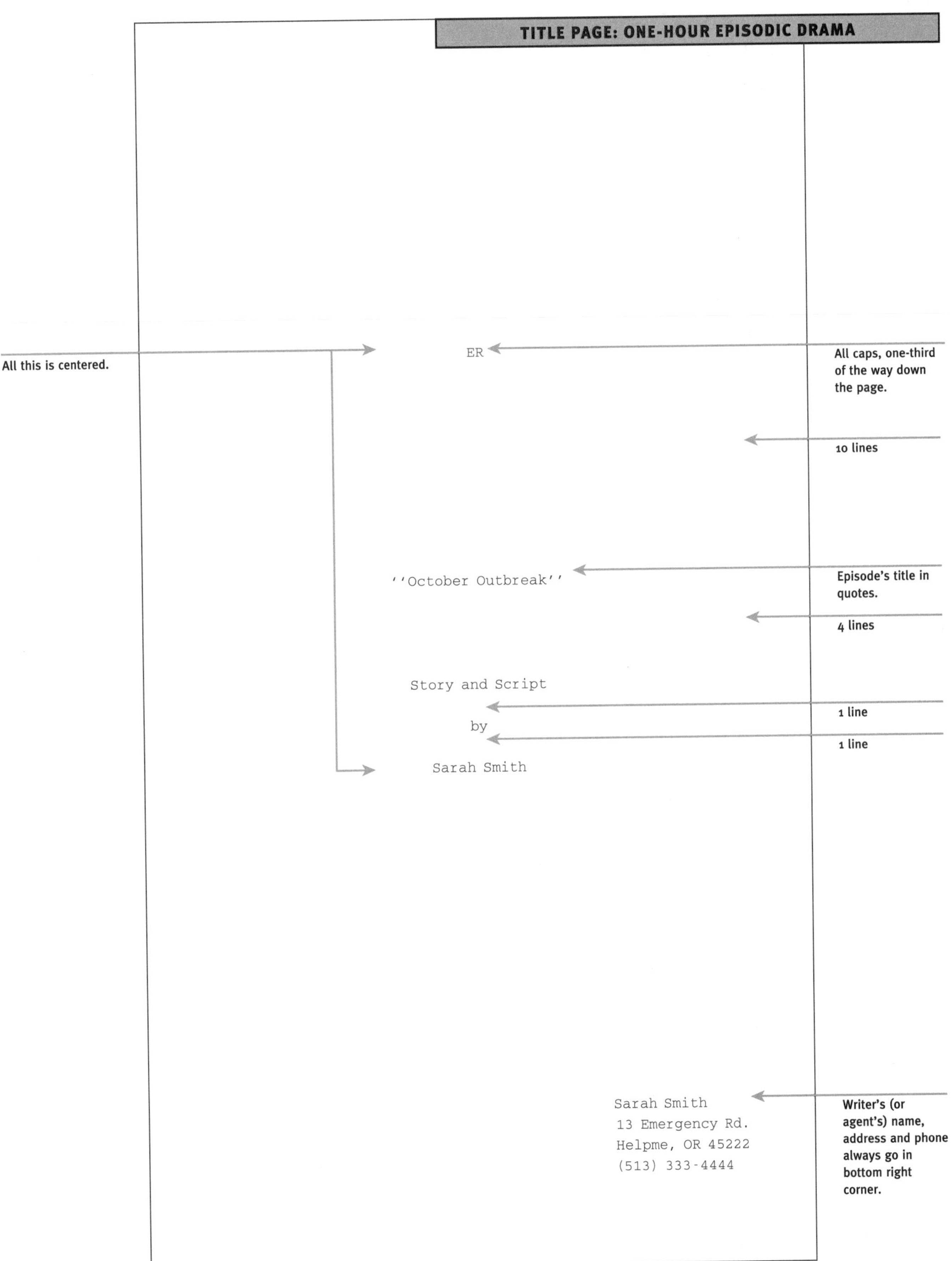
TITLE PAGE: ONE-HOUR EPISODIC DRAMA
All this is centered.
ER
All caps, one-third of the way down the page.
10 lines
''October Outbreak''
Episode's title in quotes.
4 lines
Story and Script
1 line
by
1 line
Sarah Smith
Sarah Smith
13 Emergency Rd.
Helpme, OR 45222
(513) 333-4444
Writer's (or agent's) name, address and phone always go in bottom right corner.

Soaps

A finished soap script is the result of teamwork. Because soaps must be cranked out five days week, with multiple stories going at once to carry the drama from episode to episode (for seemingly perpetuity), a number of writers, producers and executives are required to get the script in working order. The best way to keep up with such demand is the same way Henry Ford put together cars: division of labor. Soap scripts are an assembly line of sorts.

Here's how that assembly line works, as outlined in *Successful Scriptwriting* by Jurgen Wolff and Kerry Cox (Writer's Digest Books). The show's sponsor (usually a corporation, like Procter & Gamble) and the producers will meet with the show's head writer to create a yearlong, roughly sketched outline for the show. Then the head writer breaks that outline into specific weekly and daily outlines. Eventually, a short scene-by-scene synopsis (usually a paragraph or two per scene) is created for each episode; then the head writer sends the synopsis to various associate writers who write all the dialogue for a particular episode. So, most writers for soaps are associate writers who pen the dialogue for individual episodes.

The best way to become an associate writer is to send a spectacular spec script to the production company or to get an agent who represents the show's writers to also represent you (see page 184 for tips on locating the production company or an agent who represents the show's writers). One other option is to find out if the show has an apprentice program for writers (the show's sponsor usually offers this program) and, if so, enroll in it. To see if the show you wish to write for offers such a program, contact the production company.

Structure

Most soaps run for an hour, with a few that only run one-half hour. Either way, you can figure that the viewing time for a soap script is a little more than one minute per page. Therefore, a one-hour show script will run about seventy pages, and a half-hour show will be roughly thirty-five pages. Although commercial breaks will eat up some of this time, ignore them and write as if your show's either an hour or half-hour. Unlike one-hour episodic dramas and sitcoms, which have a set number of acts, soaps work in a different way because they're continually running. A soap episode is more a series of scenes than one story episode delineated into a beginning, a middle and an end.

Format

The script elements and formatting specifications for soaps is almost identical to those for motion pictures (see page 170). There are, however, a few differences you should be aware of. The primary difference is that all action directions are capitalized, appear in parentheses and get mixed in with the dialogue. Also, a soap script has practically no camera directions and relies heavily on dialogue.

One major problem with writing a spec script for a soap is that the formats vary so much from show to show. Many shows use the "standard" soap format demonstrated on page 208, but some opt for a format that looks more like a radio script:

```
JOHN: Would you please bring me some water?
MARY: I'm not your maid.
```

To determine what format the soap you want to write for uses, try to obtain back scripts from the production company. Finding the production company isn't too difficult: Tape the show, watch the credits, write down the name of the production company and get the phone number from one of the listed directories in Submitting Television Scripts, on page 183. You only need to talk to the secretary. Just say you want to write for the show and would like to obtain some back scripts. Offer to send an SASE with adequate postage. Making the call will pay off—it will be to your advantage that you're using the correct format for the show.

SOAP OPERA SCRIPT

1" margin on top and bottom.

Page number followed by a period (space 72 or flush with right margin—space 75).

5.

Transition is in all caps.

FADE IN:

HAROLD DANFORTH'S DEN. HAROLD IS SEARCHNG THROUGH HIS DESK TRYING TO FIND THE RECEIPT FOR THE NECKLACE HE BOUGHT FOR HIS MISTRESS, ABIGAIL CHAMBERS. HIS WIFE, ELIZABETH DANFORTH, WALKS INTO THE DEN.

Left margin is at space 17.

Character cue is in all caps (space 43).

ELIZABETH
(OPENS THE DOOR) Well hello, darling. (SLOWLY CLOSES AND LOCKS THE DOOR BEHIND HER)

Action is in all caps, surrounded by parentheses (except at the beginning of a scene when no parentheses are required).

HAROLD
(NERVOUSLY CLOSES THE TOP DESK DRAWER AND LOOKS UP) Hi, dear. How are you? (LOOKS BACK DOWN AND STARTS SORTING THROUGH SOME PAPERS ON HIS DESK) I'm just in here trying to find that letter from the school board. Have you seen it? (KEEPS LOOKING DOWN, SHUFFLING THE PAPERS)

ELIZABETH
(NOT RESPONDING, SLOWLY WALKS UP TO THE DESK AND JUST STANDS THERE)

HAROLD
Dear? (KEEPS SHUFFLING THE PAPERS AND THEN LOOKS UP. HE SEES HER RIGHT IN FRONT OF HIS FACE) Ah! (SCREAMS) Damn, you scared me.

ELIZABETH
I did, did I? Well what do you have to be scared about? It's only me.

Dialogue is single-spaced, upper and lowercase text (do keep blocks of dialogue short).

HAROLD
(FLUSTERED) You just surprised me, that's all. (LOOKS DOWN AND SORTS MORE PAPERS) Where is that thing? I swear I saw it here this morning.

ELIZABETH
(CALMLY PULLS THE RECEIPT FROM HER LEFT SHIRT POCKET) Oh, could this be what you're looking for, darling? (SHE LETS IT HANG IN FRONT OF HIS FACE)

Double-spaced between changes in dialogue and action lines.

HAROLD
(LOOKS UP, SEES THE RECEIPT, AND GRABS IT OUT OF HER HAND) Damn you. What the hell is this? (CRUMBLES UP THE RECEIPT)

ELIZABETH
(STARTS TO CRY) You know damn well what it is Harold. I suppose you bought that necklace for me. But why would you buy me anything? Why, you haven't bought me anything for years.

HAROLD
(STANDS UP, WALKS AROUND THE DESK) Now dear. (TRIES TO HOLD ELIZABETH'S HAND)

ELIZABETH
(PUSHES HIS HAND AWAY) Don't ''now dear'' me, Harold! For God's sake just admit you're having an affair. Please! I swear you're nothing but a weak, selfish, lying man. (SLAPS HIM AND WALKS AWAY. SLAMS THE DOOR ON HER WAY OUT)

FADE OUT

Transition to leave scene.

Movie of the Week

A made for TV movie, called a movie of the week or MOW, is similar in format to a regular motion picture, but much different when it comes to content. The primary difference is that almost all MOWs are geared toward middle-aged (and older) female viewers. That might not sound too kind or fair, but it's the reality of television movies (especially when aired on Sunday and Monday nights during football season). With that in mind, remember that all MOW scripts have a high level of emotion, are more character driven than plot driven, and contain less action and violence than your average motion picture feature.

Structure

The MOW has seven acts, runs anywhere from 90 to 105 pages, and takes up about 90 to 95 minutes of viewing time. Almost all MOWs are granted a two-hour block of time. Aside from the seven-act breaks (for commercials), a MOW has the same format as a regular motion picture screenplay (for formatting specifications, see page 170). Some writers prefer to break down their MOW script according to the seven-act breaks, with cliffhangers at the end of each act. Doing so can give you an edge because it shows the production company that you know how a MOW is structured and that you've tailored your script to work within that structure.

On the other hand, you might want to refrain from breaking down your script into seven acts for two reasons. First, all MOW production companies anticipate a MOW spec submission to arrive in the regular motion picture feature format (you won't seem like an amateur if your script isn't divided into seven acts). Second, your MOW script might actually get sold as a feature movie (in which case you'll probably get a lot more money and the seven-act breaks won't matter). After you sell your script as a MOW, you can get together with the production company to put your script into the seven-act formula.

You might still be one of those people who wants to get the act-breaking out of the way from the get go. If that's true, here are the average page lengths for the average MOW, as outlined in David Trotter's *The Screenwriter's Bible* (Silman-James Press). Notice the first act is the longest (to draw the viewer into the story), and that the rest of the acts get progressively shorter (the viewer is already hooked so why not toss in more commercial breaks?):

Act One: 18-23 pages
Act Two: 12-15 pages
Act Three: 12-15 pages
Act Four: 9-12 pages
Act Five: 9-12 pages
Act Six: 9-12 pages
Act Seven: 9-12 pages

With the end of each act comes a few commercials. As for your script, start each new act on a new page, drop ten lines, center and put the act number. Then drop three or four lines and begin the new scene. As mentioned earlier, every act except the last one should end with a cliffhanger or a moment of drama (this is done to hook viewers into sticking around for the next act, after the commercial break). The most dramatic act breaks should occur at the end of acts one and three, because these are considered the most crucial times when viewers might try to change channels. You don't want anybody changing channels when your script is on the air, and neither does the network.

QUERY LETTER TO AGENT: MOVIE OF THE WEEK

Nice, simple letterhead

Sandra K. Warren
5535 Deer Tail Dr.
San Antonio, TX
(210) 777-9999

March 16, 2000

1 line

Jack Scagnetti Talent & Literary Agency
5330 Lankerskim Blvd.
N. Hollywood, CA 91601

Addresses letter to specific agent and spells name correctly.

1 line

Dear Mr. Scagnetti:

1 line

I found the name of your agency in the *Guide to Literary Agents* and I thought you might be interested in seeing my screenplay, ''Hidden Casualties: Battles On The Homefront.'' It's about the custody battle that ensues after Sergeant Sara Raye returns home injured from service in the Persian Gulf War. While Sergeant Raye was in Saudi Arabia, her ex-husband illegally manipulated the courts in another state and stole custody of her three children. Seventeen lawyers told her that there was nothing she could do; that she had lost her children and it would take years to get them back. Citing violation of rights as stipulated in the Soldiers and Sailors Civil Relief Act, she refused to give up. It wasn't until she went public with her story that the Army, in two unprecedented moves, stepped in to right the wrong.

1″ margin

Single-spaced text

Tells where she found agency and what her script is about. She tells a lot but shows this is a timely and unusual subject. She also quickly reveals conflict and tough battle to overcome problems, and the power of not giving up—things that are appealing in a good story.

''Hidden Casualties'' is a story that will appeal to a wide range of audiences, from those interested in legal matters that bridge military and civilian life to those who served or had loved ones serving in the Persian Gulf, even to those who are serving elsewhere. Medical personnel, single parents and those concerned with women's issues and children's rights will also be interested.

Mentions the various audiences who will be interested in this story.

1 line between paragraphs

This story is changing the way the military deals with single parents, and has been discussed in meetings with military lawyers throughout the country. It was profiled on CNN and on all major networks in southern Texas.

Reveals the real-life results of the action taken by the main character.

I'm a member of SCBWI (Society of Children's Book Writers and Illustrators) and have written multiple books, an educational video and an audiocassette in the educational field. My books include four story books, activity books, a ''how to'' book, reader's theater and a poetry collection.

Tells enough about herself to show she's not a novice, and that tells me I should at least read what she's sent.

I look forward to hearing from you. I've enclosed an SASE for your response.

Sincerely,

Signature

Sandra Warren

Encl.: SASE

Comments provided by Jack Scagnetti of the Jack Scagnetti Talent & Literary Agency.

CHAPTER NINE

THE AUDIO/VIDEO SCRIPT

Audio/Video Scripts for Corporate Clients

Audio-video scripts are used to inform, usually with a goal to instruct (educational videos for corporate clients) or sell (commercials). Video presentations are essential when businesses need to educate those in-house and those outside of the company. They are most often used to train new employees, to convince another company their product is worth investing in, to tell the history and mission of the business and to explain procedural steps that go into a company's products. On the selling front, audio-video scripts are the backbone of television commercials, and advertising agencies would be lost without them.

Format Rationale

Almost all audio-video scripts demand one thing: a clear script that complements the implementation of the ideas on camera. Common elements in audio-video presentations include animation, stock footage, music, illustrations and narration. The scriptwriter directs the organization and flow of all these elements on the script's page, using an especially effective format—the two-column audio-video (A/V) format. Understanding and using the format is simple: The visual direction and description go on the left side of the page, and the dialogue and audio go on the right. While this certainly is only one way of conveying a message, it is the most effective and popular way to sell a product or communicate a message.

Corporate Programs

If you're producing a short format program to convey a business-to-business message or a business-to-consumer message, the two-column format is most appropriate because it helps clients who don't have a significant background in film or video. They can easily understand the connection between what is heard and what is seen. Also, the two-column format allows for making changes to the first drafts of your script, and ultimately makes it easier to produce.

Commercials

If you're producing a commercial, the two-column format is ideal for the same reasons explained in the preceding paragraph. Ad agencies and their customers pay thousands upon thousands of dollars for broadcast time, and many believe you have to stuff each spot with tons of information and images. A lot happens in most ten-, twenty-, or thirty-second commercials, and often most of the images are supported by a narration. It seems like some commercials have more scenes than full-length features. For these reasons, the two-column format allows everyone, even the graphic artists and editors, to know what is happening every second, if not every frame. Just be sure not to use too much video jargon; you want to make your script easy to understand for your clients.

Take a look at the following sample script page to see how to format the two-column AV script.

> **"I've found over the years that working with corporate clients requires a deep knowledge of their business goals and their market—you need to know what they are currently saying to their audience and, more importantly, how they are saying it. As far as the format for a corporate script is concerned, it seems that most clients prefer a script that clearly connects every word or phrase with a specific visual description. For those new to scriptwriting, the most important piece of advice I can offer is pretty simple—just because it sounds good on paper doesn't necessarily mean it will translate to film or video or will be understood when heard by the audience. So, read the script out loud and imagine how it will look if you had the same background and knowledge base as the target audience."**
>
> —Kurt Lex Angermeier, Writer, Panoptic Media

AUDIO/VIDEO SCRIPT

Include your company's information on the left.

Double-space information in header. Include client and project information on right.

ALL WORLD MEDIA	CLIENT: Baby Paper Products
2222 Ninth St.	PRODUCT: Happy Heinies
New York, NY 10000	TITLE: ''Christmas Diapers''
(212) 555-1111	LENGTH: 45 Seconds

Separate the header of the script and the body with a line break.

VIDEO:	AUDIO:
OPEN WITH A FROWNING BABY IN A SANTA HAT AND CHRISTMAS OUTFIT.	MUSIC: (AWFUL SOUNDING VERSION OF ''SILENT NIGHT'')
	NARRATOR: Do you want your little loved one to have a soggy Christmas?
SHOW SHOT OF INEXPENSIVE SOGGY DIAPERS COMING APART ON BABY'S BOTTOM.	(A BABY STARTS WHINING AND CRY-ING UNCONTROLLABLY IN BACKGROUND)
SHOT OF SNOWFLAKES FALLING INTO A DIAPER	MUSIC: (''I'M DREAMING OF A WHITE CHRISTMAS'')
	NARRATOR: Or a happy white Christmas?
SHOT OF SMILING BABY, FOLLOWED BY SHOT OF A CLEAN, WHITE, DRY STURDY DIAPER ON BABY'S BOTTOM	(BABY GOO-GOOS HAPPILY.)
SHOT OF UGLY YELLOW DIAPER JUXTAPOSED WITH CLEAN WHITE DIAPER	NARRATOR: It's up to you, mom and dad.
SHOT OF HAPPY BABY HOLDING HAPPY HEINIES PACKAGE	NARRATOR: This holiday season, make the right choice.
FADE OUT.	

Music directions are in all caps.

Narration and dialogue is in upper- and lower-case text, double-spaced.

Video directions are in all caps.

Sound comments and direction (other than narration) go in parentheses and are in all caps.

Indicates this script is finished.

Video always goes on the left side of the page, audio on the right. Notice the audio directions begin on the same line as the last line of the video directions.

CHAPTER TEN

THE PLAY SCRIPT

The Stage Play

Structure

Most plays contain one, two or three acts (some even have four or five acts), depending on what the playwright deems is the most appropriate length for what he or she is trying to accomplish. Using the following formatting specifics, plan on about one minute per page when performed out loud. Script lengths are generally 90 pages for a three-act play (30 pages per act), 100 to 105 pages for a two-act play (50 to 52 pages per act), and 20 to 50 pages for a one-act play.

Despite the number of acts and pages a play possesses, all plays should follow the basic "dramatic structure" and have three overarching movements—a beginning, a middle and an end. Here's a rough sketch of what the overall dramatic structure of your play should look like, as outlined in Jeffrey Hatcher's *The Art & Craft of Playwrighting* (Writer's Digest Books):

Part One (15-30 percent of the play)

Start of Play.
Introduction of characters, place, time, setting or exposition.
Introduction of the primary inciting event.
Initial point of attack or primary conflict.
Introduction of the central dramatic question.

Part Two (50-75 percent of the play)

Characters embark on journey/struggle/search for answers/goals.
Conflicts with other characters, events, circumstances.
Characters reassess situations, respond to obstacles and challenges, plan new tactics, succeed, fail, attack, retreat, surprise and are surprised, encounter major reversals (rising action).
A crisis is reached.
Characters embark on an action that will resolve the crisis and lead inexorably to the conclusion.

Part Three (5-25 percent of the play)

The major characters or combatants engage in a final conflict (climax).
The characters' goal is achieved or lost.
The central dramatic question is answered.
The actions suggest the themes or ideas of the play.
Following the climax is the resolution, in which a new order is established.
End of Play

The Title Page

The title should be in all caps, centered, about one-third of the way down the page. Drop four lines and type (depending on what you write) either "A One-Act Play by," or "A Play in Two Acts by" or "A Play in Three Acts by." Drop four lines again and type your name (if your play is written with another person use an ampersand between your names). Also, if your play is based on a novel, drop six lines and type "Based on the novel *Novel's Title*," drop two more lines and type "by Author's Name." In the lower right-hand corner, put your name, address and phone number, single-spaced, in regular text (not all caps). If you have an agent, type "Representation:," skip a line and put the agent's name, address and phone number instead of yours.

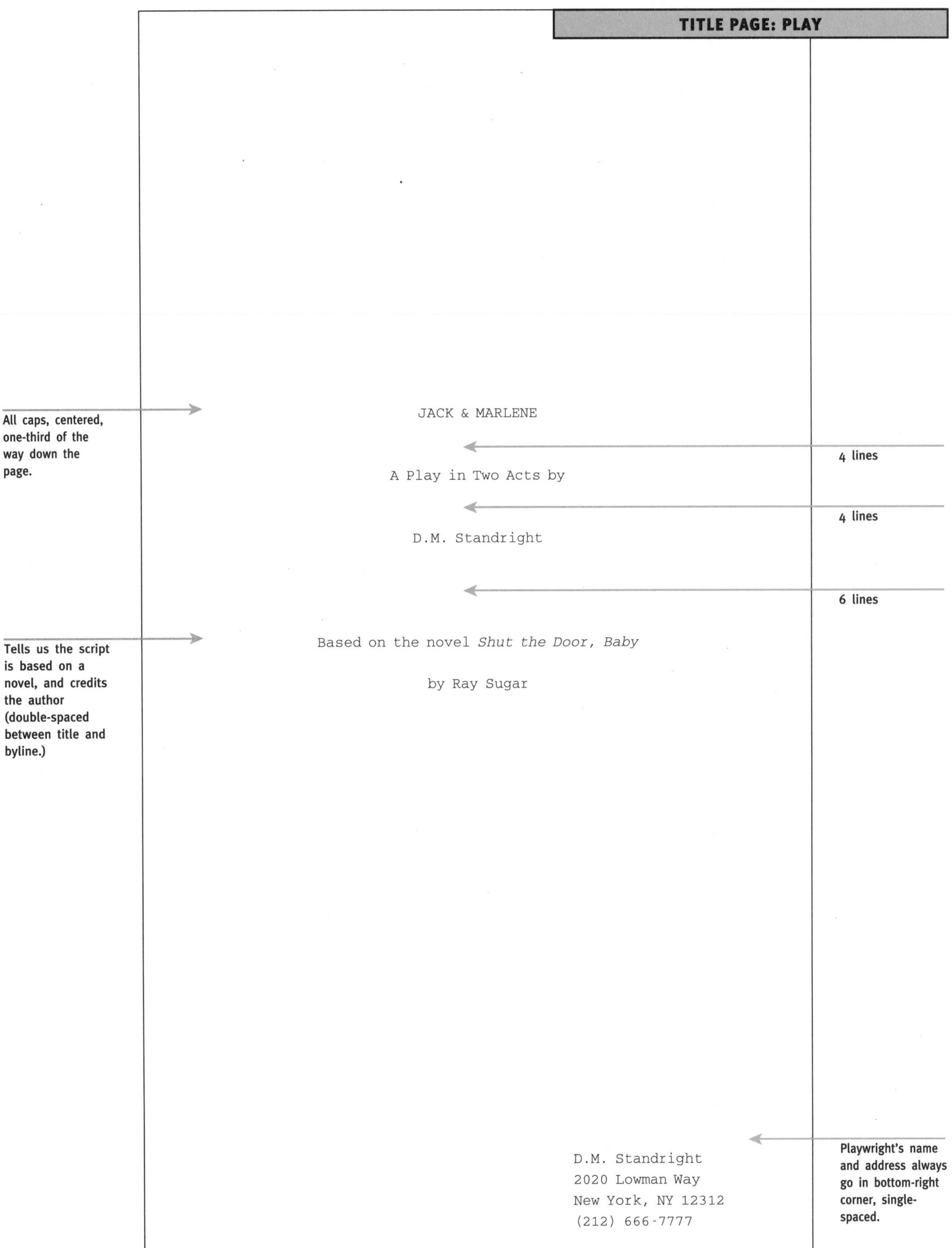
TITLE PAGE: PLAY
JACK & MARLENE
A Play in Two Acts by
D.M. Standright
Based on the novel Shut the Door, Baby
by Ray Sugar
D.M. Standright
2020 Lowman Way
New York, NY 12312
(212) 666-7777
All caps, centered, one-third of the way down the page.
4 lines
4 lines
6 lines
Tells us the script is based on a novel, and credits the author (double-spaced between title and byline.)
Playwright's name and address always go in bottom-right corner, single-spaced.

Act and Scene Breakdown Page

After the title page comes the act and scene breakdown page listing the acts and scenes. Number this page (and the first three introductory pages detailed later) with a lowercase Roman numeral i, four lines from the top of the page, flush with the right margin. Drop four lines and type the play's title in all caps, underlined and centered. Drop four more lines below the title, and on the left margin (about 1″) type "ACT ONE" in all caps, followed by a series of ellipses that move across the page to where you describe the day and date of the act. Do this for each subsequent act, triple-spacing between each line. If Act One is divided into two scenes, then the first line of the page breakdown reads ACT ONE: Scene One, followed by the series of ellipses. Scene Two appears two lines beneath the first line and looks the same.

On the left margin, 1″ from the bottom of the page, include the approximate running time of the play. The words RUNNING TIME: should be in all caps and on the next line the play's time length, including the number of intermissions.

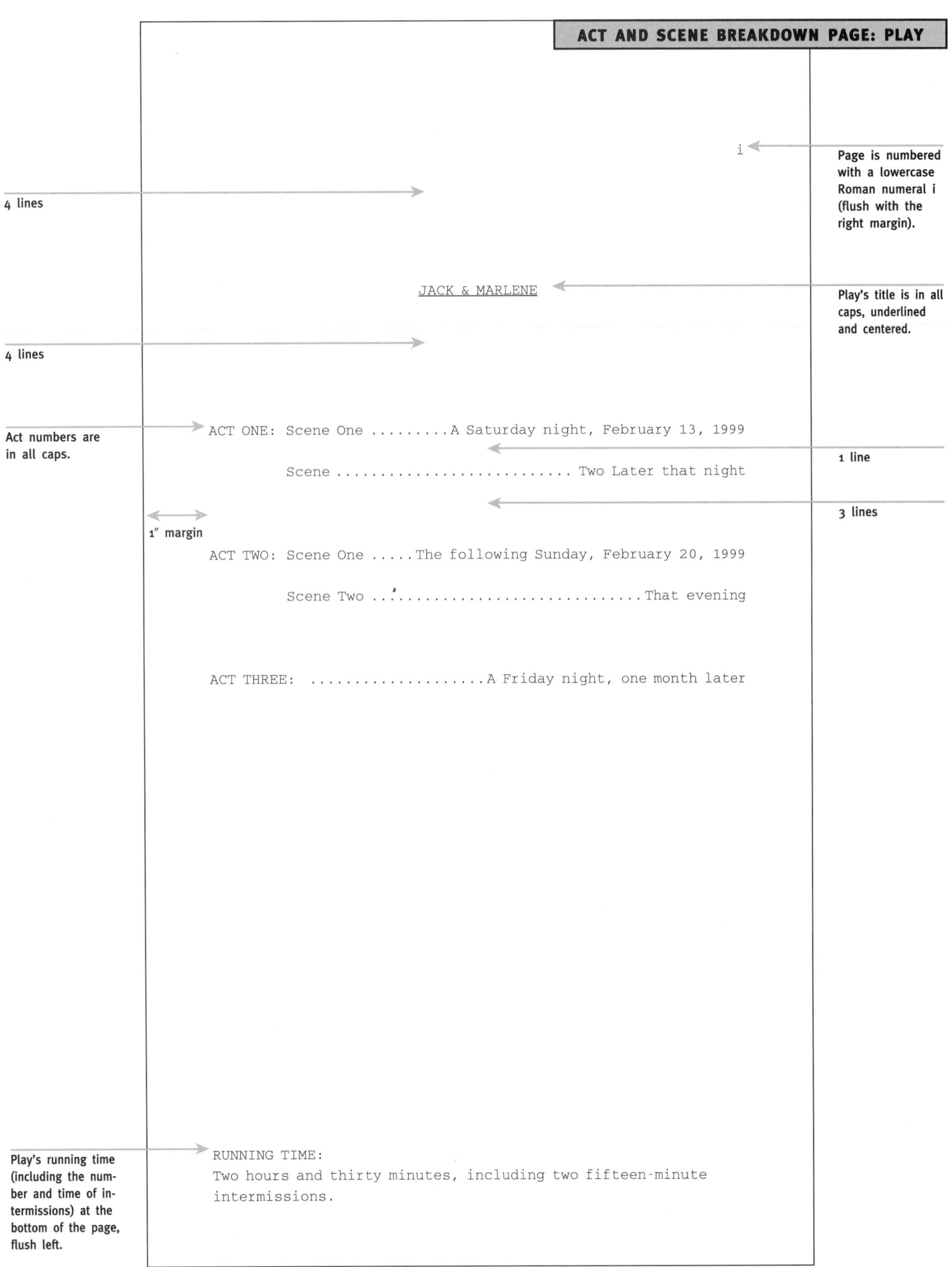
ACT AND SCENE BREAKDOWN PAGE: PLAY
i
Page is numbered with a lowercase Roman numeral i (flush with the right margin).
4 lines
JACK & MARLENE
Play's title is in all caps, underlined and centered.
4 lines
Act numbers are in all caps.
ACT ONE: Scene One ....A Saturday night, February 13, 1999
1 line
Scene .... Two Later that night
3 lines
1" margin
ACT TWO: Scene One .....The following Sunday, February 20, 1999
Scene Two ....That evening
ACT THREE: ....A Friday night, one month later
Play's running time (including the number and time of intermissions) at the bottom of the page, flush left.
RUNNING TIME:
Two hours and thirty minutes, including two fifteen-minute intermissions.

Cast of Characters Page

The cast of characters page follows the act and scene breakdown page, and of course provides information about your characters. This page should have the Roman numeral ii in the top right corner flush with the right margin. The words CAST OF CHARACTERS should be in all caps, centered, eight lines from the top of the page. Drop four lines and include each character's name; follow each name with a series of ellipses and a brief description of that character. Both the name and the description should be in all caps. The character descriptions can be simple or elaborate—whatever you think you need to include. Below the primary characters' names you can list the secondary characters who have few to no lines but will appear on the stage sometime throughout the play.

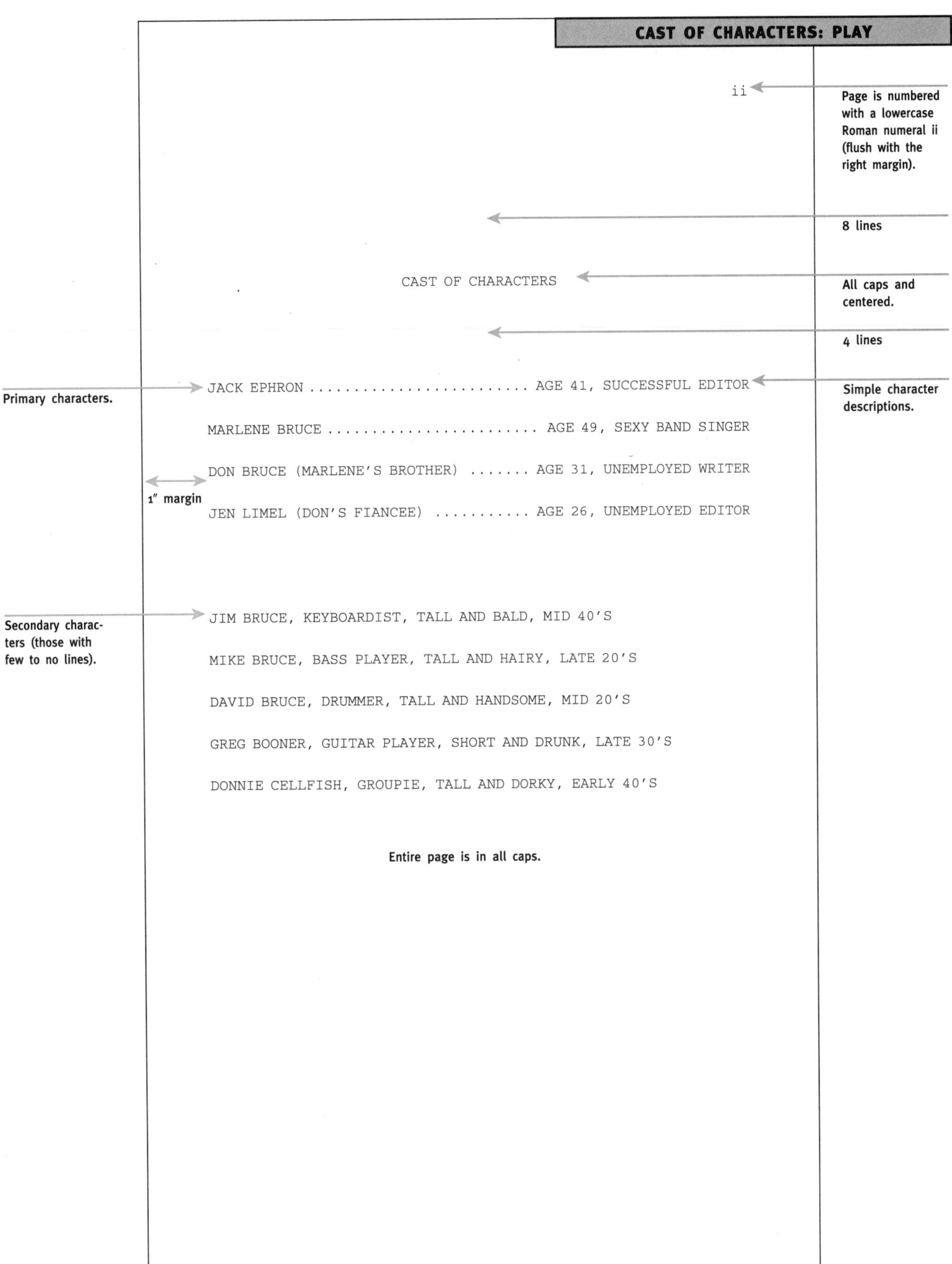
CAST OF CHARACTERS: PLAY
ii
Page is numbered with a lowercase Roman numeral ii (flush with the right margin).
8 lines
CAST OF CHARACTERS
All caps and centered.
4 lines
Primary characters.
JACK EPHRON .... AGE 41, SUCCESSFUL EDITOR
Simple character descriptions.
MARLENE BRUCE .... AGE 49, SEXY BAND SINGER
DON BRUCE (MARLENE'S BROTHER) .... AGE 31, UNEMPLOYED WRITER
1" margin
JEN LIMEL (DON'S FIANCEE) .... AGE 26, UNEMPLOYED EDITOR
Secondary characters (those with few to no lines).
JIM BRUCE, KEYBOARDIST, TALL AND BALD, MID 40'S
MIKE BRUCE, BASS PLAYER, TALL AND HAIRY, LATE 20'S
DAVID BRUCE, DRUMMER, TALL AND HANDSOME, MID 20'S
GREG BOONER, GUITAR PLAYER, SHORT AND DRUNK, LATE 30'S
DONNIE CELLFISH, GROUPIE, TALL AND DORKY, EARLY 40'S
Entire page is in all caps.

The Setting Page

The setting page details the setting of the play (you will also need to use a short setting description at the beginning of each scene) and is the last of your introductory pages (numbered page iii). The word SETTING: appears in all caps, underlined, flush with the left margin, about eight lines from the top of the page. Tab 1½″ from the left margin and begin the body of your description on the same line. Type the setting information in all caps or regular text, double-spaced. The sample on page 223 uses all caps.

Note: Some playwrights like to put the cast of characters and the setting on the same page, with the setting on the top of the page and the cast of characters below it.

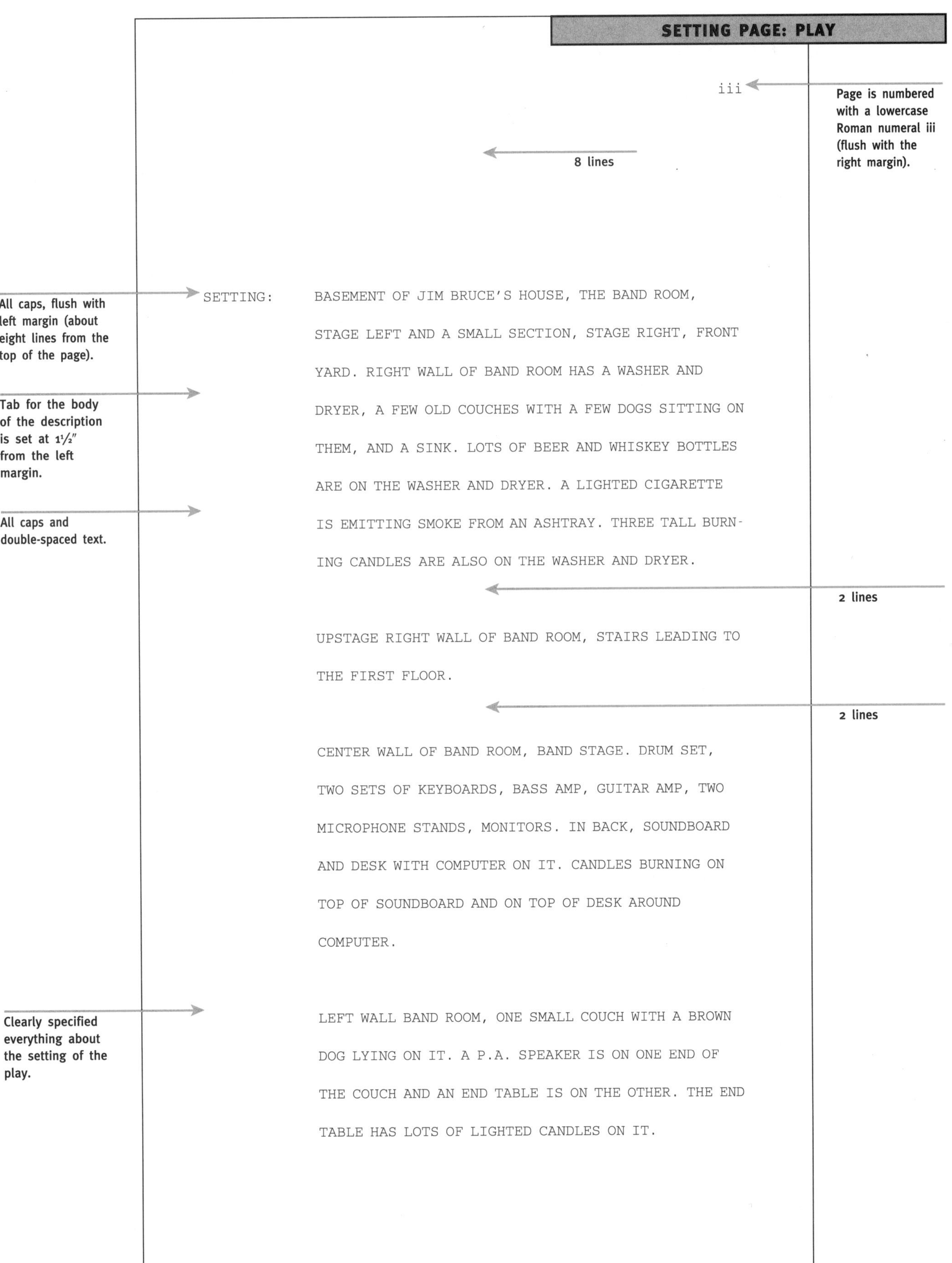
SETTING PAGE: PLAY
iii
Page is numbered with a lowercase Roman numeral iii (flush with the right margin).
8 lines
All caps, flush with left margin (about eight lines from the top of the page).
SETTING:
BASEMENT OF JIM BRUCE'S HOUSE, THE BAND ROOM, STAGE LEFT AND A SMALL SECTION, STAGE RIGHT, FRONT YARD. RIGHT WALL OF BAND ROOM HAS A WASHER AND DRYER, A FEW OLD COUCHES WITH A FEW DOGS SITTING ON THEM, AND A SINK. LOTS OF BEER AND WHISKEY BOTTLES ARE ON THE WASHER AND DRYER. A LIGHTED CIGARETTE IS EMITTING SMOKE FROM AN ASHTRAY. THREE TALL BURNING CANDLES ARE ALSO ON THE WASHER AND DRYER.
Tab for the body of the description is set at 1½" from the left margin.
All caps and double-spaced text.
2 lines
UPSTAGE RIGHT WALL OF BAND ROOM, STAIRS LEADING TO THE FIRST FLOOR.
2 lines
CENTER WALL OF BAND ROOM, BAND STAGE. DRUM SET, TWO SETS OF KEYBOARDS, BASS AMP, GUITAR AMP, TWO MICROPHONE STANDS, MONITORS. IN BACK, SOUNDBOARD AND DESK WITH COMPUTER ON IT. CANDLES BURNING ON TOP OF SOUNDBOARD AND ON TOP OF DESK AROUND COMPUTER.
LEFT WALL BAND ROOM, ONE SMALL COUCH WITH A BROWN DOG LYING ON IT. A P.A. SPEAKER IS ON ONE END OF THE COUCH AND AN END TABLE IS ON THE OTHER. THE END TABLE HAS LOTS OF LIGHTED CANDLES ON IT.
Clearly specified everything about the setting of the play.

The Script Pages

After the introductory pages comes the play script itself. The first page is numbered with the Arabic numeral 1. On this first page of the play, center the play's title in all caps, eight lines from the top of the page. Double-space after the title and put the words Act One in upper and lowercase, centered and underlined. Double-space again and put the scene number in upper and lowercase (Scene One). Skip four lines and begin the scene description/introduction, which should just be a few double-spaced lines that describe and set up the scene.

Dialogue

Following the scene description, double-space and begin the dialogue. Formatting the dialogue is simple. The speaking character's name appears in all caps, flush left and followed by a colon. Then begin the text of the dialogue. When the dialogue runs more than one line, indent five spaces (just use your tab button). The dialogue should be in regular text (not all caps) and single-spaced.

Parentheticals

Parentheticals include description, expression or direction that helps the actor or director know what you intend. There are two types of parentheticals in playwrighting:

1. A parenthetical that appears within the dialogue lines. When the direction indicates an action or emotion to occur while the character is speaking, the parenthetical is put in lines of dialogue. If the parenthetical is used to signal the character's mood or delivery, it is placed between the character's name and the first word of dialogue. All the text is lowercase.

2. A parenthetical that falls between or outside of spoken lines. When there are more detailed directions (often physical directions), the parenthetical will be set apart from the dialogue by a triple-space, and the text will have the same indented margins as the dialogue (beginning 5 spaces in from the left margin). The text is both upper and lowercase, and is single-spaced within the parenthetical. Triple-space to go back to dialogue.

Note: When a character's name is used in a parenthetical it should appear in all caps, and when a character enters a room both the character's name and the word ENTERS should appear in all caps.

The Act Ending

To end an act simply type "*Curtain Falls*" (italicize or underline it), centered, at the bottom of the page.

PLAY SCRIPT

1.

Page number with Arabic numeral 1.

Play's title, centered and in all caps.

JACK & MARLENE

1 line

Act One

Act number goes in upper and lowercase, centered and underlined.

1 line

Scene One

Scene number is in upper and lowercase (not underlined).

1 line

A PURPLE LIGHT SHINES ON WASHER AND DRYER. THE BAND BEGINS PLAYING IN THE PITCH DARK, CENTER STAGE. JACK, DON AND JEN ENTER FROM THE STEPS. A BRIGHT FLOOD OF RED LIGHTS SHINES DOWN ON MARLENE. SHE STARTS TO SING.

Briefly describes the setting for this scene.

Character cue is in all caps, flush with left margin, followed by a colon.

MARLENE:(looks up from her microphone, notices JACK in the room. She stops singing and screams) Ahhhh! Oh my God. You must be Jack.

(the music stops)

1″ margin

JIM: So Marlene, are you ready to put a bag over your head yet?

JACK: (laughing nervously, looks at MARLENE) So I guess I shouldn't ask you to marry me yet. I'll wait a few hours. (everybody laughs, JACK takes a sip of beer and looks at MARLENE)I'm just teasing of course. It is good to finally meet you.

Dialogue is single-spaced (double-spaced when a new person starts to speak).

When the dialogue runs more than one line, indent five spaces.

MARLENE: It's good to meet you, too.

JACK: Thanks. Well, you can go back to singing now. We'll just watch.

Character's name in a parenthetical appears in all caps.

(JACK walks over to the washer and dryer and starts talking with DON and JEN. The band starts up again. MARLENE begins to sing. JACK stops talking and stares at MARLENE, transfixed by her voice, her lips on the microphone and her radiating beauty.)

Parenthetical within the dialogue lines—signals the character's mood or delivery.

Parenthetical falls outside of spoken lines—more detailed directions (often physical).

JACK: (glowing with delight, yells over the music to DON and JEN) Wow. I am blown away. My God, you guys didn't tell me she was so sexy, so lively.
(They watch the band play the rest of the song. The music stops, DON, JEN and JACK clap.)

JACK: (impressed, looking in the general direction of the band) That was great. Really. (focuses in on MARLENE, smiles) A real treat.

MARLENE: (blushing) Well thank you.

(MARLENE moves from behind the microphone, stares at JACK and then walks up the steps. Stage goes black.)

Curtain Falls

Lets us know the act is finished.

Once Your Play Is Finished

When your play is finished you need to begin marketing it, which might take longer than writing it. Before you begin marketing it, however, have your script bound (two brads and a cover are fine) and copyrighted with the Copyright Office of the Library of Congress, or registered with the Writers Guild of America (7000 W. Third St., Los Angeles, CA 90048-4329, [323] 951-4000). Write either agency and ask for information and an application.

Your first goals will be to at least get a reading of your play. You might be lucky and get a small production. Community theaters or smaller regional houses are good places to start. Volunteer at a local theater. You will get a sense of how a theater operates, the various elements that go into presenting a play, and what can and cannot be done physically as well as dramatically. Personal contacts cannot be overemphasized. Get to know the literary manager or artistic director of local theaters, which is the best way to get your script considered for production. Find out about any playwrights groups in your area through local theaters or the drama departments of nearby colleges and universities. Use your creativity to connect with people who might be able to push your work.

Contests can be a good way to get noticed. Many playwrighting contests offer as a prize at least a staged reading and often a full production. Once you've had a reading or workshop production, set your sights on a small production. Use this as a learning experience.

Seeing your play on stage can help you view it more objectively and give you the chance to correct any flaws or inconsistencies. Incorporate into your revisions any comments and ideas from the actors, director or even audience members. Use a small production as a marketing tool—keep track of all the press reviews and any interviews you give.

After you've been produced on a small scale, you can take your play in several directions. You can aim for a larger commercial production; you can try to get it published; or you can seek an artistic grant. (Choosing one direction does not rule out pursuing others at the same time.) Once you have successfully pursued at least one of those avenues, look for an agent. *The Dramatists Sourcebook*, published annually by Theatre Communications Group (355 Lexington Ave., New York, NY 10017), lists opportunities in all these areas. The Dramatist Guild (234 W. Forty-fifth St., New York, NY 10036) has three helpful publications: a bimonthly newsletter with articles, news and up-to-date information and opportunities; a quarterly journal; and an annual directory that lists theaters, agents, workshops, grants and contests.

To submit your play to larger theaters you'll need to put together a submission package. This will include a one-page query letter briefly describing the play to the literary manager or dramaturg. Mention any reviews and give the number of cast members and sets. You should also send a two- to three-page synopsis, a ten-page sample of the most interesting section of your play, your resume and your press kit. Be sure not to send your complete manuscript to anyone until it is requested. For more on querying and submitting, please see pages 109-110 in Novels and page 172 in Submitting Your Screenplay to an Agent or Production Company.

Automatic Formatting Software Programs

Fortunately for scriptwriters, there are several highly competitive stand-alone and add-on software programs to help format scripts. All will save you time, all will make your writing easier and most work on both Macs and PCs. They don't take up much disk space on your hard drive, either. You should also be able to download a demo of the product from the retailer's Web site (don't buy unless you try). Find out more about these programs by contacting the developer directly, checking the individual Web sites or speaking with the people at The Writer's Computer Store (11317 Santa Monica Blvd., Los Angeles, CA 90025, [800] 272-8927 or [310] 479-7774, www.writerscomputerstore.com). Without further adieu, we will now break up these programs into their stand-alone and add-on camps, define the differences between these two types of script-aides, and offer information about each program.

Stand-Alone Programs

A stand-alone script processor does it all, all by itself—formatting, paginating, indexing, spell-checking and other chores. You do not need a word processing program to run a stand-alone program. Essentially, it works without a word processor and requires just a few keystroke commands from you and minimal hardware space from your computer. Most programs cost about the same ($250-$300), and all offer screenplay, sitcom and stage play formats. While there are individual differences among them, they all make writing scripts and organizing ideas unbelievably easy.

FINAL DRAFT (Final Draft, Inc., 16000 Ventura Blvd., Suite 800, Encino, CA 91436, [310] 636-4711, www.finaldraft.com) Final Draft offers formatting capabilities for screenplays, sitcoms or stage plays. The enter and tab keys can handle most of the commands in Final Draft. You can easily change your script from one format to another (just in case you write a sitcom but change your mind and want to turn it into a screenplay). Final Draft imports and exports scripts in both ASCII and RTF, and will export to Movie Magic Scheduling. One problem with Final Draft is that when cutting and pasting text from another program in Windows, Final Draft changes everything into all caps. However, this doesn't happen when importing an RTF file. Final Draft offers an outline view and an index card view, as well as a great spell-checker and thesaurus. For an additional twenty-five dollars or so, you can get an add-on program for television scripts that provides character names and formatting specs for many shows airing today. Manual included.

MOVIE MAGIC SCREENWRITER (Screenplay Systems, 150 E. Olive Ave., Suite 203, Burbank, CA 91502, [800] 847-8679, www.screenplay.com)

Movie Magic Screenwriter is perhaps the king of software formatting programs (Screenplay Systems was first to develop scriptwriting software, back in 1983). It offers formatting for screenplays, sitcoms, stage plays and multimedia scripts. You can do almost all your work with the tab and enter keys. You get a spell-checker, a thesaurus and a Character Name Bank containing thousands of names (in case you need some). Perhaps the most impressive part of Screenwriter is its electronic index card system that lets you build your script scene by scene. The program also controls your script length. All production features (revisions, breakdown sheets, tagging for export to Movie Magic Scheduling) are in one menu. Screenwriter also includes templates with preset margins, sets, character lists and script styles for the most television shows on the air. And it by far has the best manual of all scriptwriting programs (good technical support, too). Foreign-language dictionaries are also available for Screenwriter (Danish, Dutch, French, German, Italian, Norwegian, Spanish, Swedish or UK English).

ScriptThing (Script Perfection Enterprises, Inc., 4901 Morena Blvd., Suite 105, San Diego, CA 92117, [800] 450-9450, www.scriptthing.com)

ScriptThing is similar in terms of quality and features to Movie Magic's Screenwriter. It provides formats for motion pictures, taped sitcoms, filmed sitcoms, stage plays and multimedia scripts. You also are treated to some neat animation features. ScriptThing is easy to use (tab and enter are the two basic buttons you'll need), plays your multimedia scripts in real time, and is very mouse-friendly. The index card feature excels. You also get all the numbering and revision features included in other programs.

ScriptThing comes with a Wizard that helps you use all the program's features. You can import and export seamlessly with ScriptThing, leaving all your initial formatting in tact. In addition, ScriptThing comes with format templates for over fifty current television shows. Manual and production bible included.

Foreign-language dictionaries are available for ScriptThing that check spelling in Danish, Dutch, French, German, Italian, Norwegian, Spanish, Swedish or UK English.

ScriptWare (Cinovation, Inc., 1750 Thirtieth St., Suite 360, Boulder, CO 80301-1005, [800] 788-7090, www.scriptware.com)

ScriptWare stands out because it is the only software program with two-column AV formatting features. It also has formatting capabilities for screenplays, television shows, sitcoms and stage plays. ScriptWare created *Scriptype*, the interface now copied by most other programs—it keeps track of and fixes all margin changes, spacing changes, capitalization and punctuation. All you need to do is control the tab and enter keys. ScriptWare takes care of page breaks and scene and page numbering. You can create scene cards that let you rearrange your scenes in index card mode. ScriptWare has a clear and uncluttered menu and a functional navigation bar with speed buttons. You can export and import a range of files, too. The program's thesaurus and spell-checker are excellent. You also get the best available telephone support with ScriptWare.

Add-On Script Processors Add-on programs complement your existing word processing software (usually MS Word). Essentially, they are a bundle of macros that help your word processor process scripts. Add-ons are less expensive than the stand-alone programs listed above ($80-$175). If you regularly use your word processor and don't have much money to spend on formatting programs, an add-on is a good choice. That said, you should know that add-ons become outdated much sooner than stand-alone programs (if you upgrade your word processing software, you'll likely need to upgrade your add-on, too).

ScriptWerx (Parnassus Software, Oak Tree Press, 256 Guinea Hill Rd., Slate Hill, NY 10973, [914] 355-1400, www.originalvision.com/scriptwerx.html)

You must have Microsoft Word 6.0 or above to use ScriptWerx, which has twelve add-on templates, including feature film, live sitcom, taped sitcom and corporate video. Each template has its own set of tool bar buttons and commands that appear under a single ScriptWerx tab on Word's menu. Most formatting can be done with the enter, shift, alt and tab keys. The program can build lists of characters and locations. ScriptWerx will take care of scene numbering and basic revision. The manual is user-friendly. There's no on-line help for ScriptWerx within Word.

Script Wizard (Stefani Warren & Associates, 1517 Hillside Dr., The Woodlands, Glendale, CA 91208, [818] 500-7283, www.warrenassoc.com)

If you like working in Word 6.0 or later and you have Windows 95 or higher, you will probably appreciate Script Wizard. The program offers twelve formatting templates for screenplays, sitcoms, A/V scripts, radio scripts, soaps, interactive projects and variety award shows, and it also has most of the features found in a stand-alone program. Most work in Script Wizard can be done using control, shift and alt key combinations. Script Wizard is one of the few programs to format a series of shots (montages). It has scene numbering and revision features for shooting scripts. You can create script notes and use Word's outline view to move scenes. A manual and a book called *An Introduction to Writing Scripts* are included, and on-line help is available in Word. You can also get a free disk that has two complete scripts and samples from a shooting script.

ScriptWright(Indelible Ink, 156 Fifth Ave., Suite 1208, New York, NY 10010, [212] 255-1956)

ScriptWright is compatible with Word and is designed to format only screenplays, but it does an excellent job. Once you install ScriptWright's own menus and help files, Word won't seem the same to you. Most of the formatting can be done with the enter, tab and alt keys, but the program offers a unique Smart Enter feature that lets you easily create short macros that'll save you keystrokes. ScriptWright comes equipped with a format check and outliner to make sure your script is in order. It will also automatically adjust your margins to keep your script at the right length. ScriptWright creates a scene breakdown and character report. You also can choose menu options to determine if you want to work only in script mode (without Word features) or if you want to work within Word with script features.

SideBySide(Simon Skill Systems, Box 2048, Rancho Santa Fe, CA 92067, [619] 756-0625, www.simon1.com)

SideBySide makes multicolumn scriptwriting in Word easy. It offers ten different multicolumn formats, including audio/visual, documentary, commercials, speech, storyboard, industrial and multimedia projects. SideBySide numbers pages, provides a word count and makes on-screen editing easy. You'll also find that SideBySide creates a narration script for you automatically. This is an ideal add-on for writers working with A/V formats.

Part Four

VERSE

CHAPTER ELEVEN

POETRY

Cover Letter

Submission Tips

Until recent years, most editors didn't expect or want cover letters along with a poetry submission; however, now many editors do specify that they want cover letters.

The best approach is to read a publication's listing in *Poet's Market* and/or to request a copy of its submission guidelines (see Request for Guidelines Letter on page 23).

If you do send a cover letter, it should be brief—no more than one page, and not a tightly packed one at that. The cover letter is not to sell the poetry, which should speak for itself. Rather, you should use it to:

- Introduce the work you're submitting (i.e., enclosed are three poems . . .).
- Introduce yourself by providing a brief biography that includes listings of some of your published work, if any, and your background, including occupation, hobbies, interests or other life events that have bearing on your work.
- Note why you think the poetry you're submitting would be appropriate for the publication (this gives you a chance to show familiarity with the publication, which is always a good idea).

If you are submitting previously published work or making simultaneous submissions, mention this in your cover letter, too, provided you already have ascertained that such submissions are acceptable to the publication.

Other Dos and Don'ts

- Don't ever request guidelines in the cover letter of your submission. It's too late at this point.
- Don't ask for criticism. You may get it, but it's not the editor's job to coach you.

COVER LETTER: POETRY

Susan Sturmundrang
43 Clovernook Place
Whittier, CA 90054
(310) 555-6700
Fax: (310) 555-6283
E-mail: ssturm@e.net

January 5, 2000

1 line

Addresses a specific editor.

Ben Alleski
Poetry Review
444 Canal St.
St. Louis, MO 55435

1 line

Dear Mr. Alleski:

1 line

Introduces the work being submitted.

Enclosed are five of my poems on a theme of alienation and rootlessness in modern culture, which I believe would fit well with your review's focus on modern cultural issues.

1 line between paragraphs.

Introduces the poet, including publication credits and relevant information.

My poetry has been published in a number of literary and general-interest magazines, including *The Atlantic Monthly* and *The New Yorker*. I teach English Literature at the University of California-Riverside and have spent most of my life wandering the country in search of a place to call home.

Notifies editor of simultaneous submissions.

I understand from your guidelines that simultaneous submissions are acceptable, and I wanted to let you know that I have submitted the enclosed poems to two other publications for which I also believe they are appropriate.

Single-spaced text

Thanks very much for your time and consideration. I look forward to hearing from you.

Best wishes,

Signature

Susan Sturmundrang

Notes enclosure.

Encl.: SASE

Poem Submission

Submission Tips

In poetry above all other forms, substance supersedes format. Your submissions should be neat and correspond to the rules of the genre. You don't get any points for fancy fonts or colored paper. In fact, your submission is likely to be viewed less favorably if you garnish it in such ways.

The best approach is to read a publication's listing in *Poet's Market* and/or to request a copy of its submission guidelines (see Request for Guidelines Letter on page 23).

Generally, submit three to five poems at a time, though some editors prefer seven or more poems if they feature a poet. Again, the publication's guidelines will help here.

Formatting Specs

- Use standard white bond, laser or ink-jet paper.
- Submit each poem on a separate page, except for haiku.
- Center a title in all caps above the poem.
- Put your name, address and phone number(s) (and E-mail, if applicable) in the upper left corner.
- Fold the poems together into thirds for insertion into the envelope. Fold the cover letter separately and place it on top of the poems.
- If your poem continues over to a second sheet, start the second page with a new stanza whenever possible or applicable.
- Editor preferences vary on whether submissions should be double- or single-spaced. Check the publication's guidelines. Unless otherwise directed, single-space.
- Capitalize the beginning of each line, flush left.
- If the line of poetry extends beyond the margin, indent the second line. If you are double-spacing the entire poem, single-space the continuation of a line.
- Put in an extra space (or two, when double-spacing) before the beginning of a stanza.
- Margins will vary, depending on the poem, but generally run at least 2″-2½″ on the sides, with the poem roughly centered top to bottom on the page.
- If you don't use a cover letter, find out if the publication wants biographical information and include such information on a separate sheet under the centered, capitalized heading "BIOGRAPHICAL INFORMATION" or "ABOUT THE POET."
- For a second sheet, use a header (generally, the title or your last name) in the top left corner and a page number in the top right corner.
- Paper clip pages of the same poem together, but submit one-page poems loose-leaf, folded.

Other Dos and Don'ts

- Do enclose an SASE, which makes it easier for the editor to respond.
- Don't handwrite your poems.
- Don't use onion skin, colored or erasable paper.
- Don't put copyright symbols or information on your poem. It's copyrighted

regardless of this, and the only thing you're likely to accomplish is to insult the editor's intelligence or intentions.

- Do address your submission and cover letter, if any, by name to the poetry editor or other editor who routinely reviews poetry submission.
- Don't submit previously published work or make simultaneous submissions unless you know the publication accepts them and you note it in a cover letter.

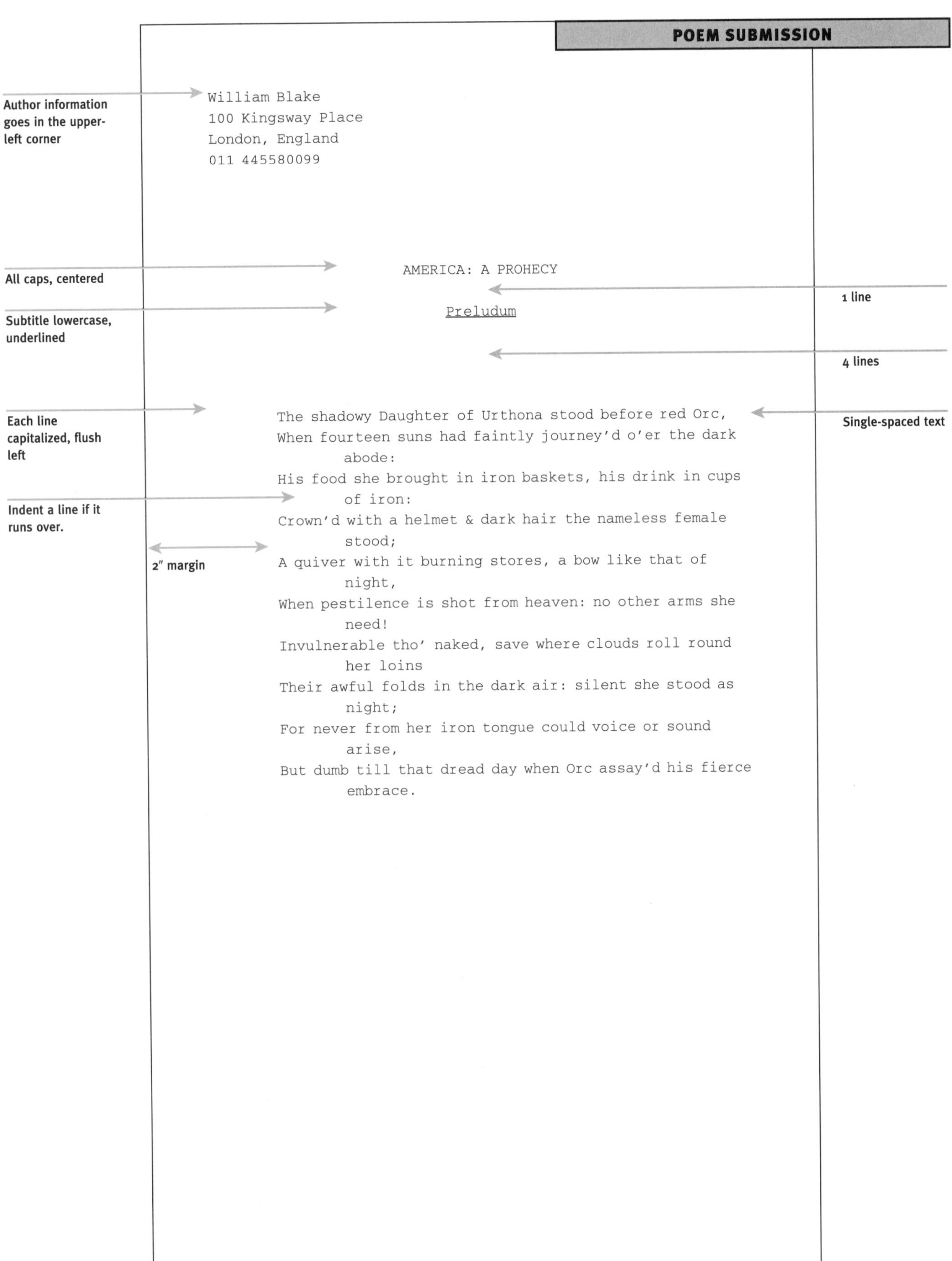
POEM SUBMISSION
Author information goes in the upper-left corner
William Blake
100 Kingsway Place
London, England
011 445580099
All caps, centered
AMERICA: A PROHECY
1 line
Subtitle lowercase, underlined
Preludum
4 lines
Each line capitalized, flush left
Single-spaced text
The shadowy Daughter of Urthona stood before red Orc,
When fourteen suns had faintly journey'd o'er the dark abode:
His food she brought in iron baskets, his drink in cups of iron:
Indent a line if it runs over.
Crown'd with a helmet & dark hair the nameless female stood;
2" margin
A quiver with it burning stores, a bow like that of night,
When pestilence is shot from heaven: no other arms she need!
Invulnerable tho' naked, save where clouds roll round her loins
Their awful folds in the dark air: silent she stood as night;
For never from her iron tongue could voice or sound arise,
But dumb till that dread day when Orc assay'd his fierce embrace.

CHAPTER TWELVE

GREETING CARDS

Greeting Cards

Submission Tips

The extremely short form of greeting card verse, concepts and gags doesn't leave much room for formatting worries. They can be submitted on anything from 3″ × 5″ cards to standard sheets of paper or electronically. The preferences of various markets vary, so contact the company and receive a copy of its submission guidelines.

Writer's Market and *Poet's Market* are good sources for contacts at a variety of specialty and niche players. The larger companies, such as Hallmark, American Greetings and Gibson Greetings, are reluctant to issue open invitations for submissions, though you can call these companies for submission information.

The basic format is similar to that for verse, in that text is centered on the page or card. Also, include your name, address and phone number on each submission.

Formatting Specs

- Center each line on the page or card.
- Margins are irrelevant for most submissions, but for versions with longer blocks of copy, follow the guidelines for poetry, with margins of at least 2″ on the side and the verse roughly centered vertically on the page.
- Capitalize or boldface the first line, then put the second line in regular up-and-down format or italicize. It doesn't matter what scheme you develop, as long as it's consistent.
- Submit one greeting card idea per page or card.
- Single-space when a line of verse needs to run on to a new line of the page. Double-space between lines of verse.
- Include a brief cover letter detailing how many card ideas you've submitted and why you think they're appropriate for the line.
- In the cover letter, mention if you are making simultaneous submissions.
- If you have illustrations or illustration ideas, outline them on a separate sheet clipped to the verse manuscript.
- Enclose an SASE for editors to respond, but make your submissions disposable. It's cheaper and easier to print them over again from your computer than it is to keep recycling paper versions.

Other Dos and Don'ts

- Do address your submission and cover letter to the appropriate contact person whenever possible.
- Do get submission guidelines in writing (using a letter similar to the Request for Guidelines Letter on page 23) whenever they're available before you submit. Preferences vary widely.
- Don't request guidelines in a cover letter along with submissions. Get the guidelines first.
- Don't make simultaneous submissions unless they're OK with the company.
- Do research the company and the line before you make your submission. When possible, visit the company's Web site and check out samples of its line in stores.
- Don't bother with putting a copyright on your submissions. They're copyrighted regardless, and the only thing you will accomplish is insulting the reader.

Electronic Submissions

Because of their brevity, greeting card verse and gags are ideal for electronic submissions. But many companies still aren't equipped to receive, track and process submissions via E-mail. Check submission guidelines or listings in *Writer's Market* and *Poet's Market* for details.

If you do submit electronically, your best bet will likely be a format similar to the print version modeled here. Essentially, your cover letter will be the E-mail, with the submission either following the letter text in the body of the E-mail message or as an attachment. If you are making several submissions, group them consecutively after the letter message or in a single attachment rather than creating the hassle of multiple attachments of very small files.

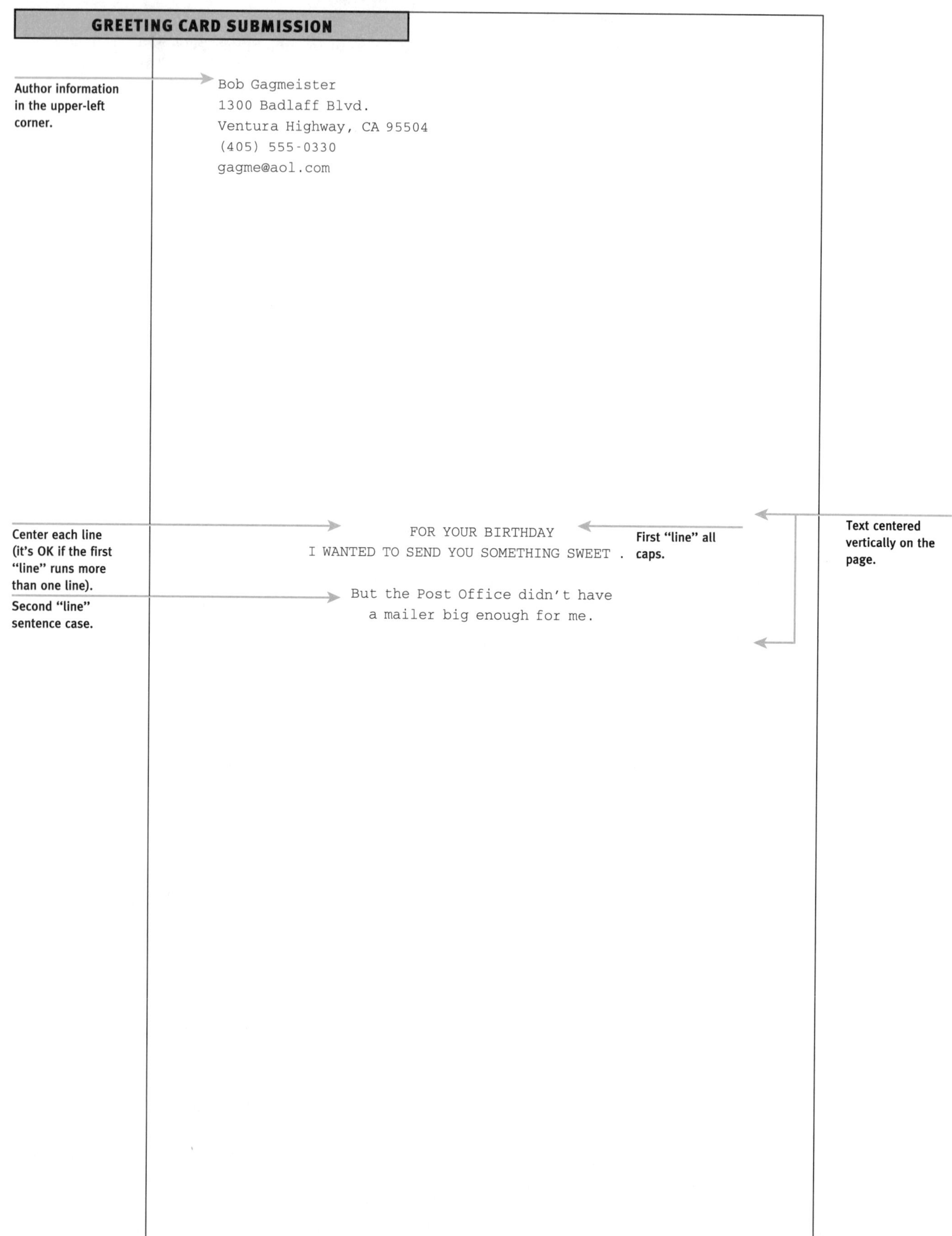
GREETING CARD SUBMISSION
Author information in the upper-left corner.
Bob Gagmeister
1300 Badlaff Blvd.
Ventura Highway, CA 95504
(405) 555-0330
gagme@aol.com
Center each line (it's OK if the first "line" runs more than one line).
FOR YOUR BIRTHDAY
I WANTED TO SEND YOU SOMETHING SWEET .
First "line" all caps.
Text centered vertically on the page.
Second "line" sentence case.
But the Post Office didn't have
a mailer big enough for me.

Appendix

Record Keeping and Forms

Some freelancers keep detailed forms tracking submissions of queries and manuscripts to publications and other markets. But the time required and paperwork generated by such efforts yields questionable value.

In the interests of saving time and forests, sensible use of your computer and other everyday records can eliminate need for tedious sets of specialized logs. With computer memory as cheap as it is today, there's no reason not to keep everything you do on your computer hard drive in perpetuity. The trick is simply organizing your hard drive in a way that will permit you to go back and grab the information when you need it. When all else fails, the Find feature found in the Start menu of Windows 95 or 98 or in the File Manager of Windows 3.1 will retrieve any information that eludes a quick browsing of your computer file folders.

The key is to keep the information you generate and back it up regularly. Even if you don't back up regularly and your hard drive crashes, the records you lose won't likely be as valuable as the time you would have wasted filling out logs. And you can usually retrieve most of the data from a stricken hard drive, anyway, with some professional help.

Following is an outline of the types of records you actually need and the most painless ways to keep them.

Submission Tracking Checklist

Your calendar/appointment book and computer should provide all the record keeping you need when it comes to queries and manuscript submissions. Here's all you need to do to track submissions:

- Keep a special folder or folders for queries, with file names descriptive enough that you'll be able to understand what they represent. When you need to keep up with how long it's been since you made a query, use the View menu of Windows to display your queries by date. A side benefit of saving your queries is having a ready supply of templates to use in creating new ones.
- Use a similar strategy for manuscript submissions by keeping a file of cover letters. If it's important to you to have a record of when a query or manuscript was accepted or rejected, the rights sold or the fee, make a notation on the query or cover letter file when you receive word.

Contact Tracking

It's a good idea to track contacts, either in the marketing or preparation of articles and books—but it's a bad idea to create mounds of paper to do this. The computer is the perfect place to keep such lists, which are constantly changing. Here are some tips on using your computer to track contacts:

- Keep files that make sense for you, such as a folder with magazine editors, book editors or editors in a particular specialized market where you work.
- Likewise, keep files of contacts for each project or a master file of all your contacts. Database programs were designed to keep this kind of information, but you may find it easier to store your contact list as a word processing file and use the find function to retrieve the names or other information you need.

Income and Expense Tracking Tips

You can track a variety of expenses several different ways. Regardless of whether you're reimbursed by a publisher for expenses, you'll need to track them for tax purposes. The IRS expects some kind of regular record-keeping system for both income and expenses, which can be through one of the many personal or professional accounting packages out there or a paper ledger system. You'll also need an auto mileage log if you use your car in your work, and you may need to log business and personal time on your computer or mobile phone to deduct equipment costs.

Here are a few tips to make tracking as pain-free as possible:

- For phone expenses, either arrange with your long-distance carrier for account codes (which is possible for all business and some home lines) or assign each publication/client to a particular carrier (for instance, your main line for your biggest market, 10-10-321 for another client, etc.).
- Keep a daily calendar or appointment book that shows what projects you're working on and who you called. You can check this against long-distance bills.
- Keep your appointment book along with your tax records each year to substantiate the business nature of long-distance calls and business use of your home office.
- If you use a personal computer for both business and personal use, keep a daily log of how many personal and business hours you spend on it. These numbers can be tallied at year-end for deduction purposes.
- If you use a mobile phone, get detailed billing, which will make the job of determining business and personal use much easier.
- Keep a separate checking account for business, and keep detailed records in your check register, recording the payer for checks you deposit and details of the expense for the checks. This can serve as a record-keeping system—or at least allow you to construct one at year-end—if you don't want a more elaborate system.

Forms, Forms, Forms

There are still a few paper forms that you will need from time to time. They include permission forms for using copyrighted material, model contracts and agreements, and release forms for photographic subjects. (Note: You don't need the latter for photojournalism-type shots in public places, but you do need these for models or when using a photograph in a home or on private property.)

Note, too, that while it always helps to have a contract or a form, many articles are written without them. You can generally write articles safely without a formal contract, and the risk is relatively slight. If you're worried, however, it doesn't hurt to send the editor a letter of agreement spelling out terms you've agreed to verbally or a model contract that you use.

Keep in mind that in the absence of a verbal agreement on rights, the default is First North American Rights or one-time use. Publishers or clients cannot make a work-for-hire agreement or buy unrestricted use without an explicit written agreement.

Publishers have their own model contracts in many cases. Keep in mind that these are negotiable, and if you see terms you don't like, you can change them at any time.

What follows are some model forms that can make your life easier.

PERMISSION TO USE COPYRIGHTED MATERIAL

I hereby grant permission to ______________________________
to quote or otherwise reprint the following:
____
____
____

From: (Publication's name)__________________________________
By: (Author's name)____

This material will be published in a ______________________
by the title ____
to be published by ____,
Address: ____
____
____

This request shall apply to all future editions and adaptations of ____.

I am the copyright holder or authorized by the copyright holder to grant this permission.

Signed:

Print name: ____
Title: ____
Date: ____

SAMPLE RELEASE FORM

Date: ____________________

I, ____________________ ,

hereby consent that my picture, portrait and/or name and reproductions thereof may be used by____________________

as (s)he may desire in connection with professional activities and may be used, exhibited or published through any or all media, including for advertising or commercial purposes. This release is irrevocable.

I am (am not) over 21 years old.

Name ____________________

Address ____________________

City ____________________ State ______ ZIP __________

Signature ____________________

Consent of Parent or Guardian

I, ____________________ ,

certify that I am parent/guardian of ____________________ ,

and hereby consent that his/her name, picture, portrait or representation may be used by ____________________

in connection with his/her professional activities and may be exhibited, reproduced, published or used through any medium in connection with those professional activities, including for advertising or commercial purposes. This release is irrevocable.

Name ____________________

Address ____________________

City ____________________ State ______ ZIP __________

Signature ____________________

LETTER OF AGREEMENT

Jack Neff
444 W. Fourth St.
Cincinnati, OH 45200
(513) 333-9000

October 12, 2000

Richard Goodwell
Greenfield Digest
101 Warsaw Parkway
Rochester, NY 10322

Dear Mr. Goodwell:

This letter is to confirm the assignment we discussed earlier today for me to write an article tentatively titled ''Brownfield to Greenfield—The Challenges Ahead'' on the following terms:

1) The article will be approximately 1,500 words, including one sidebar.
2) The article is due Nov. 15, 2000.
3) Payment of $750 is due upon acceptance.
4) *Greenfield Digest* will review and either accept or seek revisions of the article within thirty days of receipt.
5) A revised version will be due within ten days of notice, with final decision on acceptance within fourteen days of receipt of revised article.
6) *Greenfield Digest* buys First North American Rights. Electronic and reprint rights are negotiable.
7) Should *Greenfield Digest* cancel the assignment before completion, a kill fee of $325 will immediately become due.
8) *Greenfield Digest* will pay reasonable telephone, database research and incidental fees, due upon receipt of an invoice and documentation of expenses.

Thanks for the assignment and for your time. If you have any questions or concerns, please feel free to call. Enclosed is an SASE in which you can return a signed copy of this letter. You may keep the original for your records.

Sincerely,

Jack Neff

I understand and agree to the terms stated above.

Richard Goodwell, Editor, *Greenfield Digest*	Date

INDEX